STALKING
NIETZSCHE

Recent Titles in
Contributions in Philosophy

STALKING NIETZSCHE

Raymond Angelo Belliotti

Contributions in Philosophy, number 68

G
P

Greenwood Press
Westport, Connecticut • London

Library of Congress Cataloging-in-Publication Data

Belliotti, Raymond A., 1948–
    Stalking Nietzsche / Raymond Angelo Belliotti.
      p.   cm. — (Contributions in philosophy, ISSN 0084–926X ; no.
 68)
    Includes bibliographical references and index.
    ISBN 0–313–30700–8 (alk. paper)
    1. Nietzsche, Friedrich Wilhelm, 1844–1900.   I. Title.
 II. Series.
    B3317.B4266   1998
    193—dc21   98–8237

British Library Cataloguing in Publication Data is available.

Library of Congress Catalog Card Number: 98–8237
ISBN: 0–313–30700–8
ISSN: 0084–926X

First published in 1998

Greenwood Press, 88 Post Road West, Westport, CT 06881
An imprint of Greenwood Publishing Group, Inc.

Printed in the United States of America

∞™

The paper used in this book complies with the
Permanent Paper Standard issued by the National
Information Standards Organization (Z39.48–1984).

10   9   8   7   6   5   4   3   2   1

For Marcia, Angelo, and Vittoria
Ciò che non mi distrugge mi rende più forte

CONTENTS

INTRODUCTION

When I was an undergraduate, Friedrich Nietzsche was beginning to undergo a rehabilitation in the United States which was animated mainly by Walter Kaufmann's stunningly thorough scholarship of the early 1950s. Although Kaufmann viewed him as a master philosopher and psychologist, Nietzsche was more frequently portrayed as a cultural prophet with a strikingly eccentric literary style. This portrayal, however, was a step up from Nietzsche's earlier caricature as a philosopher of Nazism.

My first exposures to Nietzsche's work were typically accompanied by a host of professorial disclaimers: Nietzsche is not really a philosopher because he rarely advances arguments; his aphorisms may be stimulating but they certainly are not susceptible to critical analysis; Nietzsche is important as an historical figure, perhaps as a precursor of European existentialism, but his work is fatally flawed by pervasive self-contradictions; he embodies stylistic flair and a poetic temperament, but his writing is unrigorous and undisciplined; Nietzsche's work too often degenerates into abusive *ad hominem* arguments, genetic fallacies, and self-referential paradoxes; and he too frequently provokes and irritates readers by his rhetorical excesses and by his peculiar subjectivism.

From the standpoint of the analytic strains of philosophy dominant in Anglo-America during the 1950s through the 1990s, such charges were and are devastating. Nietzsche was permitted into the cherished enclaves of Anglo-American philosophy more as an amusing side show than as a full-fledged member.

While I often taught Nietzsche in my undergraduate classes over the past twenty years, I usually did so in introductory courses, as a way of stirring the imagination of those still untutored in analytic philosophy and as a challenge to the stultifying conformity embodied by most freshmen.

But that changed in the spring semester of 1996, when I taught an advanced undergraduate seminar on Nietzsche. Spurred on by a group of bright students and by other compulsions, I immersed myself in Nietzsche's thought, voraciously reading most of his published work and a sizeable amount of the secondary literature. My favorite books authored by Nietzsche were *Thus Spoke Zarathustra*, *The Gay Science*, and *Ecce Homo*. I do not claim these are necessarily his best writings, only the ones I enjoyed most. I found Nietzsche unique among philosophers; he was impossible to ignore.

NIETZSCHE'S LIFE

Nietzsche makes his own life an issue for examination by insisting that great philosophy is autobiographical. Born in Prussia in 1844, his father was a Lutheran minister, as were both his grandfathers.[1] He was his parents' first child and was named in honor of the reigning king of Prussia. Nietzsche sometimes claimed his paternal line descended from Polish noblemen, but that is unclear. His father became mentally ill by the time Nietzsche was four years old, and died a year later. Nietzsche's childhood household consisted of his mother, sister, paternal grandmother, and two maiden aunts. Nietzsche had apparently loved his sister, Elisabeth, deeply as a child, but as an adult often found her avid German nationalism, anti-Semitism, penchant for meddling, and husband virtually impossible to bear.

Nearsighted and often plagued by migraines, Nietzsche was an excellent student. At age twenty, he graduated from a renowned Protestant boarding school and then studied theology and classical philology at the University of Bonn. By 1865 he gave up theology and went to Leipzig, following his philology lecturer, Friedrich Wilhelm Ritschl. There he read Schopenhauer for the first time and was greatly impressed. One strain of philosophical gossip holds that Nietzsche contracted syphilis in Cologne while he was a student at Bonn, and untreated or improperly treated syphilis is what eventually drove him insane. Nietzsche was in military service from 1867 to 1868, being discharged because of an injury suffered when riding a horse.

In 1868, he first met renowned German composer and poet Richard Wagner and his wife Cosima. For more than eight years, Nietzsche extolled Wagner as a paradigm of artistic genius, and apparently was infatuated with Cosima. In 1869, Nietzsche, upon strong recommendation of Ritschl, was appointed associate professor of classical philology at the University of Basel. Soon thereafter he was awarded his doctorate by Leipzig, without examination, on the basis of his published work. In 1870 he received a leave to volunteer as a medical orderly in the Franco–Prussian War. Within less than two months, he returned to Germany with dysentery and diphtheria. Another strain of philosophical gossip holds that Nietzsche contracted syphilis while ministering to ill soldiers. In any event, Nietzsche had few sexual encounters. The most that has been claimed is that as a student he may have visited a brothel once or twice. Throughout his life, he cultivated an exquisitely polite, soft-spoken, reserved manner, and suffered poor health.

In 1872, Nietzsche accompanied Wagner on the latter's fifty-ninth birthday to the laying of the foundation stone of the Bayreuth theater, a proposed cultural center. Early in April 1876, Nietzsche traveled to Geneva and spent a few days with Hugo von Senger, a conductor whom he had met in Bayreuth. At Senger's house, Nietzsche met Mathilde Trampedach. She apparently made a stunning impression on Nietzsche: He wrote her a letter on April 11 in which he proposed marriage. She swiftly declined his invitation. In the summer of 1876, the first Bayreuth festival marked the beginning of his estrangement from Wagner. Nietzsche sensed Bayreuth was fast becoming a center of rabid German nationalism, anti-Semitism, and Christian idolatry. He left Bayreuth with Paul Ree, a friend whom he had first met in Basil in 1873. In 1878, Nietzsche received from Wagner the score of *Parsifal*, which Nietzsche derided. His friendship with Wagner had ended.

Nietzsche's classes attracted relatively few students, but several of them chronicled their high regard for him. By 1879 he had retired from the University of Basil due to ill health. For the next ten years he wandered and wrote, mostly in France, Switzerland, and Italy. Nietzsche generally stayed in hotel rooms and modest resorts. He suffered severe migraines, painful vomiting spells, near blindness, and a variety of stomach and lung ailments throughout this period. It is said that his lodgings would contain one table for his writing and another table for the numerous medicines and potions he used to moderate the symptoms of his illnesses.

In 1882, Ree met Lou Salome in Rome and apparently fell in love with her. Nietzsche later met her and was greatly impressed. Some writers claim Nietzsche proposed marriage to Lou Salome either in person or through Paul Ree, was turned down, but eventually settled for an intellectual ménage à trois. Other writers claim Nietzsche never proposed marriage to her, although Lou was apparently waiting for him to do so. In any event, it is clear that Nietzsche was attracted to her and regarded Lou Salome as uncommonly gifted. It is also clear that the two remained chaste, and by the end of 1882 Nietzsche was estranged from both Ree and Salome, partly due to the intrigues and meddling of Elisabeth.

In 1889, at age forty-five, Nietzsche collapsed in a street in Turin while embracing a horse that had been flogged by a coachman. Nietzsche's friend, Franz Overbeck, brought him back to Basel and took him to a psychiatric clinic. Nietzsche's mother soon arrived and took him to the Jena Psychiatric Clinic. In May 1890, Nietzsche was permitted to leave the clinic and live in Naumburg with his mother. There he was cared for by his mother and a maidservant. From early 1894, Nietzsche was unable to leave the house. His mother died in 1897. From the moment of his collapse in Turin until his death in 1900, he was insane.

Elisabeth, after the suicide of her husband in Paraguay where they aspired to nurture a racially pure Aryan colony, returned home to find that Nietzsche's fame was spreading. She took control of Nietzsche's care during his final three years. She also acquired publishing rights to all his work. In the last three years of Nietzsche's life, Elisabeth sometimes dressed him in flowing white robes and orchestrated showings for visitors. Ironically, Nietzsche became famous only after he had gone insane. Elisabeth nurtured the Nietzsche legend, a combination of solitary visionary and saintly prophet, as a way to earn prominence in German society. She also apparently loved her brother deeply.

After Nietzsche's death, his sister continued to exploit his fame, including editing and publishing passages from Nietzsche's notebooks, and telling Hitler that he was precisely what Nietzsche had in mind when he discussed the *Übermensch*. Although Elisabeth claimed special insight into her brother's motivations and intentions, she lacked refined analytic and critical skills. Several unscrupulous Nazi interpreters, such as the notorious Alfred Baumler, pictured Nietzsche as an apologist for the Third Reich despite the extensive textual evidence that Nietzsche despised German nationalism, anti-Semitism, and the idolizing of the state over culture. The Nazi interpretation of Nietzsche damaged his reputation in the Anglo-American world for decades.

PROBLEMS OF INTERPRETATION

To interpret Nietzsche is to invite a legion of problems. Nietzsche tells us that the philosophical is the personal: all great philosophy is autobiographical. Thus, the connection between Nietzsche's life and his work assumes an importance that is obscured in other philosophers. Also, there is an oxymoronic character to his writing. He enjoys talking, for example, about "false truths," "selfish altruism," "irreligious religion," "compassionate contempt," and the like. Such linguistic puzzles add interpretive difficulties.

Nietzsche uses a variety of literary styles and embraces a multiplicity of critical perspectives. Aphorisms, metaphors, calculated exaggerations, genealogical critiques, and personal invectives coalesce uneasily in his work. Both the forms and contents of Nietzsche's writing may strike novice readers as hopelessly contradictory. He cultivates this reaction by relishing self- referential paradoxes, passages where he seems to self-consciously contradict his earlier positions. Nietzsche tells us that multiplicity forms the core of the human spirit. Thus, according to his own conviction, there is no fixed, final way to read and interpret Nietzsche, only many plausible ways.

Writing a book that interprets Nietzsche makes it virtually impossible not to entomb his thought in a non-Nietzschean metaphysical language of explanation. An interpreter cannot make a rational system of Nietzsche's thought without falsifying Nietzsche's guiding impulse. To fulfill readers' expectations to read the "truth" about Nietzsche in unequivocal terms is to domesticate his literary style and to defeat Nietzsche's central aspirations. Readers must confront Nietzsche's work directly to experience the episodic rhythms and psychological drives that constitute his thought.

Interpreters must grapple with the relationships between Nietzsche's broad themes, his critique of mainstream philosophy, his general musings on living life, his specific background views which energize his general musings on living life, his world views which often embody warrior rhetoric, his genealogical suspicions about conventional wisdom, and his (vague) vision of the future. By his "broad themes" I mean his most fundamental recurring convictions: the inescapability of inner conflict; the perspectival nature of truth; the links between psychological types of humans and their embrace of different truth claims; the need to perceive reality from multiple perspectives; the connection between writing and life; the inability of language to capture life's complexities and fluidity; the denial of absolutism; the need to impose order and meaning on the world of Becoming; the salutary rhythms of deconstruction, reimagination, and re-creation; the need to recognize and welcome the tragedy and contingency that constitute life; replacing the task of objectively disproving truth claims with the project of casting suspicion upon their origins and the psychology of those who embrace them; the importance of self-overcoming, which includes subjecting one's own theoretical and practical commitments to the strictest scrutiny; and the call to luxuriate in the immediacy of life. These broad themes, taken as a whole, resist unambiguous doctrinal exposition.

There is also the problem of Nietzsche's avowed experimentalism. How much of what he says is provisional and discarded, implicitly or explicitly, later in his work? How much shows a mind in flux? To what extent is the central character in one of his major books, Zarathustra, a projection of Nietzsche's own thoughts and to what extent is Zarathustra only a literary character meant to represent a variety of attitudes and stages of life, some decidedly un-Nietzschean? Nietzsche has a penchant for self-parody, warns us not to regard his work as the redemptive final word, and insists that the only disciples worth addressing are those who seek to surpass, not abjectly parrot, their teacher.

Finally, to what extent are Nietzsche's *Nachlass*, his voluminous unpublished writings, admissible as evidence of Nietzsche's convictions? By far the best-known part of the *Nachlass* is a volume, *The Will to Power*, first edited and published by Nietzsche's sister, Elisabeth Forster-Nietzsche, in 1901. The volume contains selections from Nietzsche's notebooks of the years 1883 to 1888. The arrangement and numbering of selections were done by his sister, not by Nietzsche. Subsequent editions, with inclusions by various editors, were published in 1904, 1906, 1911, 1930, 1940, and 1956. Kaufmann published a version of *The Will to Power* in 1967 with the warning, "These notes were not intended [by Nietzsche] for publication in this form. . . . This book is not comparable to the works Nietzsche finished and polished, and we do him a disservice if we fudge the distinction between these hasty notes and his often gemlike aphorisms" (*WP* xv–xvi).

Some philosophers, such as Martin Heidegger, regard the *Nachlass* as the key to Nietzsche's thought. Heidegger took Nietzsche's published work to be the mask of an author who insisted on the need for disguises. The interpreters in this camp are likely to render Nietzsche more philosophically, metaphysically, systematically, and doctrinally than other interpretations see him. Other philosophers, such as Bernd Magnus, distinguish sharply between Nietzsche's published work and the *Nachlass*. Under the commonsense assumption that unpublished thoughts scribbled into notebooks during long walks should not be regarded on a par with polished, published work, such philosophers rule the *Nachlass* inadmissible. The interpreters in this camp are likely to portray Nietzsche as an early postmodern, nonrepresentational thinker who paved the way for contemporary thinkers such as Derrida, Foucault, and Rorty.

WHY I HAVE (MIS)INTERPRETED NIETZSCHE

I make use of *The Will to Power* sparingly, using selections, I hope, only when they support passages cited from Nietzsche's published work. However, I also portray Nietzsche more philosophically and systematically than postmodernists, and perhaps Nietzsche himself, would like.

Each chapter of this book begins with a relatively brief exposition of Nietzsche's writing in a particular area which raises important questions of interpretation, and concludes with a lengthy dialogue between two characters, Fegataccio and Apollonia, on those questions. Moreover, there is a subtext in which the relationship between the two characters in the dialogues and the topics they address develops in ways that exemplify and do not merely explain Nietzsche's broad themes. In this manner, the book's literary form closely tracks the broad content of Nietzsche's thought. The dialogues also engage with many classical and contemporary interpreters of Nietzsche. This method, I hope, will deepen readers' understanding and appreciation of Nietzsche's project in ways that typical books on Nietzsche do not.

This book is an introduction to Nietzsche's thought with special attention to those who, having been influenced by numerous popular renderings of Nietzsche, approach his work with grave skepticism. With the possible exception of the first chapter on perspectivism, the book is accessible to nonspecialists and does not presuppose extensive philosophical training or previous reading of Nietzsche's work. It concentrates on, and its literary style exemplifies, the connection between philosophy and living: How can reading Nietzsche change one's life? What links are there between accepting Nietzsche's broad philosophical themes and practical conduct? What lessons, if any, can Nietzsche teach us about the human condition?

I do not directly confront the radical reading, as advanced by Derrida and de Man, that Nietzsche is not defending a systematic position but merely parodying philosophy in order to eviscerate it. But the dialogues indirectly reject that position for a variety of reasons. Nor do I accept the conservative reading that Nietzsche advances and defends a substantive philosophical system. I write from the perspective that the power of Nietzsche's thought resides in his broad themes, not in specific pronouncements. While the indeterminacy of those themes irritates many interpreters, I find it liberating and challenging. Nietzsche's system is a framework of commitments and historical interpretations that counsels accelerated self-revision, robust acceptance of radical contingency, and grave suspicion of conventional wisdom.

As are all attempts to mediate Nietzsche's work for readers, mine is a (mis)interpretation. Only direct confrontation with Nietzsche's thought conveys his spirit. Still, (mis)interpretations are important because they exemplify Nietzsche's broad themes and permit communication among readers. Perhaps we can all appropriate something from Nietzsche's work for our lives, even if we cannot—as Nietzsche said we could not—freeze his ideas into doctrines, stable theories, and truths.

When I immersed myself in Nietzsche's writings, I found that I could not treat him the way I treat so many philosophers, as academic signposts in the history of ideas. Nietzsche challenges the way we live and forces us to interrogate the person we are becoming. Certainly other philosophers ask the same questions Nietzsche does, but most can still be treated in the established academic fashion: at a distance, with detachment, safely confined within the university classroom. Nietzsche, by contrast, follows me home. He screams and preens, he prods and irritates, he breaks all the rules of academia and laughs about it, and then he laughs at himself. But he will not be ignored.

I discovered there are kernels of truth in the professorial disclaimers I heard long ago, but there are other sides to the story that lay within Nietzsche's calculated deconstruction of established discourse and self-conscious flaunting of conventional understandings. This book is an attempt to tell different sides of Nietzsche's story without a happy ending; indeed, with no final solution. My hope is that Nietzsche will follow you home, too.

===

Chapter 1

SHADOWS AND CAVES

Perspectivism, Truth, and Reality

Nietzsche embraces a variety of literary styles and a multiplicity of critical perspectives. Aphorisms, metaphors, calculated exaggerations, genealogical critiques, and personal invectives coalesce uneasily in his work. Both the form and content of Nietzsche's writing may strike novice readers as hopelessly contradictory. He self-consciously abrogates the tools that have partially defined Anglo-American philosophy: clarity, simplicity, unadorned prose, and logical rigor. Indeed, Karl Jaspers claims that "self-contradiction is the fundamental ingredient in Nietzsche's thought. For nearly every single one of Nietzsche's judgments, one can also find the opposite."[1]

Although many of these self-contradictions are merely apparent—as they result from Nietzsche's calculated verbal equivocations or readers' failure to attend carefully to different contexts—others reflect Nietzsche's understanding of the complexity of reality which requires "seeing with many different sets of eyes":

Let us guard against the snares of such contradictory concepts such as "pure reason," "absolute spirituality," "knowledge in itself" . . . There is *only* a perspectival seeing, *only* a perspectival "knowing": and the *more* affects we allow to speak about one thing, the *more* eyes, different eyes, we can use to observe one thing, the more complex will our "concept" of this thing, our "objectivity," be. (*GM* III, 12)

In fact, Nietzsche's style, which inspires some while irritating others, is an integral part of his general philosophical framework. His literary style exemplifies his most fundamental themes: the inescapability of inner conflict; the perspectival nature of truth; the links between psychological types of humans and their embrace of different truth claims; the need to perceive reality from multiple perspectives; the connection between writing and life; the inability of language to capture life's complexities and fluidity; the denial of absolutism; the need to impose order and meaning on the world of Becoming; the salutary rhythms of deconstruction, reimagination, and re-creation; the need to recognize and welcome the tragedy and contingency that constitute life; replacing the task of objectively disproving truth claims with the project of casting suspicion upon their origins and the psychology of those who embrace them; the importance of self-overcoming, which includes subjecting one's own theoretical and practical commitments to the strictest scrutiny; and the call to luxuriate in the immediacy of life.[2]

PERSPECTIVISM

In this chapter, I begin with an account of Nietzsche's perspectivism regarding truth-claims. In sum, Nietzsche denies the existence of absolute transcendent truths and affirms the need for perspectival interpretation. "Everything the philosopher has declared about man is, however, at bottom no more than a testimony as to the man of *a very limited* period of time. Lack of historical sense is the family failing of all philosophers. . . . There are *no eternal facts*, just as there are no absolute truths" (*HAH* 2).

He understands that some propositions become embedded in language and common sense and earn the honorific title of "truth," but he denies that our way of speaking about the world necessarily reflects an independent Reality. Instead, our language and conventional understandings of truth mirror the needs, interests, and general psychology of different human types. Those understandings that flow from the masses reflect the leveling mindset of the "herd." Although Nietzsche sharply disparages the mediocrity, banality, and muted will to power, as well as the attitudes of *ressentiment* and revenge that typically accompany the judgments of the herd, he sometimes acknowledges the refinements to human possibilities that the herd has produced.

Nietzsche unsqueamishly accepts that our beliefs are false, at least when judged by the humanly created standard of absolute truth. Instead of being preoccupied with transcendent standards of absoluteness and unconditionality, however, we should embrace this life fully by accepting the contingency and fallibility of the perspectives we advance. "The falseness of a judgment is for us not necessarily an objection to a judgment. . . . The question is to what extent it is life-promoting,

life-preserving, species-preserving, perhaps even species-cultivating"
(*BGE* 4).

Perspectives are not merely particular sets of coherent beliefs.[3] Nietzsche accepts that there can be untrue beliefs in a perspective; indeed, he often asserts the need for "falsity" in life and within one's perspective. Moreover, one could adopt a perspective, even self-consciously, and not believe all the truths implied by it. Nietzsche also holds that statements can be true in certain perspectives but not in others, but he does not hold that our believing something establishes truth, even within a perspective. Embracing a perspective is related to coping and comprehending the world, to imposing order related to one's character, experiences, and powers. This process includes both social and individual dimensions: Churches, cultures, states, communities, races, individuals, and so on all adopt and create perspectives.[4] Thus, a particular person is influenced by numerous, often conflicting perspectives. Where there are loci of power, where there is life, perspectives are generated.[5]

The relationship of perspectives, reality, facts, and truth is at the heart of Nietzsche's philosophy. If Nietzsche is correct, we have no bare facts—facts independent of our perspectival interpretations—to which we can appeal for foundational justification of our truth-claims. Thus, there is no particular account that uniquely captures the complexities of physical reality or that unequivocally discovers a natural order in the universe. Indeed, Nietzsche's most strident rhetoric is directed against the prevalent philosophical view of his time that there are things-in-themselves which stand above space, time, and human notions of causality.

For Nietzsche, a thing-in-itself is an incoherent concept because all things must have properties and all properties are relational in the sense that they are effects of a thing on other things. Given such a view, the concept of an unrelated, pure entity which somehow exists independently of other entities is nonsense. He does not, however, subscribe to a crude idealism which accepts only a mind-dependent world. Instead, he embraces a Heraclitean world of inherently undifferentiated chaotic flux. Rejecting an independent, objective world structure, Nietzsche takes the project of human life to be imposing order, interpretation, and evaluation on the world of Becoming and on our own characters. Through the structure of our language we reflect our conceptions of the world.

His view of the world underwrites Nietzsche's perspectivism. Because the world is inherently undifferentiated flux, it lacks stable, independent metaphysical attributes which could objectively measure human evaluations. No particular perspective can rightfully claim to capture the world as it really is or to be the best possible rendering of the world, because the world is inherently unstable and reality is nothing more than a name for the entire range of institutions, theories, and conventions humans select and impose. Thus, there are no bare facts, there are only interpretations. "Against that positivism which stops before phenomena, saying 'there are only *facts*,' I should say: no, it is precisely facts that do not exist, only *interpretations*" (*WP* 481).

As a result, the distinction between truth and error is much fuzzier than generally imagined. The human quest to impose order and meaning must be undertaken without metaphysical guarantees; no particular perspective can portray the world as it really is because undifferentiated flux resists further description—there are no fine details to describe. Nietzsche writes the following:

It is no more than a moral prejudice that truth is worth more than mere appearance. . . . There would be no life at all if not on the basis of perspective estimates and appearances; and if . . . one wanted to abolish the "apparent world" altogether—well supposing *you* could do that, at least nothing would be left of your "truth" either. Indeed, what forces us at all to suppose there is an essential opposition of "true" and "false"? Is it not sufficient to assume degrees of apparentness and, as it were, lighter and darker shadows and shades of appearance? (*BGE* 34)

Perspectivism highlights the role that human evaluations, interests, purposes, and goals play in the formation of "truth." Moreover, perspectivism underscores the part historical struggle among interest groups plays in establishing the social conventions that become enshrined as common sense: There is no available Archimedean point, no all-encompassing master perspective, no available unsituated vantage point from which humans can discern the Truth.

Moreover, adopting particular perspectives is not a matter of immediate choice. At birth we find ourselves in one social setting, with a certain range of possibilities, with a circumscribed set of life prospects. We are socialized into certain worldviews which often embody the seeds of their own destruction. Conversions to new perspectives require accepting new arrangements of life that resist simple commitments of will. Only great effort, revised self-images, and personal re-creation can animate such conversions.

None of this troubles Nietzsche because, if he is correct, things could hardly be otherwise. He is distressed, however, at the way perspectives often masquerade as more than what they are, how they arrogate to themselves the trappings of absolute truth, universal authority, and timeless necessity. When perspectival interpretations assume such imperial self-understandings they wrongfully renege on the contingency of life.

When we interpret from a perspective we select and simplify. Because Nietzsche claims there is no world in itself and no aperspectival rendering of reality, human selection and simplification underscore the necessarily partial nature of all perspectival interpretations. Once we abrogate the pretension to transcendent truth, truth that stands above human interests and purposes, we can only impose order and meaning on the world through simplifications that are motivated by the needs and desires of particular peoples at particular times. Moreover, peoples will be (largely) unaware of the precise motivations that fuel their specific world visions. In sum, perspectival interpretations both reflect and constitute modes of life that promote particular types of people in specific historical contexts.

Perspectivism's self-conscious partiality has several dimensions: There is no final, fixed best perspective *simpliciter*; different peoples embracing conflicting modes of life will impose different perspective understandings on their worlds; reinterpretation, reevaluation, and recreation are not only possible but also salutary; we will be mostly unaware of the precise ways we have simplified the world and of the motivations and values that underwrote those simplifications; and the pretension to universal authority is a dangerous illusion which can artificially limit human possibilities.

Perspectivism's partiality contrasts with absolutism or dogmatism— the view that certain truth-claims pertain to all humans in all contexts at all times; that at least some of these claims are discoverable by human reason; and that once discovered and validated these claims are fixed and final and can thus serve as epistemological foundations. Dogmatism of this sort is typically supported by a commitment to objective metaphysical structures such as Kantian things-in-themselves, Platonic forms, or the Judeo–Christian–Islamic Supreme Being.

Nietzsche, clearly and consistently, rejects all versions of dogmatism. When describing "philosophers of the future" he says, "Are these coming philosophers new friends of 'truth'? That is probable enough, for all philosophers so far have loved their truths. But they will certainly not be dogmatists. It must offend their pride, also their taste, if their truth is supposed to be a truth for everyman—which has so far been the secret wish and hidden meaning of all dogmatic aspirations" (*BGE* 43).

Yet, in typically Nietzschean style, his rejection of dogmatism is not one-sided, but admits reversal and subtlety:

Without accepting the fictions of logic, without measuring reality against the purely invented world of the unconditional and self-identical, without a constant falsification of the world by means of numbers, man could not live— that renouncing false judgments would mean renouncing life and a denial of life. To recognize untruth as a condition of life—that certainly means resisting accustomed value feelings in a dangerous way; and a philosophy that risks this would by that token alone place itself beyond good and evil. (*BGE* 4)

Perhaps his message here is that our notions of objectivity and transcendence are themselves ingenious human creations that are in some sense necessary to life. But they are neither metaphysical facts nor aperspectival depictions of the world. Instead, they are one kind of human myth, one type of human interpretation and evaluation. Thus, our notions of objectivity and transcendent truth are not pure foundations for absolutism; although they may present themselves in that fashion, at bottom they are no more than one interpretative schema among many. Nietzsche's clearest and most poetic denunciation of absolute truth is in "On Truth and Lie in an Extra-Moral Sense":

What, then, is truth? A mobile army of metaphors, metonyms, and anthropomorphisms—in short, a sum of human relations, which have been enhanced, transposed, and embellished poetically and rhetorically, and which after long use seem firm, canonical, and obligatory to a people: truths are illusions about which one has forgotten that this is what they are; metaphors which are worn out and without sensuous power; coins which have lost their pictures and now matter only as metal, no longer as coins. . . . To be truthful means . . . the obligation to lie according to a fixed convention, to lie herd-like in a style obligatory for all.

Nietzsche's views on truth and perspectivism connect with his views on life. The construction and application of concepts and (falsifying) language are part of the basic human activities: creation and evaluation. The structures of dogmatism—a transcendent world, things-in-themselves, objective truth that must be discovered, universal valuations, the quest for certainty—strike Nietzsche as limiting and suffocating. At bottom, humans are creative artists (in a broad sense) who must impose meaning and order on their world of Becoming. Worse, the structures of dogmatism embody a no-saying attitude toward our world and a craven aspiration for a transcendent pain-free world. They constitute a denial of a favorite Nietzschean theme: reimagination and re-creation accompanied by conscious celebration of contingency and personal mortality. Moreover, dogmatism and absolutism wrongly assume that what is good for some is good for all. As such, dogmatism and absolutism falsely sanctify the conclusions of the herd—judgments which reflect the needs and desires of the masses of mediocrities—and deny the order of rank among humans.

Healthy strong humans are not paralyzed by radical perspectivism, but rather rejoice in increased creative opportunities. The moment of

nihilism—when all seems up for grabs because recognition of the lack
of metaphysical foundations is widespread—prepares the way for delight in human artistic achievements as passion, reason, and experience create new values and modes of life. Indeed, creativity is largely
unconscious and instinctual. The learned academician, scrupulously
laboring on perfecting theoretical projects, is more likely to mirror current social and cultural contexts than to create subversively and to legislate new values and cultural practices.

But all this is put too simply. In fact, it is probably impossible not to
oversimplify when outlining Nietzsche's work. But even this underscores broader Nietzschean themes. Simplification and falsification
invariably accompany the imposition of meaning and order on the
world of Becoming; if perspectivism is persuasive then there are inevitably numerous conflicting ways to interpret Nietzsche's own work.
Thus, powerful literary works create numerous interpretations and
confusions. Within each of us, multiple conflicting perspectives vie for
supremacy. Nietzsche often talks of the inherent multiplicity of the self.
Fundamental conflict is at the core of one's internal life and external
relations. By highlighting that the self is not a natural unity, Nietzsche
reminds us that we all embody internal battlegrounds where our conflicting drives fuel conflicting perspectival frameworks. To forge a unity
out of inner conflict, to give style to one's character, and to create out of
oneself new values and perspectives are the missions of the philosophers of the future.

Some of Nietzsche's more strident passages on perspectivism suggest a virulent noncognitivism, an apparently outright rejection of the
possibility of rational discernment of truth and value. He seems to conceive of reason as the mere instrument of deeper physiological forces
which generate goals.[6] His insistence that the philosophers of the future must create new values that do not merely replicate existing arrangements and his emphasis on interpretation may suggest he
implicitly endorses an abject relativism which cannot distinguish among
competing perspectives.[7]

John Wilcox, however, points out that "some interpretations have
merits that others lack. . . . They rise above the ordinary."[8] According to
Nietzsche, interpretations and entire perspectives can be graded on
the basis of their scientism, logical consistency, being supported by sensory evidence, subtleties, openness to revision, recognition of fallibilism,
comprehensiveness, style, unity, honesty, and reflection of healthy and
strong origins.[9] Satisfying such criteria counts in favor of interpretations. Thus, Nietzsche's perspectivism is safe from charges of abject
relativism and irrationalism. Wilcox describes Nietzschean truth as
"this-worldly, fallible, hypothetical, perspectival, value-laden, histori-

cally developed and simplifying truth—which we might call, using Nietzschean hyperbole, 'erroneous' truth."[10]

Some commentators have claimed that Nietzsche adopts a pragmatic theory of truth: A proposition is true if it works or is useful and false if it does not.[11] But there is much textual evidence against this claim. In the context of considering the view that what makes people happy or virtuous is true, Nietzsche says, "Happiness and virtue are no arguments, But people like to forget—even sober spirits—that making unhappy and evil are no counterarguments. Something might be true while being harmful and dangerous in the highest degree" (*BGE* 39).

Nietzsche underscores his conviction in the separability of effects and truths when he says, "[Those who say] it does not matter whether a thing is true, but only what effect it produces [manifest] an absolute lack of intellectual integrity" (*WP* 172). He also makes clear that usefulness to life is no proof of truth: "*Life no argument.*—We have fixed up a world for ourselves in which we can live—assuming bodies, lines, planes, causes and effects, motion and rest, form and content: without these articles of faith, nobody now would endure life. But that does not mean that they have been proved. Life is no argument; the conditions of life could include error" (*GS* 121).

Nietzschean perspectivism, however, does confront a powerful puzzle: the paradox of self-reference. Nietzsche seems to hold that there is no uniquely correct interpretation of the world; that there is no uniquely correct interpretation of any particular thing; that there are only a variety of interpretations that are correct only from within their own perspectives, the frameworks that serve as the totality of reference points; and there is no such thing as a thing-in-itself. All these and other Nietzschean claims present themselves as "real truths," as insights that correct the mistakes of dominant cultural perception, as clear improvements over the judgments of the herd, and as salutary reminders of the rank among human types and the need to wholeheartedly embrace the flux that is the world and the contingency and conflict that define human existence.

The paradox of self-reference calls into question the status of Nietzsche's own assertions: To assert perspectivism—"all truth is perspectival" or "there is no absolute truth"—may undermine perspectivism because the assertion's claim to be true is unsettled by its own propositional content. To put the matter differently, if P ("all truth is perspectival") is itself a knowledge claim, then P is either a case of perspectival knowing or a case of aperspectival knowing. If P is a case of perspectival knowing then it lacks unconditional power and the possibility of aperspectival knowledge remains. If P is a case of aperspectival knowing then P itself is true unconditionally and P undermines its own truth-claim. In either case, it appears that P cannot be asserted consistently.

There is some textual evidence suggesting Nietzsche was aware of the paradox of self-reference and choose to underscore the conditionality of his own interpretation that all interpretation was conditional. For example, he concludes a section of criticism with this sentence: "Supposing that this [Nietzsche's exposition] also is only interpretation—and you will be eager enough to make this objection?—well, so much the better" (*BGE* 22). Moreover, when describing philosophers of the future, he adds, "'My judgment is *my* judgment': no one else is easily entitled to it—that is what such a philosopher of the future may perhaps say of himself" (*BGE* 43). Nietzsche also has Zarathustra say, "'This is *my* way; where is yours?'—thus I answered those who asked me 'the way.' For *the* way—that does not exist" (Z III, "On the Spirit of Gravity," 2). At times, Nietzsche also hints at the paradoxes that confront a seemingly unconditional denial of absolutism: "Every morality is . . . a bit of tyranny against 'nature'; also against 'reason'; but this in itself is no objection, as long as we do not have some other morality which permits us to decree that every kind of tyranny and unreason is impermissible" (*BGE* 188).

Nietzsche further suggests the need for a new fusion of the objective and subjective dimensions of knowledge:

To see differently in this way for once, to *want* to see differently, is no small discipline and preparation of the intellect for its future "objectivity"—the latter understood not as "contemplation without interest" (which is a nonsensical absurdity), but as the ability *to control* one's Pro and Con and to dispose of them, so that one knows how to employ a *variety* of perspectives and affective interpretations in the service of knowledge. (*GM* III, 12)

But such fragments are strikingly inconclusive, and Walter Kaufmann is undoubtedly correct when he says, in the context of the self-referential puzzles of Nietzsche's conception of the will to power, "Nietzsche was not at his best with problems of this kind: he never worked out an entirely satisfactory theory of knowledge, and most of the relevant material remained in his notebooks and did not find its way into a more coherent presentation in his published works."[12]

Accordingly, numerous questions linger: What, if anything, is Nietzsche's theory of truth? Can his perspectivism resist or overcome the paradox of self-reference? Is his literary work merely the mischief of a calculated ironist? Or must his style exemplify Nietzsche's broad themes, those about which he is most confident? Is Nietzsche merely a provocateur, laughing up his sleeve at the pedants of the future who will oversimplify his thought? Independently of Nietzsche's particular motives and intentions, can contemporary readers expropriate his rhetoric and ideas for their own purposes?

THE FIRST DIALOGUE

In a shopping mall in New York, a discussion of Nietzsche's work is taking place while the parties eat deep-dish pizza prepared by the local unit of a national fast food chain. There are many books piled on the table.

Apollonia: It amazes me that you can take Nietzsche seriously, Fegataccio. His work is fatally ensnared by self-referential paradox. As much as he rails against dogmatism and absolutism, he ends up advancing his own positive theses—indeed he must—as if they were unconditional insights. So he presents his convictions—"all truths are conditional," "there is no aperspectival truth," "there are no things-in-themselves," "the world is inherently undifferentiated chaos," "the judgments of the herd nurture mediocrity," and all the rest of his views—as if they are "really" true. He underscores what he himself takes to be the stench of unconditionality when he asserts them with such self-promotion and such rhetorical stridency.

Fegataccio: Apollonia, you and the other sycophants of Anglo-American analytic philosophy are prisoners of your own creations: The paradox of self-reference, the genetic fallacy, the fallacy of abusive ad hominem, and all the other tricks of bivalent logic are your knee-jerk reactions, your conceptual bludgeons, with which you attack any position that threatens your dominance. You pose as the voice of objective Reason, you mask your haughtiness with apparent dispassion, and you conceal the origins—the powers—underwriting your views. You are the most dangerous of them all, Apollonia, because you are so cool, so above the fray.

Apollonia: That was a splendid, dramatic expression of your discontent, Fegataccio, but what has it to do with my claims? How does it rehabilitate Nietzsche?

Fegataccio: Okay, I will play your game. First, you beg the question against Nietzsche, your very presuppositions rule out his views. Don't you like that, Apollonia, an appeal to "begging the question?" You assume that stability of meaning, explaining away conflict, the principle of identity, and the entire objective world are the framework within which Nietzsche must work to convince you. How could he possibly do that, at least through Reason, when he denies from the start all those presuppositions? Of course, from within your language games Nietzsche's views will seem deficient, for it is precisely the metaphysical and logical basis of those language games that Nietzsche calls into question.

But let me enter into your game from another angle, perhaps one more acceptable to you. Nietzsche understands well the conditionality of his own views; he does not hold them as aperspectival or absolute truths. His multiple literary styles, his appreciation of ambiguity, his calculated reversals of meanings—which you would call equivocations—his embrace of flux and conflict as definitive of life, all exemplify his most deeply held convictions: the need for self-overcoming, institutional deconstruction and re-creation, and going beyond one's own current convictions. His real message, I think, is not in specific recommendations, but in these broad themes. He is not a closet absolutist seeking to impose fixed doctrines on humanity; he remains the apostle of contingency.

Apollonia: Well, at least you have calmed down a bit. Although I don't believe that the basic principles of logic constitute just another language game among many, I will leave that issue for now. It strikes me that it is Nietzsche who begs the question, not me. By ruling out, virtually by fiat, the reality of an external world not of our making, the possibility of truths that transcend perspectives emanating from human desire, and all the rest, he immunizes himself from critical attack by mainstream philosophers and thereby trivializes his own position. His followers can always say, as you have, that we cannot criticize him (without begging the question against him) from the typical standpoints because those are the very standpoints he wishes to deny. But that only reveals the desperation and vacuity of Nietzsche's position.

Moreover, if I accept your view that Nietzsche was aware of the conditionality of his own position, then that undercuts his persuasiveness. If Nietzsche's own themes are merely perspectival renderings emanating from Nietzsche's "will to power," as molded from his historical and social contexts, then I have little antecedent reason to be swayed from my own views.

Fegataccio: You assume that "persuasion" is equivalent to "rational demonstration in accord with bivalent logic." Remember, Nietzsche's views are always tied in with ways of life. One should not be persuaded to Nietzsche's view because it is demanded by Reason; that itself would be un-Nietzschean. Nietzsche does not seek disciples from commonplace minds or abject hero worshipers. At bottom, he does not want his views to be mainstream, for that would suggest that the herd mentality is compatible with those views. He pitches his case to the few, those of aristocratic temperament who can joyfully and eagerly welcome the realization that conflict, contingency, and instability prevail in life. Perspectives are not merely belief structures, they reflect and affect entire ways of life.

Your refusal to be open to Nietzschean themes, Apollonia, tells me much about who you are! It tells me you prize stability and false authority, that you resist ambiguity and nuance, and that you live in a black-and-white-world. You are rigid, Apollonia! Open yourself to the possibilities of life; revel in human powers of creation.

Apollonia: I should have known that your calm and reasonableness would be short-lived. Let's be frank, Fegataccio. You are saying that by refusing Nietzsche's invitations I reveal myself as yet another anal-retentive, fearful member of the herd. But that won't do. It is just another self-serving, question-begging epithet to be hurled at those who see through Nietzsche's self-contradictions.

Furthermore, Nietzsche's self-conscious acceptance of the contingency of his own views remains problematic. Why should I think, even under Nietzsche's own views, that they are anything more than a reflection of Nietzsche's psychology? And, if so, why would I want a life—and I use the term loosely—such as Nietzsche's? He was a recurrently ill, isolated, alienated writer who went insane, possibly from syphilis he contracted during one of his few sexual encounters! Perhaps he could write a good life, if one views him charitably, but he surely could not lead one!

Fegataccio: Ah, Apollonia, who is the hothead now? I must have struck a nerve! It is my turn to insist that we return to the topic. Nietzsche has no *theory* of truth; he isn't really playing that language game. He means only to undermine the absolutism of one of our second-order beliefs (one of our beliefs about our beliefs) about truths, the belief that our truths are rationally required for all peoples. He clearly does not hold the idiotic views that "every view is as good as every other" or that "believing something to be the case is sufficient to make it the case." Those are fictions—strawperson views created by analytic philosophers who need adversarial bobos to immolate easily.

In a Nietzschean understanding, we can still have strong convictions and beliefs while acknowledging the fallibility of those beliefs. This is especially the case when we recognize that such convictions and beliefs are necessary for life and that aperspective truths are unavailable to humans. Nietzsche is interested in the relations of power that generate our discourse of truth or falsity and what effects that discourse itself generates.

So he doesn't try to prove his conclusions through the fixed methods of deductive logic, for then he would really have a self-referential paradox: establishing broad themes of contingency, flux, and perspectivity through narrow categories of necessity, fixed meanings, and absolutism! Instead, he casts suspicion on the origins and modes of life embodied by mainstream views and invites us to a special dance: deconstruction, reimagination, and re-creation in the service of new ways of life.

Apollonia: You move too quickly and confidently through a morass of problems. Although Nietzsche may not want to assert a theory of truth—and given the contradictions and equivocations that define his writing, who can blame him?—he does take certain things to be true, at least perspectively, and he sure sounds like a dogmatist when he brays his conclusions with such stentorian bravado. The question remains: What is truth for Nietzsche?

Furthermore, I would agree easily that no one *wants* to be in the ridiculous position of claiming that every view is as good as every other or that believing something to be the case is sufficient to make it the case. Clearly, there are few, if any, sophisticated thinkers who would self-consciously assert views which cannot be stated coherently, much less lived. But that is not the important issue. The real question is whether Nietzsche's corpus of work implicitly reduces to those views even though neither he nor anyone else would self-consciously assert them. In other words, does Nietzsche's work end up placing him in a theoretical position he does not explicitly desire?

Finally, the relationship between our beliefs and our beliefs about our beliefs is not as simple as you suggest. Whether we believe that our beliefs about, say, justice, fairness, and equality are objectively grounded is paramount to the fervor with which we hold and express them. You need only look to the history of religious fanaticism to see this: holy wars, grand inquisitions, suicide missions, martyrdom, centuries-old feuds over allegedly sacred land, intractable policy differences, and the like. To cast suspicion upon our second-order beliefs has a profound effect on the way we perceive our first-order beliefs.

Fegataccio: There you go again, Apollonia, trotting out all the stock-in-trade moves of analytic philosophy! How banal! How commonplace! How uncreative! Worse, how very misguided!

Why do you think that Nietzsche would disagree with your point about first- and second-order beliefs? He is undermining our second-order belief in the absolutism of our beliefs because he wants to have "a profound effect on the way we perceive our first-order beliefs." He suggests that people of greatness, those mentally and physically capable of transcending the herd mentality, will find their creative energies animated by the joyous embrace of radical contingency. Are you too dull to get the point?

You also assume too smugly that belief in objectivity is necessary for robust convictions. Doesn't Nietzsche himself demonstrate that such is not the case? Doesn't he have firm convictions, held fallibly? Can't we recognize the revisability and finitude of our beliefs, yet still express them strongly? Why think that dogmatism and absolutism must underwrite our thoughts and practices?

And remember that Nietzsche cannot, once we understand his broad themes, advance any theory of truth as a fixed doctrine. He is more interested in painting a picture, demonstrating a dance, singing a song. We will be drawn to his aesthetics (in a broad sense), we will be repelled, or we will be indifferent. Our reactions, contrary to the obtuse understandings of analytic philosophers, will result not from differing applications of the humorless, prosaic categories of bivalent logic, but from differing temperaments and ways of life.

Apparently I must repeat this because it hasn't penetrated your thick skull: Nietzsche does not seek universal acceptance of his convictions; indeed, such acceptance would be the clearest refutation of his thoughts because it would signal their cooptation by the herd. Insofar as the categories of logic demand universal assent they falsify the fluidity and rank order of life.

Nietzsche is simply not, indeed cannot be, interested in providing neat theoretical structures for his convictions. Again, given his broad themes, to do so would be fatal. He knows that he cannot hope to refute mainstream philosophy by employing its own conceptual tools. He is pleased that the minions of the mainstream and the sycophants of academia are unconvinced by his words.

Apollonia: Your response on behalf of Nietzsche is so typical. Talk about banalities! If I disagree with Nietzsche that actually confirms his broadest themes and establishes what he (and you) so arrogantly presuppose: I accept mainstream philosophical argumentation so I must be temperamentally and intellectually deficient. If I point out the puzzles and problems within Nietzsche's thought, then all Nietzscheans rejoice because it shows that he has succeeded in provoking the herd mentality, in unsettling its confidence, and in exposing life's paradoxes. For you Nietzscheans, your guru does not have to resolve paradox and conflict. Instead, he must only raise doubts, manifest contingency, and cast suspicion on the mainstream. To fascinate, provoke, fragment, and deconstruct become the core of the "philosopher of the future"— the philosopher as performative artist.

But aren't the tools of your trade themselves suspicious? You insulate yourselves from criticism by calling it disguised affirmation and by defensively hurling abusive ad hominems freely and thus irresponsibly. You exonerate yourselves from seeking resolutions while taking solace in your self-conferred sense of superiority? You seek attention by tweaking and sputtering, and then dare to impugn the alleged "pretensions to imperialism" of the "absolutist" mainstream. Isn't Nietzsche just the Dennis Rodman of philosophy?

Fegataccio: You, too, do your fair share of what you decry. Your ad hominems may be more disguised, more mendacious, but they are just as real (or just as illusory). Indeed, the adversarial sparring which defines Anglo-American philosophy is little more than combat for physical cowards. Those who would turn up their noses at war, fistfights, and the like, sanctimoniously labeling them "brutish," gleefully engage in verbal disputes that mask their psychological origins by calling themselves "dispassionate pursuits of truth." What a lie! Just as there are bullies, coercive gangs, and physical assaults in schoolyards, there are intellectual equivalents in higher education. And the most vengeful practitioners are found among those analytic philosophers who shroud their motives with high-minded talk. The philosophical arguments of the mainstream are rarely anything more than linguistic power plays of the physically enfeebled. I do not rail against the exercise of these arguments, but only against the motives which support mendacious self-understanding.

Also, notice how you have blatantly falsified Nietzsche's thought by depicting him as a mere deconstructionist. You fail to highlight his main quest: cultural reimagination and re-creation. Of course, style is important for Nietzsche because he sees the link between the writings of the great philosophers and their lives. If he is correct—if all writing is autobiographical in some sense—then we cannot neatly separate evaluations of "form," "content," and "author's rank in the human hierarchy."

You have also falsified Nietzsche's critique of mainstream philosophy. He does not subscribe simply to the proposition, "If X is a mainstream analytic philosopher then X is a mediocre transmitter of the herd mentality." On the contrary, he recognizes a range of motivations which correlate to the rank order of humans.

Apollonia: Well, I obviously disagree with your portrayal of philosophical argument. (Are we engaging in a power play and in combat now?) You are correct, though, about my simplification of Nietzsche. But am I not allowed, in fact encouraged, to do that by some of his own broad themes? Isn't life falsification, simplification, and imposition of order and meaning on chaos? Given that the chaos that is Nietzsche's thought exemplifies the macrocosm, I must make all those nasty conceptual moves according to his own broad themes. Savor the irony: I am truer to Nietzsche in this regard than are you! You want to impose an orthodoxy and fixed meanings on your master. Shame on you!

But I want to return to Nietzsche's lack of a theory of truth, his ensnarlment in the paradox of self-reference, and his view of bivalent logic. How can one make numerous truth claims while simultaneously ignoring theories of truth? Furthermore, how can Nietzsche escape the paradox of self-reference?[13]

Fegataccio: Nietzsche is wary of theories of truth because he suspects the motives and impugns the historical uses which they have served. Theories of truth have been vessels for evading responsibility for our beliefs, social practices, and personal actions. Worse, they are the prime collaborators with dogmatism in nurturing uniformity of belief.[14] Thus, they deny the rank order of life by appealing to universality, objectivity, and impersonal (or supernatural) authority. Moreover, notions of truth obscure the fluidity of the world and the "dynamical importance of ideas as vehicles for promoting and stultifying various forms of life."[15] Nietzsche treats his own ideas as experiments, as transitory, and as robustly conditioned by his historical context. He understands fully that he cannot advocate that everyone should ahistorically abrogate the notion of unconditional truth.[16] The herd mentality, part of which involves wholesale acceptance of unconditional truth generated from supernatural sources, is fine for those who are (inherently?) members of the herd. What Nietzsche resists is the herd mentality's resentful and vengeful claims to universality, its hostile quest to impose itself on everyone forever. If the herd is successful, then the result is widespread mediocrity which minimizes the development of great individuals and cultural breakthroughs. At his core, Nietzsche is more concerned with promoting possibilities for refined ways of life than he is with abstract renderings of allegedly eternal truths.[17]

In general, Nietzsche resists binary logic and dualistic thinking, at least in some sense. He places more faith in different degrees of one underlying phenomenon and different types of people and ways of life. So truth and falsity, for Nietzsche, are not dualisms, but differences of degree; different people, although all possessing the will to power, express their power in different measures of refinement which manifest their various types and specific ways of life. Nietzsche's warm embrace of radical contingency undermines the fixed categories of binary oppositions.

Apollonia: Wait right there! Nietzsche consistently uses just such dualisms: Apollonian/Dionysian, decadent/refined, slave/master moralities, crude/sublimated passions, life-denying/life-affirming, and I could add a dozen more.

Fegataccio: But he uses them in specialized ways. He tries to demonstrate their essential unity, how they emanate from the same fundamental drives, how they serve as reference points on a continuum rather than as true opposites, and how they are and can be used strategically to underwrite different ways of life.

Earlier I said that Nietzsche resists binary logic and dualistic thinking *in some sense.* What I was holding open is that he accepts them in another sense, as historically indispensable to the project of ordering and imposing meaning on the world of flux. Although he is suspicious of the motives supporting their self-understanding as ahistorically privileged categories, he nevertheless recognizes the historical role they have played in facilitating certain human ends.[18] As always, though, Nietzsche calls into question the origins of our categories of logic and examines their relationship to the paramount projects of reimagination and re-creation.[19]

Apollonia: While I appreciate your reversion back to a professional tone, Fegataccio, your musings on behalf of Nietzsche hardly satisfy my original points. To make a vague attack on binary logic and dualistic thinking, accompanied by an equally vague reminder that Nietzsche's—as is typical—reverses his attack to some degree, combined with reminders of Nietzsche's suspicions of the origins and motives of the notion of truth, cannot evade charges of self-referential paradox.

Fegataccio: Again, I must point out that you will inevitably have an advantage in this part of our discussion. I am accepting your categories for the moment, but only for the sake of argument, and will try to formulate possible resolutions in those terms on behalf of Nietzsche. By trying to discuss Nietzsche's thought within your language game, I immediately assume a probably insurmountable disadvantage. But I'll give it a try, actually several tries, because I am not sure which of these strategies, if any, will appeal to you.

Perhaps I can evade the problem of self-reference by restricting the domain of perspectivism. If perspectivism applies only to first-order specific theories about the world and not to second-order metatheories about first-order theories (e.g., perspectivism itself), then the self-referential paradox evaporates.[20] Thus, the proper scope restrictor can salvage perspectivism even within the confines of your language and logic categories.

Apollonia: But that seems ad hoc to me, an afterthought for a special purpose. You would be saying that as a metatheory perspectivism is true absolutely, which implies that it could still deny any unconditional claims of first-order worldviews. But what vantage point permits such a move? Can you access any ground, other than wishful thinking, that would allow you to make that distinction while remaining loyal to Nietzsche's broad themes?

Fegataccio: I must admit that the efforts I'll make to answer your question may not reflect any intentions of Nietzsche. Frankly, I think in some sense he thought it was sufficient merely to admit the conditionality of his own views: to accept the contingent perspectivism of his perspectivism, to highlight the inevitability of conceptual conflict in human thought, and to underscore the experimentalism of his own thought. These thoughts would be amicable with, indeed they partly constitute, Nietzsche's broad themes. But from within your logical categories I suspect they inadequately finesse the paradox.

But remember that Nietzsche does not completely reject logic and reason. In fact, his own thought, as it must, embodies patterns; a logic of deconstruction, reversal, and rehabilitation; and appreciation of the historical role of mainstream rhetoric. What he objects to is the dogmatism of first-order worldviews. I'm not sure Nietzsche needs to "access [special] ground" to restrict his perspectivism, as I have suggested. He would not necessarily be asserting that perspectivism as a second-order metatheory *was* absolutely true, only that it could possibly be absolutely true. Such a stance would preserve the core of his broad themes yet permit him to sidestep the paradox of self-reference.

Apollonia: I think we have both lost our bravado and have reached common ground: mutual uncertainty. The move still seems blatantly ad hoc to me, with the potential to undermine Nietzsche's view (or the view you have imposed on him for argument's sake) on perspectivism as critique of the unconditional claims of first-order worldviews. Let me put it this way: If perspectivism as a second-order metatheory could be absolutely true, then why can't (some? most? or all?) of the claims of particular first-order worldviews possibly be absolutely true? I grant that if perspectivism is absolutely true as a second-order metatheory then the claims of first-order worldviews could not be absolutely true, but then I would relodge my inquiry about the vantage point from which the absolute truth of the metatheory could be made (consistent with Nietzsche's broad themes). But if you finesse my original complaint by resorting to the mere possibility of perspectivism being absolutely true as a second-order metatheory, then I suspect that I can resuscitate the possibility of the absolute truth of at least some first-order worldviews. Unless and until we could resolve the respective possibilities, Nietzscheans and mainstreamers might be left with a rhetorical stalemate.

Fegataccio: I am not so sure the stalemate, if we are indeed left with it, is fatal to Nietzsche. I would recharacterize it as a tacit recognition of contingency: We would never "resolve" the situation you describe, and the ebb and flow of mutual possibilities might manifest the rank order of life. Remember, Nietzsche does not want us all to think and act alike, and does not desire universal acceptance of his thought. In fact, I can put the matter more strongly: He does not want *any* abject disciples! We must overcome not only ourselves and our cultural inheritance (to the extent possible), but also Nietzsche's own thought. The notion of self-overcoming may well be the quasi-foundational foil that binds Nietzsche's broad themes together.

But let me try a slightly different move. I'll begin by pointing out that all philosophies and perspectives necessarily depend on presuppositions. Nietzsche's perspectivism, as a second-order metatheory, revels in the rank order of life. It denies that we can measure all people by a single scale, and it denies the neutrality of first-order perspectives.[21]

Apollonia: The metaphor of "self-overcoming" seems strained. Have I "overcome" Nietzsche's thought? I have never believed much of it. The crux of your claim, which is advanced by Alexander Nehamas, is that perspectivism does not claim that every view is necessarily an interpretation and thus perspectivism cannot be disproved by showing that it is possible that some views are not interpretations. Such a showing suggests only that perspectivism is possibly false, not that perspectivism is false. Thus, to disprove perspectivism one would have to show that some views are not in fact interpretations, not merely that it is possible that some views are not interpretations.[22]

If Nietzsche—or, more accurately, you on Nietzsche's behalf—insists that perspectivism is actually true (first-order belief) although it may possibly be untrue (second-order belief), I don't see how that helps him. That puts us right back where we were quite a while back: What standard permits Nietzsche to make such a claim? Isn't he just begging the question? Aren't we back to Copleston's fundamental criticism and my suspicions regarding the relationship between first- and second-order beliefs? I think Nehamas's argument provides nothing new. It only puts our previous discussion in explicitly modal terms.

Fegataccio: I'll leave self-overcoming for another day, but I think the argument does emphasize important aspects of our discussion. First, it may well be critics such as yourself who are begging the question by implicitly viewing perspectival interpretation as an ersatz form of understanding. Second, while perspectivism cannot compel its own acceptance under this argument, that correlates well with Nietzsche's denial of dogmatism, his refusal to seek universal agreement, and his constant reminder that different interpretations of the world flow from different kinds of people.

I concede straightaway, in concert with Nietzsche's broad themes, that I cannot convince everyone (that is, there is no neutral method antecedently binding on all) and that Nietzsche's perspectivism escapes self-referential paradox. To think otherwise is to reinstate dogmatism. All I can do is cast suspicion on the beliefs of those who insist that Nietzsche's perspectivism is clearly refuted by self-referential paradox. I can call into question their motives. I can undermine the genealogy and the value of the life forms partially generated by their foundational beliefs. Or I can do what I am doing now: I can enter the favored categories and language games of the critics and make the case that their proofs fail. I cannot, however, within those categories and language games, prove that Nietzsche's perspectivism is untouched by self-referential paradox or that perspectivism must be accepted.

Apollonia: There is something about the laws of thought that strikes me as purely formal and necessary. Why aren't they "neutral"? They do not inherently recommend any particular form of law. While their origins *may* lie in the human need to impose order and meaning, that correlates with Nietzsche's broad themes. Why do you keep referring to them as my "language game" or as mainstream "categories?"

Fegataccio: From a Nietzschean perspective, the laws of thought and formal logic are particular ways of carving up the world. They may be "necessary" for us, but only given the people we are and the historical legacy we have inherited. While they do not, say, imply any particular moral or political structure—they aren't part of a democratic conspiracy or a communist plot—their binary and dualistic prejudices may well nurture dogmatism and artificially limit possibilities. If there are numerous possible ways to categorize the world of flux, then the structures of bivalent logic are themselves only one among many possibilities. Thus, their claims to ahistorical necessity would be false.

Within your own mainstream there are multivalent logics which deny the necessity and practical viability of binary oppositions. Multivalent logics see the world as ambiguous and filled with conflicts. They take "paradoxes of self-reference [to be] *half-truths*. Fuzzy contradictions. A AND not-A holds but A is true only 50% and not-A is true only 50%. The paradoxes are literally half true and half false. They reside at midpoints of fuzzy cubes, equidistant from the black-and-white corners."[23] Much Eastern thought, for example, sees the world filled "with things and not-things, with roses that are both red and not red, with A AND not-A."[24] Multivalent logics hold that the proof techniques of binary logic falsify the world. More important, such logics have proved superior to binary logics in a host of practical contexts.[25] So in what way are the standard Western "categories of thought" ahistorically necessary? Certainly, robust ways of life have been formed without them.

Apollonia: I think they are presupposed in our discourse and that you (and Nietzsche) must depend on them even to mock them. I also think that "fuzzy logics" must depend on the standard categories of thought to make their probabilistic claims.

Fegataccio: It may seem that way, but only because Nietzsche and I need to make ourselves intelligible in standard discourse to communicate with mainstreamers. Nietzsche realizes that changing the paradigms of philosophical discourse requires the positing of new criteria and new presuppositions, but he also knows he cannot escape from all elements of established paradigms. Indeed, these paradigms form the context from which Nietzsche critiques and from which (at least to some extent) he will be evaluated. Perhaps Nietzsche's pattern of deconstruction, reversal, and re-creation is tacit admission of all this. However, Nietzsche's project is fundamentally practical, not theoretical; it concerns action not reflection.[26]

Your criticism is better directed at my clumsy explanations than at Nietzsche's own work. On Nietzsche's behalf, I would make three points. First, the brunt of his suspicion is cast at bivalent logic, not all logic. For example, Nietzsche wonders "what forces us at all to suppose that there is an essential opposition of 'true' and 'false'? Is it not sufficient to assume degrees of apparentness and, as it were, lighter and darker shadows and shades of appearance—different 'values,' to use the language of painters? . . . Shouldn't philosophers be permitted to rise above faith in grammar?" (*BGE* 34).

Second, he retains some appreciation for even bivalent logic as a means of ordering the inherent chaos that is the cosmos. Third, although Nietzsche is suspicious of the way bivalent logic can lure us into accepting Platonic realism, he takes (multivalent?) logic to be a presupposition of thought and perhaps of life. Thus, Nietzsche does not wage a wholesale assault on logic as such but, typically, only against certain effects and second-order beliefs encouraged by a particular form of logic. And, again typically, he tries to unsettle those effects and second-order beliefs because of the ersatz attitudes toward life they allegedly nurture.

Apollonia: At times I think your pattern is one of strident critique, followed by retreat (after I have pointed out the extremes in your view), followed by apologies for Nietzsche! By the way, do you have any more to offer on the self-referential paradox?

Fegataccio: There are numerous ways of trying to confront the paradox, of trying to undermine its imperialism, and of trying to soften its effects and appeal without disproving its applicability. The force of the self-referential paradox depends on a dogmatic acceptance of bivalent logic and an interpretation of perspectivism that forces it to make the claim that every assertion bears a truth value that is perspective-specific. I have tried to cast some suspicion on the claims of bivalent logic to ahistorical necessity. Let me now make a move in the other direction.

One might claim, on behalf of Nietzscheans, that while virtually all assertions bear truth values that are perspective-specific, a few assertions bear the same truth values in all human perspectives.[27] This version of perspectivism may evade self-referential paradox because a statement of its own truth may be one of those few assertions that is true in all human perspectives. In fact, this version of perspectivism can claim that the only assertions that are true in all human perspectives are assertions about perspectivism's own truth and whatever else Nietzsche requires as a quasi-foundation for his philosophy—his broad themes and the presuppositions required to assert his broad themes.

The beauty of this move is that it neither reinstates absolutism nor seriously compromises Nietzsche's broad themes of radical contingency and self-overcoming. We could view the convergence of truth claims across all human perspectives as historically but not ahistorically necessary. In other words, perspectivism itself is not objectively true in the sense of being embedded in nature or of being decreed by a nonhuman legislator of truth. Instead, it could be viewed as merely historically necessary given the peoples now inhabiting the earth and the modes of life they have constructed. Such a view would permit Nietzsche to retain the falliblism of second-order beliefs while strategizing in mainstream language games.

Let me repeat: I do not claim that Nietzsche himself would make this move. In fact, I think, given his practical orientation, that he would not be troubled much by the paradox of self-reference.

Apollonia: I don't see this as a new exciting response. It strikes me as a repackaged version of the same old tired ad hoc strategy you used earlier: Exempt Nietzsche's assertions about the truth of perspectivism itself from perspectivism's own critical bite.

What basis would you have for selecting your favored few across-perspectives truths? From distinguishing truths that are and are not perspective-specific? The only ground you suggest is Nietzsche's desperate need to exempt some of his assertions in order to evade a self-referential paradox. Since when is "desperate need" a sound criterion of categorization?

Furthermore, your latest effort looks like an inverted Nehamas move, so I'll make a Nehamas-inspired response: It is not enough to claim that perspectivism itself, Nietzsche's broad themes, and the presuppositions needed to make those broad themes may be across-perspectives truths. You need to demonstrate in an independent fashion that they are across-perspectives truths. The mere claimed possibility that these favored few assertions are across-perspectives truths is insufficient to evade the lingering presence of self-referential paradox.

And how could you possibly establish independently that your favored assertions are across-perspectives truths? Surely, you cannot appeal to cross-cultural descriptions of actual perspectives, for that would undermine your strategy. Such an appeal would show that virtually all actual "perspectives" in the world take themselves to be objective or ahistorically necessary, not contingent, historical, perspectival renderings.

Finally, your attempt to savage the falliblism of second-order beliefs may well impinge on the efficacy of the distinction between the truth-specificity of "virtually all" assertions and the across-perspectives truth of your favored "few" assertions.

Fegataccio: You keep trying to get me into your language and logic games more deeply. Remember, I am not trying to prove that Nietzsche's views can be interpreted in a way that escapes the claws of the prized strategy of bivalent logic, the self-referential paradox. I am only trying to loosen its grip and soften its pressure. In fact, to prove that perspectivism is immune from the paradox would be untrue to Nietzsche's broad themes. Accordingly, any criticisms from mainstreamers that "demonstrate" my inability to prove what I do not intend to prove are misguided.

Moreover, the self-understandings—the dogmatism and absolutism—of numerous perspectives refer to their second-order beliefs. My offering on behalf of Nietzschean perspectivism concerns first-order perspectives themselves. Obviously, I would never refer to the actual self-under-standings of extant perspectives as evidence for my interpretation. Most of Nietzsche's work calls those self-understandings into question as its fundamental project.

A key distinction under my interpretation is "between something being true *in all* [human] perspectives and something being true *out-side of all* perspectives."[28] Nietzsche must deny the latter because it is an implication of his anti-metaphysical position: his rejection of things-in-themselves, divine legislators, inherent order in the universe, and neutral vantage points. Nietzsche, if I am correct, can accept the former because it is compatible with his broad themes. Thus, across-perspectives truths have no special metaphysical status, even though they are true in all human perspectives. There would remain, for Nietzscheans, no extra-perspectival truths.

Remember, for Nietzsche, perspectives are action-guiding, life-molding, evaluative understandings of a world of undetermined flux. The world becomes a product of perspectival interpretations. I have self-consciously, for the sake of argument, overly unified and simpli-fied Nietzsche's notions of truth.

Apollonia: Be careful how you link perspectivism and life. As a sec-ond-order belief about the status of our first-order beliefs, perspectivism does not entail any particular moral or political views. Thus, while perspectives may connect to different ways of life, perspectivism itself does not.

You dance quite well, Fegataccio. But hand waving and two-stepping don't satisfy me. All your words amount to is a claim that there is an ad hoc move available to Nietzsche—something he can say but not dem-onstrate—that holds out the possibility that his perspectivism is not fatally harmed by self-referential paradox. You add to this the alleged compatibility of the ad hoc move with Nietzsche's broad themes. But it seems to me that your ad hoc move is not obviously compatible with Nietzsche's broad themes. Isn't your move redolent with what Nie-tzsche would take to be the stench of absolutism and dogmatism?

Fegataccio: If so, I don't think it is a dangerous sort of dogmatism. The dangerous kind of dogmatism takes what is good for some peoples at some times as metaphysically mandatory for all peoples at all times. My strategy is compatible with a contingent historical convergence of all hu-man perspectives. But this holds open the possibility of new human

types and new human contexts whose perspectives would not con-
verge with the established across-perspectives truths. This possibility
preserves and highlights Nietzsche's broad theme of self-overcoming.
Thus, the "dogmatism" that you detect is benign; it neither depends
on accepting metaphysical foundations nor posits timeless truths.
Nietzscheans could therefore retain their second-order belief in
falliblism.

Although Nietzsche attacks the metaphysician's search for foundational truths as revealing moral weakness and fear of contingency, he
also praises intellectual rigor as a refusal to accept received opinion
unquestioningly. He subscribes wholeheartedly to the critical impulses
of the will to truth, but rejects its yearning for eternal foundational
grounds. His point is that the critical impulses of the will to truth undermine acceptance of the foundationalists' quest. Thus, the will to
truth, when understood honestly, must conclude against one of its own
aspirations: foundationalism.

Apollonia: But my main point lingers: Your suggestion is ad hoc and
insufficient to escape the force of the self-referential paradox. Of course,
you will agree to this and reverse it, using my remark to illustrate one
of Nietzsche's broad themes or to underscore one of your aspirations
on behalf of Nietzsche. So I won't press the point any further.

But I want to return to your second-order belief in falliblism. Isn't it
disingenuous? Don't you just trot it out when it is convenient—when
you are criticized my mainstream philosophers—as a way of softening
the attack? Don't Nietzscheans, especially, announce their conclusions
in the strongest terms? Don't they act as if their pronouncements are
dew drops of wisdom cascading from the mountaintop of Eternal Truth?
Isn't second-order falliblism a disguise, a sham?

Fegataccio: The core of Nietzschean perspectivism is not any specific conglomerate of views and evaluations, but the broad theme that
numerous clusters of views and evaluations are possible and apt for
different peoples. Although, for the sake of argument, I have been presenting Nietzschean themes in simplified rigid form, he understood
that he could not describe, advance, and defend his views in the standard manner. We have talked constantly about Nietzsche or
Nietzscheans "asserting" this or that; we have suffocated Nietzsche's
thought by divorcing it from his literary style and by artificially forc-
ing it into propositional form. Our dialogue is an ersatz imitation of
Nietzsche's thought that too often fails to highlight another one of his
broad themes: He must exemplify rather than assert his views and
evaluations. He must embody them and manifest to others—but only
a few others—their possibilities for facilitating new modes of life. Readers must then ask themselves, "What type of person do I want to become?" and "Am I able to become such a person?"[29]

Again, I must underscore a few of the broad themes that you and I have obscured: Nietzsche understands that perspectivism cannot be proved, he does not and cannot claim that all others are required by reason to embrace it, he gives psychological explanations of why some people are attracted to perspectivism while others are not, and he pitches his presentation to rare, superior types who can become legislators, not merely reflectors, of values.

Apollonia: Your remarks are useful for understanding why you and I must differ. But I hope you understand why, from my perspective (pun intended), I am repelled by the themes you just adumbrated. The self-conscious acceptance of the inability to prove one's thesis encourages self-indulgence and wrongly turns nonrigorous speculation and rhetorical excesses into virtues. The psychological accounts and explicit appeals to "aristocratic" audiences reek of elitism and nurture ad hominem attacks: If you don't agree with me, if you aren't attracted to my views, then you must be a lowly herd animal. The call to legislate new values from the "abundance of one's life" risks degenerating into reliance upon force: might makes right.

Fegataccio: Life *is* a series of risks. I suspect that unscrupulous types, wrongly supposing themselves to be a higher breed, may wrongly try to invoke Nietzsche's work as an imprimatur for their indefensible aspirations. Indeed, history shows this can occur.

But surely you don't assume that the pet tricks of philosophers and logicians can honestly transcend such risks. What those masters of illusion are more likely to do is to conceal the origins and purposes of their work and to deny the autobiographical elements of their thoughts. But in their more sober moments they understand that even our most useful scientific theories are underdetermined by the evidence and that the evidence itself is not pure: It is "infected" by our theories; our language cannot reflect reality but instead manifests our interests, purposes, desires, and power; and the rules of rationality themselves cannot be independently justified because they themselves determine what should count as a good reason or a sound justification. Thus, what theories we prefer is mainly a function of interests and powers, and what theories prevail in a society is mainly a function of what groups have the most power to instantiate their interests.

All this is lost, however, when we accept the illusions you cling to so frightfully: the objectivity of knowledge; the ahistorical understanding of reason and institutions; the refusal to examine the genealogy—the history—of how things, including standards of reason, became as they are; the disinclination to see power for what it is; and the inclination to mask the role of social conflict in establishing truths.

I am not bemoaning the phenomena I described. On the contrary, Nietzscheans aspire to embrace life fully and eliminate much of the sham and pretense, to live life fully without appeal to absolute truths, and to see life for what it is and live it honestly.

Apollonia: It seems to me that you Nietzscheans are a bit deceived about your own motives and the genealogy of your own views. Don't you tacitly yearn for metaphysical certainty and transcendental standards, but when such certainty and standards cannot be independently established conclude there is only nihilism? You detect limitations and fragility in the mainstream criteria of logic, language, and morality, and then conclude radical indeterminacy and contingency are all-pervasive. At bottom you accept the polarities of either metaphysical realism (the view that numerous truths about the world are mind-independent: embedded in the universe and discoverable by human reason) or radical contingency (the view that there are many incommensurable, conflicting paradigms, theories, and life forms). These polarities, however, exude vitality only if we share the conviction that the two alternatives define the range of possibilities. I think that those who share that conviction are unwitting collaborators in the same discourse, not true adversaries. Furthermore, I think that Nietzscheans are therefore closet metaphysical realists who have merely lost their faith.

Fegataccio: I must admit there is something in what you say. But you wrongly fail to distinguish Nietzsche from the run-of-the-mill apostle of radical contingency. He never stops at "either metaphysical realism or radical contingency." He exemplifies how the philosophers of the future, as legislators of values, can overcome the nihilistic moment and use radical contingency for practical advantages. His view can be better described as metaphysical realism or radical contingency or recurrent deconstruction–reimagination–reinvention. Moreover, different types of humans will embrace different "solutions" to the problem of human life: The herd will still cling to versions of metaphysical realism, the severely alienated will wallow in nihilism and be overwhelmed by radical contingency, and the higher types will gratefully luxuriate in deconstruction–reimagination–reinvention.

Apollonia: Aren't you confusing how one will or should practically respond to the metaphysical realism–radical contingency polarity with the alternatives of the polarity themselves? Perhaps Nietzsche tacks on a different way to respond to radical contingency, but that does not negate my point that he still accepts the basic terms of the polarity itself. He still tacitly thinks that undermining metaphysical realism leads directly and inexorably to radical contingency.

Fegataccio: I suppose within the confines of your favorite logical categories you score a point. But remember, Nietzsche does not separate theoretical and practical concerns so neatly.[30] Jaspers, for example, emphasizes the fluidity of truth for Nietzsche, how even what we are saying now about what is true must itself evaporate. He also underscores the connection between theoretical knowledge and practical action and how one's theoretical commitments can vivify one's lifestyle. He explains how Nietzsche's thoughts on truth seem to conflict because, in your terms, they struggle with self-referential paradox.[31]

Again, we see the recurrent need to overcome forms of truth in the service of creating new possibilities for life. Also, philosophers of the future must overcome the "spirit of gravity" whose unbearable heaviness threatens to keep us rooted in familiar contexts and institutions: "To Nietzsche laughter is an expression of this truth that cannot be communicated. . . . The rank of a philosopher is determined by the rank of his laughter."[32]

Apollonia: Jaspers projects his own existential philosophy onto Nietzsche's thought, it seems to me. But I think we return—and don't we always return—to the same old impasse of our different presuppositions and categories. I am surprised, however, that you did not use the Jasper quotes as a springboard for another didactic discourse on Nietzsche's literary styles, multiplicity of impulses, and musings on language.

Fegataccio: I'll take that as an invitation! With regard to language, Nietzsche warns us of its inherent function to mislead, to present itself as mirroring reality while in fact it partially constitutes a way humans have imposed meaning and order on the world of Becoming. Because of the limitations of language, truth and reality itself must remain ineffable. As we impose seemingly fixed categories and doctrines, we simplify and falsify. None of this is horrifying, it is just part of the human condition.

Nietzsche's conception of language fits well with his general understanding of theories and doctrines. Instead of asking what features in the world make a doctrine true, he asks what types of needs, interests, desires, and distribution of powers exist (or must be created) to underwrite the doctrine. Thus, Nietzsche ties in theory with modes of life. And that is why he thinks we cannot distinguish thinkers from their thought. All writing is autobiographical because philosophy must be lived prior to being disseminated, it must be exemplified instead of being aridly taught. Because there are numerous human types and numerous modes of life, Nietzsche refuses to subscribe to second-order dogmatism and absolutism.

Apollonia: Let me repeat yet another time: I don't see from what vantage point Nietzsche can confidently make such claims given his own perspectivism. But by now I know what your response will be, so please spare me the rehash!

I find the point about autobiography and philosophy interesting. For years I've thought that book reviews, especially in philosophy, reveal more about the psychology of the reviewers than about the books being evaluated. I'd bet that a good psychologist could sketch quite accurate profiles of reviewers from five or six of their reviews. I hadn't made the wider connection between one's philosophical writings and one's psychology, but as I ponder it now there is a lot to it. In fact, the point seems obvious. How much one tolerates ambiguity, how community minded or individualistic one is, what elements most fully constitute one's sense of identity, one's personal and familiar history—how could these not greatly affect, perhaps even determine, a philosopher's acceptance or rejection of various philosophical positions that embody various images of these influences?

So you can call me a Nietzschean on this small point. But remember, I would still separate the reasons one might accept a position from the underlying truth of that position.

Fegataccio: But we can't oversimplify all this. We are making it sound as if univocal, transparent psychological profiles of authors can be easily extracted from perusing a few pieces of their work.[33] Nietzsche celebrates the multiplicity of drives that constitute humans. Profound spirits do not deny their inner conflicts or seek solace in the homogenizing labors of mainstream analytic philosophy which disguises then renounces the contradictions partially constituting the human condition. Instead, Nietzsche sees the quest for fixed unambiguous doctrines, social practices, and values as decadent and as symptoms of decline.

Apollonia: Yes, I've heard these paeans to Nietzschean multiplicity before. They make a terrific excuse for unrigorous thought and a wonderful self-serving exoneration from the self-referential paradox. Even I must admire the sheer arrogance of viewing Nietzsche's own contradictions and obscurantism as indicators of the "truth" of his general philosophical themes, all in the name of sophisticated irony!

Fegataccio: Well, we do seem to be continually going around in circles, Apollonia. And I feel a bit embarrassed about this entire exercise: I have been an accomplice in the oversimplification of Nietzsche's thought. In order to indulge ourselves in your favorite type of adversarial discourse, we have had to impose some seemingly fixed meanings, theories, and doctrines on Nietzsche thought. In the name of the spirit of gravity, we have destroyed his invigorating fluidity and sense of life. I must advise you to read his work rather than relying on our conspiracy to domesticate his thought. As you read and interpret Nietzsche, you may find that what he says resonates with your experiences more than you might suppose.

Apollonia: You sound as if you think we have reached the end of the line on our discourse on Nietzschean perspectivism. Not so fast! My mainstreamer's need for philosophical closure has not been satisfied.

I am struck by how Nietzscheans are constrained by language, how you cannot truly articulate your perspectivism coherently from within the confines of our language. As such, Nietzsche cannot avoid sounding, at times, as if he is an absolutist and dogmatist. Even using parables, aphorisms, narratives, and the like will be of only temporary help because, after years of interpretive commentary, they will also assume a range of conventional meanings. At least part of the self-referential paradox must involve the limitations of our language. And, believe it or not, although I am not a Nietzschean I am also not simpleminded enough to think that language mirrors Reality in a pure way.

Fegataccio: I'm happy to hear you coming around to my view. All cultural critics face the puzzle of trying to undermine established institutions and practices from within the confines of those very structures. While most structures contain the seeds of their own destruction, it is still often difficult to articulate radical switches of worldviews in ways acceptable to the established paradigms.

Apollonia: I am not coming around to your view. I don't think everything Nietzsche said was wrong: Even a blind squirrel finds an acorn occasionally!

My purpose, however, is wider. I want to sketch five aspects of our language that reveal themselves in argument. Call them "rhetorical strategies," "modes of thought," or "dialectical categories," I don't care. My claim is that if you track philosophical arguments you will see these dialectical categories employed to different degrees by the interlocutors. The participants will be most deeply engaged when they both speak from the same category or from similar categories. The participants will experience their deepest mutual frustrations and gravest sense of incommensurability when they speak from dissimilar categories.[34]

Fegataccio: I'll hear you out, but I prefer the term "rhetorical strategies." That term has an aura of Nietzschean fluidity about it. So, what are the five rhetorical strategies?

Apollonia: I'll call the first the analytic strategy, my favorite. This is the strategy of classical logic and argumentation: deductive, inductive, analogical, and practical. The validity and soundness of argument are adjudicated by universal laws of reason, while intellectual inconsistency, ignorance, and falsity are understood as the primary adversaries of truth. The analytic strategy has much confidence in theoretical explanations and, often, justifications of established social doctrines and practices. This strategy self-consciously embodies what you sneer at as a second-order dogmatic belief.

Although Nietzscheans distrust this strategy deeply, they must still at times use it to try to articulate and defend their own beliefs. At those times, Nietzscheans run their greatest risks. As you admit, they sound a bit like dogmatists themselves, their thoughts seem fixed and doctrinal, and their avowed fluidity and radical contingency are momentarily arrested. And as I said earlier, the use of parables and aphorisms as forms of expression ameliorates but cannot escape this problem.

Fegataccio: Certainly, Nietzsche must have recognized this at some level. If so, that would explain his need to exemplify much more than articulate his thought, his recognition that your logical categories are in some sense indispensable, and his occasional reversal of his own historicism.[35]

Apollonia: Perhaps, but I want to move on to the second rhetorical strategy, the intuitive. I think we have both noticed how participants in normative and epistemological debate, when pressed thoroughly, must resort to "primitives": self-evident principles, undefended axioms, and allegedly universal practices as the foundations of their theories. These are appeals to intuitions which, at bottom, rest on the authority of tradition, faith, or social conventions. Such appeals cannot interrogate their own starting points, but, instead, accept the facticity or givenness of established methodologies, privileged texts, and institutional practices.

Fegataccio: I take it that you are not positing a special faculty of the intellect called "intuition," but, instead, use the term to cover a hodgepodge of dimly understood ways through which we arrive at worldviews. These ways typically have a deep social genesis and can include psychological conversions and gestalt switches.

Apollonia: I surely am not relying on any unique faculty of mind, but I am not sure your description is quite accurate. We can have intuitions on relatively small matters that need not implicate an entire worldview. Also, I doubt whether all intuitions have a "deep social genesis," but you did say "typically," so we probably have no real argument on this issue.

Let me push on to the third rhetorical strategy, the pragmatic. This strategy typically celebrates community and conversation and is skeptical of totalizing schemes and critiques. It often attacks the analytic rhetorical strategy for its dualism and proclivity to freeze fluid distinctions into inflexible polarities. The pragmatic strategy champions the flux and pluralism of social life and opposes the projects of foundationalists. Furthermore, the pragmatic strategy privileges falliblism and marginalizes the solitary reasoner as well as ideal reasoning situations.

Fegataccio: Surely the notions of pluralism, falliblism, fluidity, antisystematization, and antifoundationalism are amicable to Nietzsche's thought. And that is why some commentators conclude that Nietzsche was a pragmatist. Nietzsche was, of course, interested in ideas and perspectives as instruments for achieving various purposes. But, clearly, Nietzsche did not subscribe to the pragmatic theory of truth that a proposition is true if and only if it is useful or works in some sense. The term "pragmatist" has so many related meanings in the literature that even savvy commentators sometimes get confused.

Moreover, it is also clear that Nietzsche does not fully accept the pragmatic rhetorical strategy. He would suspect that "community" and "conversation" could easily degenerate into the herd mentality. Nietzsche, however, would embrace community and conversation among higher human types as prerequisites for higher cultures. Also, I think he would have more appreciation for solitary reasoners, at least those of the proper type, than the pragmatic strategy suggests.

Apollonia: You are making my point. Nietzsche did not employ only one of these rhetorical strategies, he employed all of them to different degrees. And most thinkers use at least several, I think. But I'll return to this point later.

Fegataccio: Exactly! Notice how that fact conforms to Nietzsche's broad theme of multiplicity of drives and conflicting passions.

Apollonia: Oh, brother, I set you up for that didn't I? Let me push on. The fourth rhetoric strategy is the substructuralist. This strategy posits nonrational, often total, explanations for choices of social practices, perspectives, and settled doctrine. The substructural strategy does not take the claims of reason at face value. It highlights experience and practice, while devaluing the primacy of reason.

Here are a few examples of substructural strategies: Marx's reliance on contradictions among the forces and relations of production as the engine of social change, Weber's understanding of bureaucratic organization, and Freud's reliance on the unconscious. Recall Marx's claim that the economic base gives rise to an ideological superstructure that serves to "legitimate" the base from which it arose. Here we can see the core of a substructuralist strategy, a critique of capitalist arrangements as a viciously circular process of legitimation which mirrors underlying reality (actual economic conditions) in a false fashion (as ideology which unconsciously masks its own origins and presents itself as independent justification).

Fegataccio: I suppose Nietzsche's reliance on will to power, which I hope we can discuss sometime, can be viewed as a substructural rhetorical strategy.

Apollonia: I would think so. Finally, we have the most notorious rhetorical strategy: the deconstructive. This strategy seems closely connected with style. It often deliberately offends and irritates mainstream sensibilities as it strives to advance the "unpresentable" in the "presentation" itself. The deconstructive strategy often seems to be deliberately mocking the pretensions of other strategies while advocating an anything-goes form. It opposes all totalizing ambitions and purposefully breaks the rules of ordinary discourse. The deconstructive strategy rejects the quest for a universal audience and common ground and, instead, celebrates the irony of difference, discontinuity, and disjuncture.

Fegataccio: We can discern some of this in Nietzsche's literary styles, in his joy at irony, in his rejection of a universal audience, and in his glee at pushing over tottering mainstream structures. Perhaps we can now account for those critics who wrongly see Nietzsche as an apostle of nihilism: They have been lured to this view by their preoccupation with his use of the deconstructive rhetorical strategy and by their failure to attend sufficiently to his frequent uses of the other strategies.

Apollonia: You may have something there, but I want to draw some morals from my story. Although it is possible for incommensurability to arise between participants speaking in the same rhetorical strategy and for engagement to occur between participants using different strategies, incommensurability typically arises when speakers are using significantly different strategies.

Speakers shift among the different strategies. Rarely does any theorist speak systematically from one rhetorical strategy. Perhaps those who speak from within the analytic strategy come closest to achieving complete consistency because that strategy is clearly dominant. But even from those speaking predominantly from within the analytic strategy we will almost always find invocations of the intuitive and pragmatic modes.

Fegataccio: This may account for the impasses between Nietzscheans and analytic philosophers. For example, analytics often assume that in order for Nietzscheans to advance valid claims they must project the same kinds of interpretive and theoretical presupposition as those projected by analytics. If a Nietzschean is trying to assert (or exemplify) substructural claims, the force of his or her position will be obscured by an analytic philosopher's reformulation of those claims as analytic, a reformulation which itself depends on an intuitive strategy. An analytic philosopher's assumption that all valid claims flow from the analytic is itself an implicit reliance on an intuitive commitment which privileges that philosopher's own intellectual sources.

Apollonia: We must be careful to remind ourselves that we are not doing anything illicit, illogical, or even undesirable as we shift among rhetorical strategies. To different degrees we all tend to use whatever cognitive and rhetorical tools are available to address the instant problem. Rhetorical shifts constitute a clash of paradigms of discourse which may itself be healthy and progressive. There is a certain irony in all this: The extent and degree of rhetorical shifting often results in more immediate incommensurability but long-term testing and progress of discourse as the various rhetorical modes refine themselves.

Fegataccio: But my Nietzschean impulses must insist that this is not to say that we will ever reach the point of everlasting equilibrium, where rhetorical shifting ceases and discourse stabilizes once and forever. This observation should not alarm: Because of audience fragmentation, it is highly unlikely that any system of discourse can guarantee communicative transparency.

I can put another Nietzschean gloss on your sketch of rhetorical strategies. Perhaps we can reconceive theoretical debates as the relentless, often incommensurable competition of rhetorical strategies. That would fit in wonderfully with Nietzsche's general themes!

Apollonia: Don't get carried away with yourself or with Nietzsche. The analytic mode is unquestionably the dominant strategy of discourse, in philosophy and generally. It often successfully domesticates and assimilates the apparent insights of the other strategies. I take this to be a socially necessary hygienic which mediates the dissonance in our life and language.

Fegataccio: My take is much different. In my judgment, the analytic strategy remains supreme by coopting and reformulating the potentially unsettling effects of the other strategies. I regard this as a politically pernicious effect of the intellectual rule of certain types of philosophers.

Apollonia: I suppose that flows from your intuitive privileging of certain of these rhetorical strategies over others, a particular rank ordering to which I do not subscribe. Regarding the politics of the matter, while rhetorical strategies, of themselves, may not seem to have any necessary political implications, they do have a few tenuous contingent connections. Political centrists will most frequently employ analytic and pragmatic strategies, conservatives will most frequently employ intuitive and analytic strategies, and leftists will most frequently employ substructural and deconstructive strategies. Again, these are generalities which admit significant variation.

Fegataccio: I am shocked by your analysis of rhetoric strategies. I think it shows you have a bit of Nietzschean flair after all! More important, I think it can aid in understanding our own discourse on perspectivism and the self-referential paradox. Wouldn't it be great to go back and analyze our discussion, to see when and why we each used particular rhetorical strategies, to discover when we slyly reformulated claims from one strategy to another strategy because it served our purposes, to pinpoint moments of incommensurability and engagement, to figure out why those moments occurred, and to see if the account of rhetorical strategies can provide a common understanding of the sources of our disagreements in fundamental convictions and worldviews?

Apollonia: Fegataccio, I thought I was supposed to be the pedant! Our discourse has been exhausting enough. Let's leave the deeper scholarship for another time.

With this, Apollonia and Fegataccio left the table. Apollonia strode quickly toward a major sporting-goods store that was advertising a once-in-a-lifetime sale, while Fegataccio heard the numbers five, six, eight, and ten buzzing in his head.

Chapter 2

MADMEN, JESTERS, AND WANDERERS
Genealogy, Nihilism, and Morality

Nietzsche's denial of dogmatism and his acceptance of perspectivism led him to mock the ahistorical pretensions of much mainstream philosophy. The main subject of this attack was morality. As always, Nietzsche sought to cast suspicion on the dominant understanding of morality by revealing its origins and describing its history. His critical project is therefore a genealogical inquiry: interpreting the human desires, needs, and passions that were reflected and which sustain the institution of morality; determining which human types are advantaged and disadvantaged by different moral theories and practices; revealing the relations and struggles of power that underwrite moral discourse; contrasting the contemporary meaning and use of morality with an explanation of morality's origin; and showing the limitations of the contemporary meaning and use—in sum, manifesting the collective psychic and cultural structures that must be overcome in the service of higher life forms.

His genealogical approach is also connected to his understanding of philosophy as autobiographical and of morality as a signifier of emotions. Thus, Nietzsche writes

It has become clear to me what every great philosophy so far has been; namely, the personal confession of its author and a kind of involuntary and unconscious memoir; also that the moral (or immoral) intentions in every philosophy constituted the real germ of life from which the whole plant had grown. (*BGE* 6) and

There are moralities which are meant to justify their creator before others. Other moralities are meant to calm him and lead him to be satisfied with himself. . . . Some moralists want to vent their power and creative whims on humanity; some others . . . suggest with their morality: "What deserves respect in me is that I can obey—and *you* ought not to be different from me."— In short, moralities are also a *sign language of the affects*. (*BGE* 187)

Critics of Nietzsche interrogate his genealogical approach from several angles. First, the method must escape charges of "genetic fallacy," the fallacy of concluding that a proposition, argument, theory, or social practice is proved false or unsound by impugning its origins. Charges of genetic fallacy, a standard tool of critique of analytic philosophy, flow from the conviction that propositions, arguments, theories, and practices must be evaluated on their own terms because their truth or soundness is independent of who asserts them and how they emerge.

Nietzsche is aware of the critical powers of the genetic fallacy. Thus, he says

The mistake made by the more refined [historians of morality] is that they uncover and criticize the perhaps foolish opinions of a people about their morality, or of humanity about all human morality—opinions about its origin, religious sanction, the superstition of free will, and things of that sort—and then suppose that they have criticized the morality itself. But the value of a command "thou shalt" is still fundamentally different from and independent of such opinions. . . . Even if a morality has grown out of an error, the realization of this fact would not as much as touch the problem of its value. (*GS* 345; see also *WP* 254)

Still, in other passages he suggests that we should link the origins of morality and its value:

We need a *critique* of moral values, *the value of these values themselves must first be called into question*—and for that there is needed a knowledge of the conditions and circumstances in which they grew, under which they evolved and changed . . . a knowledge of a kind that has never yet existed or even been desired. (*GM*, Preface, 6; see also *GM*, Preface, 3)

The appeal to such well known passages is, therefore, inconclusive. The charge of genetic fallacy must be analyzed further.

Second, critics can question the specific genealogical account of morality Nietzsche provides. Is it historically sound? Is it the best, the only, available interpretation of the origins of morality? Does it beg the question (tacitly assume from the outset what it should have to prove)

against the dominant views of morality? Third, critics can wonder whether Nietzsche's specific genealogical account reproduces the very structures he aspires to revise. Fourth, critics can press Nietzsche regarding the vantage point from which he makes his genealogical assessments. Given his perspectivism and his own historical context, how can he ascend to a vantage point which allegedly permits him to see what others cannot?

MASTER AND SLAVE MORALITIES

Nietzsche's specific genealogical account invokes the images of master and slave moralities. The master morality equates "good" to worldly success: achieving one's goals of conquest, fame, wealth, and adventure, and embodying pride, strength, passion, and guiltless joy. Nietzsche relishes the master morality's limit-breaking activities and robust nobility. Moreover, the master morality prefigures some of Nietzsche's broad themes: the need to transcend present contexts and create values out of the abundance of one's life and strengths; the desire to creatively use passion; the joyful affirmation of this world; the manifestation of self-possession; the lack of repressed hostility; and the production and honoring of higher human types.

The master morality, which for Nietzsche symbolizes the Greeks of the Homeric age, did not perceive itself as unconditional or universal. This morality did not prescribe how others (nonmasters) should conduct their lives and understood explicitly that its evaluations pertained only to a certain type of human. In that vein, masters sought friends and adversaries only from members of their own rank.

The master morality was dominant and ruled over slaves. These slaves, however, developed their own version of morality. Slave morality reflected and sustained what was beneficial for the masses or herd of men. The slave morality's notion of "good" applied to the actions and intentions of men, instead of their character. Because the herd is inherently mediocre, its values celebrate sympathy, kindness, and general benevolence, virtues that serve the weak and aspire to widespread equality. The values of masters—such as power, self-assertion, and world success—are retranslated in slave morality as vices. While the masters were essentially indifferent to slaves, viewing them as different human types, slaves bear *ressentiment* toward masters.

Prior to the slave revolt in morality which led to the end of the domination of master morality, the "bad conscience" emerged. When humans become enthralled with society, civilization, and peace, the will to power turns back on itself as instincts are not discharged externally. This process culminates in self-hate and self-destruction:

"The man who, from lack of external enemies and resistances and forcibly confined to the oppressive narrowness and punctiliousness of custom, impatiently lacerated, persecuted, gnawed at, assaulted, and maltreated himself" (*GM* II, 16; see also *GM* II, 17–19). The bad conscience, although at first blush the facilitator of repression and internal division, can be creatively used by the excellent few to control, sublimate, and integrate their multiple drives.

In contrast to masters who act on their emotions and then forget their past grievances against others, slaves repress their hostile feelings because of their fears, which stem from their relative powerlessness. For Nietzsche, forgetting exhibits strength because it opens the way to self-overcoming and re-creation:

[Forgetting] is an active and in the strictest sense positive faculty. . . . To close the doors and windows of consciousness for a time; to remain undisturbed by the noise and struggle of our underworld of utility organs working with and against one another; a little quietness . . . to make room for new things, above all for the nobler functions . . . that is the purpose of active forgetfulness. (*GM* II, 1)

Ressentiment is bottled-up hatred and aggression caused by repressing one's hostile feelings. Although masters are the source of the slaves' hostile feelings, slaves are afraid to confront their superiors. Accordingly, the slaves' intense humiliation and hostility are internalized. These hostile feelings, however, are eventually expressed in cunning fashion: They produce the slave morality whose cleverest trick is the revaluation of master morality.

The slave revolt in morality begins when *ressentiment* itself becomes creative and gives birth to values: the *ressentiment* of natures that are denied the true reaction, that of deeds, and compensate themselves with an imaginary revenge. While every noble morality develops from a triumphant affirmation of itself, slave morality from the outset says No to . . . what is "different" . . . and *this* No is its creative deed. This inversion of the value-positing eye—this *need* to direct one's view outward instead of back to oneself—is of the essence of *ressentiment*. (*GM* I, 10)

Accordingly, the pursuit of sex, power, overt aggression, and conquest become refashioned as immoralities, while chastity, humility, obedience, and meekness become the cornerstones of "morality." Slave morality also extols the unconditionality and universality of its own perspective, it attempts to undermine the character advantages and superiority of masters by labeling them "evil." These strategies are indispensable to the success of the slave revolt: Unless slaves could universalize their values, their leveling efforts would be unsuccessful and slaves would still be vulnerable to the greater powers of masters.

Slave morality, then, is fundamentally reactive and fueled by fear and hostility. To solidify its powers of revaluation, slave morality appealed to a transcendent world ruled by a supernatural being. Thus, the triumph of equality, deprecation of this world, and celebration of fixed values in the West was begun by the Jews and refined by Christianity: "The Jews have brought off that miraculous feat of an inversion of values. . . . Their prophets fused 'rich,' 'godless,' 'evil,' 'violent,' and 'sensual' into one and were the first to use the word 'world' as an opprobrium. . . . They mark the beginning of the slave rebellion in morals" (*BGE* 195; see also *GM* I, 7–8). Nietzsche also writes the following:

Christianity has been the most calamitous kind of arrogance yet. Men, not high and hard enough to have any right to try to form *man* as artists; men, not strong and farsighted enough to *let* the foreground law of thousandfold failure and ruin prevail, though it cost them sublime self-conquest; men, not noble enough to see the abysmally different order of rank . . . between man and man—such men have so far held sway over the fate of Europe, with their "equal before God," until finally a smaller, almost ridiculous type, a herd animal . . . has been bred. (*BGE* 62)

Invoking the imperatives of a supreme being solidified several themes of slave morality: the equality of all humans despite their obvious factual differences; the vision of this world as an ersatz copy of a transcendent world; the assurance that a final judgment of all human actions will constitute perfect justice; and the full meaning and consequences of the terms "guilt," "personal responsibility and moral autonomy," and "good and evil."

A series of dualisms underwrite these themes of slave morality. The herd privileged the soul over the body, reason (carefully circumscribed by religious authority) over the passions, and the transcendent world over this world. In this fashion, according to Nietzsche, the slaves' *ressentiment* culminates in revenge: the revaluation of the masters' judgments. Thus, slaves reduce the importance of robustly living this life for "the meek will inherit the earth"; they minimize the pursuit of worldly success for "it is easier for a camel to pass through the eye of a needle than for a rich man to enter heaven"; they elevate pity and sympathy, sentiments permitting herd members to wallow in their weakness, to virtues; and they deny currency to factual human differences in deference to the virtues of modesty, deference, and humility. In this insidious manner, and especially through the connivance of the priestly class and its God, people of excellence become unwittingly collaborators in the undermining of the social conditions under which they had flourished.

For Nietzsche, the slave morality, particularly its glorification of pity and sympathy, encourages a life of minimal exertion and avoidance of risk. Nietzsche judges moralities, cultures, and people in part by the way they confront suffering and the tragic dimensions of life. The robust life requires self-mastery through confronting obstacles, overcoming suffering, and affirming tragedies. Greatness and excellence require creative confrontation with suffering and pain; surmounting obstacles is the core of the will to power.

Instead of reveling in the adventure that is life, however, the slave morality aspires to eliminate pain and to nurture limited vulnerability and few demands: The "good" person is merely one who assiduously avoids proscribed actions. Worse, the celebration of pity and sympathy stems from weakness and timidity. Nietzsche writes, "Pity . . . is a weakness, like every losing of oneself through a *harmful* affect. It *increases* the amount of suffering in the world. . . . Supposing it was dominant even for a single day, mankind would immediately perish of it" (*D* 134), and "The noble human being, too, helps the unfortunate, but not, or almost not, from pity, but prompted more by an urge begotten by excess of power. . . . [He] delights in being severe and hard with himself and respects all severity and hardness. . . . Such a type of man is actually proud of the fact that he is *not* made for pity" (*BGE* 260).

Moreover, at least three dubious metaphysical assumptions about humans support slave morality: Humans embody a free will that permits independent moral choice; human motives and intentions for action can be discerned and evaluated comparatively; and humans are morally equal. These three assumptions lead to further conclusions about the institutions of morality: Individuals are responsible for their actions; they deserve to be either rewarded for good actions or punished for evil actions; and the application of moral institutions is universal.

Nietzsche resists the three metaphysical assumptions and the conclusions they generate. First, he denies the notion of free will as a wrongful reification of cause and effect, as mistaking conventional fictions for metaphysical explanations, and as positing an underlying substance called "will" which can be free or determined:

The Error of Free-Will. At present we no longer have any mercy upon the concept "free-will": we know only too well what it is—the most egregious theological trick that has ever existed for the purpose of making mankind "responsible" in a theological manner . . . to make mankind dependent upon theologians. . . . Wherever men try to trace responsibility home to anyone, it is the instinct of punishment and of the desire to judge which is active. Becoming is robbed of its innocence when any particular condition of things is traced to a will, to intentions and to responsible actions. (*TI*, "The Four Great Errors," 7; see also *BGE* 17, 21, 213; *D* 148; *WP* 484)

For Nietzsche, just as there are no things-in-themselves there are no substantial selves. We are merely our passions, past experiences, drives, instincts, and other dispositions which language seduces us into attributing to the individual subject. Each human embodies similar basic drives whose intensity varies from person to person.

Second, Nietzsche questions our ability to discern and evaluate motives and intentions for acting:

The origin of an action was interpreted . . . as origin in an *intention*; one came to agree that the value of an action lay in the value of the intention. . . . We immoralists have the suspicion that the decisive value of an action lies precisely in what is *unintentional* in it. . . . We believe that the intention is merely a sign and symptom that still requires interpretation—moreover, a sign that means too much and therefore, taken by itself alone, almost nothing. (*BGE* 32; see also *GS* 335; *D* 119, 129; *WP* 291, 294, 492)

Third, Nietzsche holds adamantly that values serve particular interests at particular times, that humans have strikingly different interests, and that universalizing moral judgments of the slave mentality under such circumstances itself promotes the interests of the herd: "Every unegoistic morality that takes itself for unconditional and addresses itself to all does not only sin against taste; it is . . . one more seduction . . . and injury for the higher, rarer, privileged. Moralities must be forced to bow first of all before the *order of rank*" (*BGE* 221; see also *BGE* 43).

Finally, the three metaphysical assumptions about humans that support slave morality betray a misunderstanding of the complexity of the world of Becoming. These assumptions posit a dualistic world of good/evil, altruism/egoism, love/hate, and so on which wrongly denies the interdependences between the posited elements. Oppositional dualisms trouble Nietzsche primarily because they renege on life's complexity. They fail to appreciate the interdependences of our motives and the genealogy of our practices: how morality flows from immorality, selflessness emerges from selfishness, truth blossoms from illusion, and good from evil. For Nietzsche, everything valuable once depended on a seemingly opposed value.

Evil.—Examine the lives of the best and most fruitful people . . . and ask yourselves whether a tree that is supposed to grow to a proud height can dispense with bad weather and storms; whether misfortune and external resistance, some kinds of hatred, jealousy, stubbornness, mistrust, hardness, avarice, and violence do not belong among the *favorable* conditions without which any great growth even of virtue is scarcely possible. (*GS* 19; see also *BGE* 2, 229; *GS* 21, 121; *GM* I, 8)

Furthermore, Nietzsche resists the conviction that certain actions or beliefs are inherently good or bad. Context and perspective are required for evaluation. Thus, humans endow drives, activities, and beliefs with value according to the group interests that emerge victorious in social struggle. Humans have always done this, although the will to objectification has often led them for strategic reasons to present their values as transcendent.[1]

Despite his occasional disclaimers to having preferences, it is clear that Nietzsche prefers master morality to slave morality. But, as usual, simple statements such as this one are too crude to capture Nietzsche's full evaluation. First, Nietzsche accepts slave morality as appropriate for the herd. He is upset only by the slave morality's pretensions to dogmatism and universalism which deny the rank order among humans and undermine social conditions necessary for excellence. Thus, it is not the existence or even the content of slave morality that triggers Nietzsche's concern, only the scope of its application and its metaphysical underpinnings. Second, the master morality consists of unrefined, unsublimated passions which too often lead to brutality instead of higher culture. Third, Nietzsche recognizes that the slave morality introduces a cleverness, cunning, and mendacity to humans that was lacking in the crude master morality. He writes, "It was on the soil of . . . the priestly form, that man first became an *interesting animal*, that only here did the human soul in a higher sense acquire *depth* and become *evil*—and these are the two basic respects in which man has hitherto been superior to other beasts!" (*GM* I, 6), and "A race of such men of *ressentiment* is bound to become eventually *cleverer* than any noble race; it will also honor cleverness to a far greater degree" (*GM* I, 10).

CULTURAL ANALYSIS AND NIHILISM

In perhaps his most famous parable, Nietzsche announces the death of God:

Have you not heard of that madman who lit a lantern in the bright morning hours, ran to the market place, and cried incessantly: "I seek God! I seek God!"—As many of those who did not believe in God were standing around just then, he provoked much laughter. . . . The madman jumped in their midst and pierced them with his eyes. "Wither is God?" he cried; "I will tell you. *We have killed him*—you and I. All of us are his murderers. But how did we do this? How could we drink up the sea? Who gave us the sponge to wipe away the entire horizon? . . . God is dead. God remains dead. And we have killed him. How shall we comfort ourselves, the murderers of all murderers?" . . . At last he threw his lantern on the ground. . . . "I have come too early. . . . My time is not yet. This tremendous event is still on its way, still wandering; it

has not yet reached the ears of men. Lightning and thunder require time."
(*GS* 125; see also *GS* 108, 343; Z IV, "Retired"; "The Ugliest Man")

The "death of God" parable consists of several messages. The news is spread in the market place, the center of commerce and the focus of modern life. The bearer of the news is a madman because such a denial of God's efficacy in a Europe dominated by Christian religion would strike the masses as madness. The news itself is not a banal assertion of atheism but rather an observation of historical trajectory: The notion of God either is or will soon be unworthy of belief even if the masses are unaware that cultural conditions no longer support fervent religious belief and practice. The dramatic, poetic conclusion that we have wiped "away the entire horizon" underscores Nietzsche's contention that without fervent religious belief and practice our standards of truth, foundations of meaning, and understanding of transcendent redemption evaporate: Without God the world of Being collapses, only the world of Becoming which precludes inherent meaning remains. We have all "murdered" God in the sense that we constitute a culture in which integrity, intellectual cleanliness, and pursuit of truth undermine continued religious belief. The "scientific conscience," which in its quest for objectivity, absolute truth, and universal application is a sublimated form of the "Christian conscience," fuels the death of God. Thus, with typical irony, Nietzsche claims that God was "murdered" by the very slave morality that originally needed to invoke Him.

You see what it was that really triumphed over the Christian god: Christian morality itself, the concept of truthfulness that was understood even more rigorously, the father confessor's refinement of the Christian conscience, translated and sublimated into a scientific conscience, into intellectual cleanliness at any price. Looking at nature as if it were proof of the goodness and governance of god; interpreting history in honor of some divine reason, as a continual testimony of a moral world order and ultimate moral purposes . . . that is *all over* now. (*GS* 357)

With the death of God comes the evaporation of meaning and the specter of nihilism, the condition of the spirit which occurs after we recognize that the highest values have devalued themselves. With the further recognition that there are no foundations for inherent meaning, values seem arbitrary, goals lack purpose, and horizons of understanding dry up. How shall we reconstruct ourselves without God? What new myths will be necessary? Must we become our own gods?

One possible reaction is self-destruction: the decline and retreat of the will to power to abject passivity. As Nietzsche writes

And I saw a great sadness descend upon mankind. The best grew weary of their works. A doctrine appeared, accompanied by a faith: "All is empty, all is the same, all has been!" And from all the hills it echoed: "All is empty, all is the same, all has been!" . . . In vain was all our work; our wine has turned to poison; an evil eye has seared our fields and hearts. We have all become dry; and if fire should descend on us, we should turn to ashes; indeed we have wearied the fire itself. (Z II, "The Soothsayer")

This mood of indifference masquerading as despair defines passive nihilism. But it bears currency only for those who insist that humans need transcendent foundations, supernatural authority, and preestablished suprahuman meaning. For those courageous enough to cheerfully reject that conviction, the death of God promises creative opportunities: the recurring cycle of reimagination, re-creation, and self-overcoming. An active nihilism can rejuvenate the will to power, not by returning to an historically obsolete master morality, but through celebration of contingency and creation of new values. The best of us can become our own gods.

GOING BEYOND GOOD AND EVIL

To understand the directions Nietzsche prefigures for those strong enough to undertake them, I will review the aspects of conventional morality that he resists. The unpalatable elements of slave morality embody suspicious origins, contents, metaphysical presuppositions, effects, and second-order beliefs. The origins reside in *ressentiment* and reaction; the contents consist of evaluating particular actions, of glorifying pity, of downplaying earthly success and life, of submitting to external authority, and of imposing a false equality; the metaphysical presuppositions include belief in a supernatural being, free will, independent moral choice, the transparency and assessibility of human motives and intentions, and the fixed opposition of good and evil; the negative effects include leveling all humans to the standards of the herd, postponing gratification, marginalizing nobility, stifling human creativity, deflating human instincts and passions, viewing contentment and tame happiness as primary goods, and sanctifying social conformity; the pernicious second-order beliefs are the universalism, dogmatism, and absolutism required to sustain the entire program.

It is reasonable to conclude that any form of morality which embodies such elements will repel Nietzsche. Although he will be indifferent to slave moralities as such, their harmful second-order beliefs and negative effects upon culture and standards of excellence ultimately prevent their coexistence with higher forms of life: By their very nature they cannot restrict their tenets and convictions to the herd. Thus, slave moralities devalue cultural health, higher forms of life, and numerous expressions of power.

Accordingly, Nietzsche's attacks on morality are criticisms of these undesirable elements rather than efforts to alter all present evaluations of right and wrong actions. In fact, Nietzsche says

I also deny immorality: *not* that countless people *feel* themselves to be immoral, but that there is any *true* reason so to feel. It goes without saying that I do not deny—unless I am a fool—that many actions called immoral ought to be avoided and resisted, or that many called moral ought to be done and encouraged—but I think that the one should be encouraged and the other avoided *for other reasons than hitherto. (D* 103)

Moreover, Nietzsche does not prescribe the end of all evaluation; on the contrary, the imposition of meaning, order, and value on a world of Becoming is a paramount creative activity. To "go beyond good and evil" involves, among other things, recognizing truth as perspectival, refusing to submit to notions of equality, understanding suffering as necessary for creative greatness, and honoring the rank order among humans (see, for example, *BGE* 4, 44, 56, 260). Moreover, the transvaluation of slave moralities requires robust self-affirmation and joyous overcoming of passive nihilism. The suspicious origins, contents, metaphysical presuppositions, effects, and second-order beliefs of slave moralities must be rejected, at least by higher human types, in the service of cultural health, refined life forms, and intense expressions of the will to power.

Nietzsche suspects that the more we venerate the transcendent Judeo–Christian world, the less we regard ourselves. Part of the "ascetic" mindset is a lingering sense of the inferiority of this world and its creatures when judged against the imagined perfection of the other world.

Although the nihilistic moment—during which the death of God is seen as the termination of all foundational meaning and fixed interpretive horizons—generates immediate chaos and social breakdown, it also offers fruitful possibilities for personal and cultural reimagination and re-creation. Also, to go beyond good and evil requires affirmation of this world and everything in it: its transitoriness, one's own mortality, the tragedy and suffering that partly constitute life, the interdependence of posited dualisms, and the radical conditionality of relationships and institutions.

Great character and healthy self-regard animate the transvaluation of slave moralities:

What is noble? . . . It is not actions that prove him—actions are always open to many interpretations, always unfathomable—nor is it "works." . . . It is the *faith* that is decisive here, that determines the order of rank . . . some funda-mental certainty that a noble soul has about itself, something that cannot be sought, nor found, nor perhaps lost. *The noble soul has reverence for itself.* (*BGE* 287; see also *BGE* 260; *GM* I, 10; *WP* 876)

The thrust of Nietzsche's thought is that we can formulate entirely new modes of evaluation that correspond to new, higher forms of life. The value of humanity is established by its highest exemplars and their creations. The higher human forms are extremely fragile and rare: self-control, mastery of inclinations, resisting obstacles, experimentation, and forging a unified character require recurrent destruction (and re-creation) of self: "All great things bring about their own destruction through an act of self-overcoming: thus the law of life will have it, the law of the necessity of 'self-overcoming' in the nature of life—the law-giver himself eventually receives the call: [submit to the law you your-self proposed]" (*GM* III, 27).

We can never transcend our conditionality and the lack of inherent meaning in the world of Becoming, but at least a few of us can loosen the limits of contingency, fully experience the multiplicity of our spir-its, forge a coherent unity from our internal conflicts, and learn to over-come ourselves and our institutions: Theoretical insight can be turned to practical advantage.

THE SECOND DIALOGUE

Apollonia had made several purchases at the sporting-goods store. She re-turned to the mall's food court for a scheduled afternoon meeting with Fegataccio, who had purchased only a copy of the night's program for the local harness racing track. Both felt drained from their lunch, previous discussion of Nietzsche's perspectivism, and shopping activities. However, once they were fueled by several cups of fruit juice, they decided to resume their discourse on Nietzsche's thought.

Apollonia: (Noticing Fegataccio's racing program folded in his back pocket) Well, I see you are up to no good! Why are you so attracted to gambling?

Fegataccio: I don't gamble, I invest. The difference is a matter of knowledge and skill. (Noticing Apollonia's new sporting apparel). I see that you are keeping up with the latest trends!

Apollonia: Just "fashioning a unity out of my character," giving a little Nietzschean style to my life!

Fegataccio: That's an interesting twist—Nietzsche as precursor to Gucci! But that isn't exactly what Nietzsche meant by style.

Apollonia: Let's get back to Nietzsche, then. One problem I have always had with his work is the way he blatantly commits the genetic fallacy, how he assumes that he can disprove a belief or practice by impugning its origins. In fact, even if his genealogy is true—his stories about master and slave moralities—nothing follows about the truth or soundness of the beliefs, conclusions, and practices of those moralities.

Fegataccio: I've been waiting for this. Earlier you invoked the fallacy of abusive ad hominem and the paradox of self-reference; could charges of fallacy of genetic fallacy be far behind? These are the three horsemen of analytic philosophy, three supposed trump cards—yes, I am mixing my metaphors, but so what?—played by mainstream philosophers when they are threatened by a potentially subversive thinker. Such a banal charge, Apollonia! And I thought you were making progress!

Apollonia: Impressive intensity, Fegataccio, but your vitriol does not engage my criticism. Again, why should I be swayed by a thinker who self-consciously triggers the genetic fallacy?

Fegataccio: I'll begin with my own attack on the notion of genetic fallacy. Even on its own terms, the genetic fallacy is only effective against one type of flat-footed deductive argument: conviction C originates from X, X is dubious or unreliable, therefore C is false. The genetic fallacy does not touch probabilistic arguments that assume, quite reasonably, that the source of a belief or practice provides evidence for or against the belief or practice. Such probabilistic arguments don't aspire to prove truth or falsity only on the basis of genesis, but they do take origins to be relevant to assessment. Or, to put a finer point on my claim, I have greater reason to believe a scientific claim, S, asserted in a treatise by Enrico Fermi than I do if S is asserted by Daffy Duck in a cartoon. The genetic fallacy, at best, only points out that, taken abstractly, S is true or false independent of who asserts it. But the genetic fallacy is a feckless analytic tool, even under its own terms, for assessing what is reasonable to believe under conditions of uncertainty. In fact, if the genetic fallacy claims that the genesis of a view is irrelevant to whether the view should be believed, then I think the genetic fallacy destroys itself.

Apollonia: You slide from truth and falsity to what is reasonable and unreasonable to believe quite quickly. To the extent that one is making truth claims—which Nietzsche is doing despite disclaimers to the contrary—the genetic fallacy is still relevant. Is Nietzsche really talking about what is reasonable to believe or is he asserting, inconsistently with his metaperspectivism, that slave moralities are truly inferior?

Fegataccio: Remember, Nietzsche is not proving anything, at least not in the sense of deductive demonstration. He is, instead, casting suspicion on dominant doctrines by undermining their dogmatic self-understandings and by illustrating their emergence from social struggle. Nietzsche recognizes that revealing the suspicious origins of a practice is insufficient to disprove the practice. The conclusion of Nietzsche's project is not "slave morality is false"—recall that he is indifferent to slave moralities if they are limited only to those of herd mentality— but rather that cultural adherence to slave morality carries a horrible price: the marginalization of excellence and fewer great people. For someone such as Nietzsche, who is convinced that the justification of humanity in a world lacking inherent meaning must emerge from the highest human exemplars, that price is too high.

Apollonia: Nietzsche's underlying assumption about the value of the "highest human exemplars" strikes me as unsupportable, but we can leave that for another time.

Fegataccio: Let me continue. Nietzsche is, at least, also pointing out that once a culture must abrogate the sustaining foundation of a practice then that culture must find a new foundation or radically question the practice. If "God is dead" and if belief in a transcendent world animated slave morality, then we must either find a new nontranscendent mooring for slave morality or radically question slave morality's self-understanding (particularly its dogmatism). Nietzsche claims that a nontranscendent mooring is unavailable. Thus, he writes for the few who are capable of radically questioning slave morality without falling into the abyss of passive nihilism.

Apollonia: I can't believe you constructed a deductive argument. My, you are becoming so mainstream, Fegataccio! You deftly evade charges of genetic fallacy by claiming that Nietzsche was not trying to prove the falsity of slave morality as such, but I can reinstate the charges by claiming that he was trying to prove the falsity of what you call slave morality's "self-understandings." And if the proof of those falsities depends only on appeal to suspicious origins, then the force of the genetic fallacy returns.

Fegataccio: Sometimes I think you are simply dense! If I have said this once I have said it a dozen times: Nietzsche is not trying to prove deductively, he is only trying to undermine dominant assurances and to unsettle received opinions. He understands that defaming the origins of a practice is insufficient.

Because Nietzsche linked moralities with the interests that emerge from social struggle, revealing the origins of slave moralities helps uncover the types of people whose interests are advanced by slave moralities. Nietzsche then assesses moralities and their self-understandings—which are, after all, partially constitutive of the moralities themselves—on the basis of the types of people they serve.[2] Accordingly, he does not commit the genetic fallacy because he never goes directly from the ersatz origins of X to the falsity of X.

Apollonia: If I accept that view then I can invent a fallacy to hurl at Nietzsche. I'll call it the "aristocratic fallacy": arguing from the belief that a practice allegedly advances the interests of "people of excellence" to the conclusion that the practice is desirable or true or superior to alternatives. I am tempted to name it "the fallacy of Fegataccio's folly," but you might think that was a cheap shot.

Fegataccio: I wonder why I would think it was a cheap shot? Yet again, truth has nothing to do with it. Nietzsche never argues that master morality or any other imaginable form of morality is true. As for "desirability and superiority," he would claim that aristocratic moralities are better suited for aristocrats, whom he admires, but certainly not that they are superior as such. I thought our discussion of perspectivism made clear that for Nietzsche the notion of "better as such" is meaningless: context and vantage point are the keys. So your new fallacy is not a fallacy at all, at least for Nietzsche, because he is not trying to play your deductive, truth-establishing, dogmatic games. On the contrary, Nietzsche only reveals his own aristocratic perspective, which holds that our dominant (slave) values lack the timeless and supernatural authority they claim.

Apollonia: I think we are starting to go around in circles again. Although Nietzscheans announce their findings with stentorian bravado, as soon as they are challenged by rigorous logical analysis they retreat to mealy mouthed defensive posturing: "it is only our perspective," "we aren't making truth claims," "no evaluation is good or bad as such," and so on.

Fegataccio: Your nastiness is really starting to irritate me! We have covered this ground before, haven't we? I think that those who speak from radically different horizons of meaning will always, if they go back far enough in their presuppositions, end up begging the question against one another. So every debate between a Nietzschean and a committed analytic philosopher can be taken back ultimately to a referendum on perspectivism. We have traveled that road and I thought we did as much as we could to illustrate the problems. I think what I have just said about ultimately begging the question happily exemplifies some of Nietzsche's broad themes.

Apollonia: Let me see if I can anticipate your response: Nietzscheans can say that the charge of genetic fallacy is itself contaminated by the herd mentality because it rules direct links between origins and value out of order.[3] Moreover, the genetic fallacy assumes what Nietzscheans deny, that descendents can go beyond the genetic contributions of their ancestors. Therefore, for Nietzscheans the genetic fallacy is yet another device insulating slave moralities from radical reassessment.

If this is your stance I find it philosophically repugnant, empirically false, and inconsistent with your precious Nietzschean "broad themes." First, Nietzscheans would be endorsing, ironically, a doctrine of original sin: If the original ancestry of a belief or practice is dubious then the belief or practice is tainted forever. Such dogmatism suggests a pedestrian determinism that coalesces uneasily with his broad themes of radical contingency, self-overcoming, reimagination, and re-creation. Second, the doctrine is empirically false, and it is poor history. We observe descendents surpassing the accomplishments and prospects of their ancestors in every imaginable way. The entire immigrant mythology in the United States falsifies the doctrine. You and I are prime illustrations, Fegataccio! Third, the doctrine reneges on your previous defense of Nietzsche. Earlier you claimed that the origins of a belief were relevant for determining whether we could reasonably accept that belief. But now you would be saying that the origins fully determine whether we should accept a belief. That is a giant leap of illogic!

Fegataccio: You are some piece of work, Apollonia! You put an entire doctrine into my mouth and then destroy it. Don't you analytic philosophers call that immolating a straw person, constructing an easy target for your own destructive purposes? I must admit that I am uncomfortable with Nietzsche's most strident passages connecting ancestry and value. I prefer to stress the broad themes of multiplicity, self-overcoming, and re-creation. But your attack assumes, once again, that Nietzsche aspires to universal prescriptions. He doesn't. He speaks from an explicitly aristocratic vantage point to others of his kind. From that perspective most of what you say is not a criticism of the aristocratic mentality but merely a restatement or description of it with the added flourish of "isn't that nasty!"

Apollonia: I think that is a shallow attempt to insulate Nietzsche from criticism. When your back is against the wall, you resort to "well, we just beg the question against each other." Of course, I expect your predictable response to be "you are simply not an aristocrat, Apollonia." I am proud that I am not!

Fegataccio: I can say a bit more than that. You have oversimplified Nietzsche's genealogical account. The account is not designed to uncover one simple explanation for complex phenomena, nor does it prove or disprove the value of beliefs and practices. Instead, genealogy aims at uncovering the diverse power struggles that generate the different interpretations that eventually constitute a social practice.[4] Nietzsche's account is particular and can undermine or sustain understandings about the origins of our practices. Ultimately, Nietzsche evaluates those practices in relation to whether they nurture ascending life, the creation of higher types of humans, and excellence. His overall purpose is genealogy in the service of life, rather than history for the pursuit of abstract truth.

Apollonia: Here are a few more questions: Is Nietzsche's account supposed to be accurate history or mythological reconstruction? How does Nietzsche escape his context in a way that permits him to see what others cannot? How can Nietzsche consistently assume that his account is superior to other possible accounts given his broad theme that data underdetermine theory?

Fegataccio: I think that Nietzsche's main aim is, as always, the undermining of dogmatism. By showing how social practices emerge from power struggles, he unsettles the conviction that our practices and values are embedded in the rationality of nature. Recognizing the perspectival character of values and practices also promotes our reimagining and re-creating them. Nietzsche cannot claim his genealogical accounts are pure dispassionate descriptions. His own aristocratic commitments, psychological understandings, and personal interests intrude freely, as they must. As with all explanatory accounts, Nietzsche's presents itself as accurate history while masking its own mythological and psychological origins. This is mainly the result of the limitations of our language and categories of logic, the issues we discussed earlier.

Nietzsche cannot claim that he escapes his context, he only nourishes the subversive seeds contained therein. Given his commitments to his broad themes, he cannot claim that his genealogical account is the only available interpretation of the "data" or that it emerges from an impartial vantage point. His account must be self-consciously partial and a product of his own will to power.[5]

Apollonia: But then Nietzsche cannot claim superiority for his account. He gives us one admittedly biased rendering of the origins of dominant morality that he hopes will resuscitate aristocratic fervor.

Fegataccio: But we have gone over this when we talked about perspectivism. Nietzsche knows that he cannot undermine dogmatism directly by meeting it on its own logical grounds and by using its own criteria of acceptable argument. Those grounds and criteria presuppose dogmatism, so any attempt to employ them directly to undermine dogmatism will ultimately reinstate the "necessity" of dogmatism. That is precisely how charges of self-referential paradox gain their currency. Instead, Nietzsche must chip away at dogmatism indirectly: through self-consciously partial genealogical accounts, by demonstrating dogmatism's unprovable presuppositions, by appealing to different pictures of life, and by dancing a different dance.

What Nietzsche does is show the poverty of the fact–value distinction. As corollaries of perspectives and power relationships, values cannot inhabit a logical category separate from facts. If Nietzsche's genealogical account is successful, it will not establish a new fixed understanding of the origins of our dominant values, but will instead stimulate the creative interpretive and practical activities of others.[6] Once again genealogy returns to and substantiates the power of Nietzsche's broad themes!

Apollonia: What about Thrasymachus in Plato's *Republic*? Remember, he claimed that our notions of justice were established by the strongest in the society, by those able to effect their will because of their social position and overall power. They set the terms of existence because they had the might to do so and, over time, those terms became codified in concepts of "justice" and "right." Nietzsche advances a different view: Justice is in the interests of the weakest elements in society, the herd. Here we have two different genealogies of morality advanced by two figures who agree broadly on the connections between value and power.

Fegataccio: Are they so different? Remember, for Nietzsche the highest types are also the most fragile. They are strongest in the sense of physical, mental, and spiritual creativity, but it does not follow that they are more likely than the herd to be preserved. On the contrary, they are more likely to perish in explosive self-annihilations.

Let me open my book and read what Nietzsche says passionately in *Twilight of the Idols*:

Great men, like great ages, are explosive material, in which a stupendous amount of power is accumulated. . . . The age in which they appear is a matter of chance. . . . Every kind of exhaustion and of sterility follows in their wake. . . . The genius—in work and in deed—is necessarily a squanderer: the fact that he spends himself constitutes his greatness. The instinct of self-preservation is as it were suspended in him; the overpowering pressure of out-flowing energy in him forbids any such protection and prudence. . . . He flows out, he flows over, he consumes himself, he does not spare himself. (*TI*, "Skirmishes in a War with the Age," 44)

So which is the stronger, the herd or the nobility? The answer must be typically Nietzschean: There is no stronger as such, only stronger in relation to specified criteria. In regard to creative genius and cultural excellence, the nobility is stronger; in regard to numbers and survival instincts, the herd is stronger. Moreover, if Nietzsche is correct, the herd supplements its strength by invoking supernatural authority and the promise of eternal happiness—if you toe the herd's line! Thus it is reasonable to see some convergence between Nietzsche and Thrasymachus: "Justice" is in the interests of the strongest. But what they take to be the criteria of "strongest" differs. From a Nietzschean perspective, Thrasymachus failed to understand how those with social power—at least in the ages of democracy, socialism, communism, and the major religions—have already been deeply infected with herd mentality. Alternately, one can read Thrasymachus as tolling Homeric themes and as recalling a time when leaders set the terms of existence in accord with master morality because they ruled prior to the ages of our mainstream religions and politics. Under either interpretation, Nietzsche and Thrasymachus have much in common.

Apollonia: I'll drop the Thrasymachus–Nietzsche comparison, but much of my critique persists. Under your own rendering, Nietzsche presents one of many possible genealogies of mainstream morality, he aspires only to provoke creative responses, he cannot truly claim superiority for his interpretation in any noncircular fashion, he appeals only to those of his "kind," and ultimately he cannot establish his aesthetic preferences rationally but only through seductive art and manipulative rhetoric. This picture, dance, song—whatever you want to call it—does not attract me. While I suppose that reveals to Nietzscheans my peasant origins and unredeemable herd allegiance, to me it shows the poverty of Nietzschean prattle and bluster.

Fegataccio: Remember, for Nietzsche those types of persuasion are all that are available to us. If he is correct, we have always established "truth" through seduction, manipulation, and power struggles. He isn't advocating any truly new fashions, but is merely laying bare what must be. He then counsels those who can bear it to use this recognition for practical advantage rather than for retreating from life.

We keep returning to perspectivism, don't we? Have we forgotten the lessons of our agreement on the nature and function of rhetorical strategies? Why do we keep returning to the same tired impasses and dissonance? Is it something about us, about life, or about Nietzsche?

Apollonia: Probably a measure of all three. I do know that I dread you, Fegataccio, in the fullest Kierkegaardian sense. I am simultaneously attracted and repelled by your words and character. Maybe you are only a trigger, though. Perhaps my deepest anxieties and, strangely, exhilarations emerge when I sense myself confronting an emptiness, a void, that cannot be vivified by aesthetic pleasure or ethical rule-following. Maybe my reactions to you are surrogates for a dread that is at its core objectless.

Fegataccio: So serious and existential, Apollonia. Do I detect a Nietzschean, not really Kierkegaardian, moment? Are you confronting a world without inherent meaning, without immortality, without fixed foundations? Is that your "emptiness," your "void?" Is your "dread" a mixture of panic as you recognize the pervasiveness of contingency and excitement as you tacitly bid *addio* to a transcendent world well lost? Are you in the throes of nihilism, Apollonia?

Apollonia: I never learn, do I? I try to share a personal moment with you, Fegataccio, and you mock my feelings while ignoring my deeper message. Did you ever wonder, Fegataccio, why you always do this as a reflex against personal, as opposed to philosophical, engagement? What hopes and fears lurk beneath your audacity and bellicosity? What demons animate your revulsion at the conventional? What illusions energize your aspirations to superiority? But why waste my time. You will respond to such queries only with sardonic wit and dismissive posturing.

Fegataccio: I am not the villain you portray me to be, Apollonia. Sometimes my tone, my hard edge, gets in the way, I know.

Apollonia: Your "apology" is accepted. If I thought you were a villain we wouldn't be having this conversation. Let's consider our exchange a small step toward emotional engagement. I hope we can continue it at a more appropriate time.

But let's get back to Nietzsche. You mentioned nihilism, and this may be a good time to discuss that much misunderstood notion, or I should say series of notions. The term is used in so many ways that serious discussion is often precluded. Let me start with a catalog of nihilisms. I'll give them my own names, in the spirit of Nietzschean creativity, of course.

Spiritual nihilism captures the convictions of Eastern religions such as Buddhism and Hinduism: This world is illusory and our attachments to it intensify our suffering. Our souls undergo a recurring cycle of death and birth, and the only way to escape reincarnation and arrive at Nirvana is through spiritual purification accomplished through discipline and detachment from the sensory imprisonments of our environment.[7]

Existential nihilism concludes that no religious or philosophical system provides firm guidance for human life or assurances that values are adequately grounded. Human life is at its core meaningless because the cosmos is purposeless. Our recognition of all this exacerbates the "absurd" human condition: the confrontation between rational humans and an indifferent universe. The world does not care about our hopes, fears, dreams, and experiences. While suicide is one possible response, it admits weakness and incapacity. A better response is human pride and rebellion, accompanied by human solidarity, which rejects despair in a self-conscious revolt against cosmic purposeless. We should contemplate and defy our absurd situation in order to maximize life's intensity. Humans give meaning to their existence not by eliminating the absurd, for that is impossible, but by refusing to yield meekly to its effects. Although the absurd prevents a fully satisfying existence, it does not prevent the creation of meaning through rebellious activity in the name of justice and human solidarity.[8]

Skeptical nihilism claims to be a belief in nothing. I say "claims" because I would argue that the belief in nothing is itself a belief. The self-referential paradox lives! Skeptical nihilism emerges from the recognitions that fuel existential nihilism, but it refuses to substitute a program of pride, rebellion, and solidarity as a prescribed alternative. Thus, skeptical nihilism denies that any alternative can ameliorate in any sense the human condition: Continued human existence is not even a sham immortality; it merely multiplies zeros by more zeros.[9]

Anarchistic nihilism is closely related to skeptical nihilism. This version concludes from the lack of inherent cosmic meaning and value that humans are free from all rules and ideals: anything goes, all is permitted. The only limits upon humans are their own physical and mental deficiencies.

Epistemological nihilism occurs when our highest values and foundations of meaning devalue themselves; when cultural conditions, largely caused by taking those values and foundations seriously, ultimately no longer sustain fervent belief in them. Epistemological nihilism is often the trigger—because it heightens the sense of inherent cosmic purposelessness—for one or more of the other forms of nihilism we are adumbrating. Epistemological nihilism is accompanied by a sense that no future human "discovery" can produce lasting values and foundations of meaning.[10]

Moral nihilism is a specialized form of epistemological nihilism. Moral nihilism occurs when the dominant moral values collapse, either by devaluing themselves or from external pressure. Clearly, moral nihilism could occur in the absence of more general epistemological nihilism.

Passive nihilism is a paralyzing pessimistic inertia once one confronted by inherent cosmic purposeless. Passive nihilism is often accompanied by the belief that life embodies no good, or that the path of least resistance and minimal effort is a prescribed response to the human condition: avoiding suffering, banal contentment, and easy acceptance become paramount.

Active nihilism accepts inherent cosmic purposeless as the springboard to creative possibilities: Reveling in radical contingency, embracing the human condition fully while recognizing its tragic dimensions; understanding the process of deconstruction, reimagination, and re-creation; and rejoicing in liberation from imposed values and meanings are at the heart of active nihilism. Instead of minimizing the importance of any particular lifetime, as does spiritual nihilism, active nihilism places paramount value on this life.

These, then, are a few uses of the term "nihilism." I don't claim this list is exhaustive. Some of the uses detail the loss of inherent cosmic meaning, some are reactions to that loss, some are mainly philosophical or theoretical doctrines, while others track psychological moods or movements. Most of those who are nihilists in any one of these senses are also nihilists in other senses.

Fegataccio: Also, I think that some of these may be of only temporary use. For example, anarchistic nihilism may be a fruitful first reaction to epistemological or moral nihilism, but it cannot serve as a fixed doctrine. And I agree with you—you'll be surprised to discover—that skeptical nihilism is life denying unless we restrict it to belief in nothing that claims transcendent authority.

Apollonia: You know what I am leading up to: Which, if any, of these forms of nihilism is acceptable to you Nietzscheans?

Fegataccio: We have both been using "Nietzscheans" too facilely. Remember that Nietzsche did not want disciples, at least not in terms of his specific convictions. Instead, refined interpreters of Nietzsche subscribe to his broad theme of overcoming Nietzsche himself. We "Nietzscheans" cannot merely parrot the words of a master—indeed, we cannot even if we want to, given the fluidity of his writing and his resistance to fixed doctrines. We must go beyond Nietzsche's thought and win our own "truths."

Apollonia: We both understand all that. So we have been using "Nietzscheans" loosely, but even that, it seems to me, should be acceptable to a Nietzschean as a sort of irony. But I'll rephrase the question: Which, if any, of these forms of nihilism would Nietzsche embrace?

Fegataccio: I'll take a shot at answering by proceeding down your list in turn. Nietzsche denies the emptiness of spiritual nihilism. It turns away from this world to preoccupation with Nirvana, a fusion with the Absolute that destroys individual identity. Spiritual nihilism is fueled by the conviction that this world should have inherent order and purpose. When that conviction is disappointed, spiritual nihilism advances a program of self-annihilation that begins by anesthetizing us to the tragic dimensions of life. Although it does involve a type of self-overcoming and internal disciple—themes amicable to Nietzsche—spiritual nihilism degenerates because it reneges on its understanding of inherent cosmic purposeless. It retains the distinction between this illusory world and an ultimate Reality, thereby ensuring a no-saying attitude to human life.

Nietzsche would find much acceptable in existential nihilism: the emphasis on pride and rebellion, the full acceptance of inherent cosmic purposeless, the refusal to degenerate into passivity and despair. But existential nihilism retains an allegiance to moral (as contrasted with functional) evaluation and aspires to humanistic solidarity, themes that are resonant with the vestiges of the herd mentality.[11]

I have spoken earlier about skeptical and anarchistic nihilisms. At best, they represent temporary initial reactions to a full understanding of inherent cosmic purposelessness. They both require refinements and qualifications if they are to play any role in the process of re-creation of meaning.

Epistemological and moral nihilisms represent two senses in which Nietzsche can accurately be termed a nihilist. But I think many insightful contemporary thinkers, including classically trained analytic philosophers, are nihilists in these senses.

Active nihilism represents the Nietzschean psychological mood of embracing life with all its tragedies and joys and with full understanding of its transitory nature:

The ideal of the most high-spirited, alive, and world-affirming human being who has not only come to terms and learned to get along with whatever was and is, but who wants to have *what was and is* repeated into all eternity, shouting insatiably [from the beginning]—not only to himself but to the whole play and spectacle, and not only to a spectacle but at bottom to him who needs precisely this spectacle—and who makes it necessary because again and again he needs himself—and makes himself necessary. (*BGE* 56)

Passive nihilism, on the contrary, in either its pessimistic or easy-contentment forms represents an anti-Nietzschean reaction, a no-saying response to the understanding of inherent cosmic purposelessness. In its easy-contentment form, the prescriptions of minimal exertion and avoidance of suffering resound with the shallowness of Nietzsche's "last men," narrow egalitarians who pursue a superficial "happiness" that disconnects their possibilities for intense love, creation, longing, exertion, and excellence:

"We have invented happiness," say the last men, and they blink. They have left the regions where it was hard to live, for one needs warmth. One still loves one's neighbor and rubs against him, for one needs warmth. Becoming sick and harboring suspicion are sinful to them: one proceeds carefully. A fool, whoever still stumbles over stones or human beings! A little poison now and then: that makes for agreeable dreams. And much poison in the end, for an agreeable death. One still works, for work is a form of entertainment. But one is careful lest the entertainment be too harrowing. One no longer becomes poor or rich: both require too much exertion. Who still wants to rule? Who obey? Both require too much exertion. . . . Everybody wants the same, everybody is the same. . . . "We have invented happiness," say the last men, and they blink. (Z I, "Zarathustra's Prologue," 5)

The highest ambitions of last men are comfort and security. They are the extreme case of the herd mentality: habit, custom, indolence, egalitarianism, self-preservation, and muted will to power prevail. Last men embody none of the inner tensions and conflicts that spur transformative action: They take no risks, lack convictions, avoid experimentation, and seek only bland survival. Nietzsche is not describing the middle-class mentality of his day, but rather the banality of the possible classless society of the future.

So Nietzsche is a nihilist in certain senses, Apollonia, but his entire project, indeed his life, aspires to overcome the most virulent and decadent nihilisms: spiritual, skeptical, anarchistic, and passive. An existence focused on idleness, contemplation, detachment, and asceticism reflects and sustains a pessimistic rejection of recurring creation. Such an existence denies life. The philosophers of the future, those who transcend decadent forms of nihilism, will focus on reshaping themselves and the world.

Apollonia: Bravo, Fegataccio! You have shown what I have always suspected: Loose talk about Nietzsche's nihilism fails to distinguish carefully among the different uses of the term. I agree fully with your understanding of Nietzsche on nihilism. I am not, of course, an epistemological, moral, or active nihilist because I do not accept the alleged inherent cosmic purposelessness that triggers these forms. But, regardless, I appreciate your analysis of where Nietzsche stands.

Fegataccio: We have shown where Nietzsche stands on nihilism, Apollonia. Your categorization was indispensable to the demonstration.

Apollonia: Thanks, Fegataccio, but before this turns into a lovefest—and I know you wouldn't like that—I want to turn to other matters. So far we have spent most of our time on metaphilosophical issues: perspectivism, nihilism, exegesis of genealogy, and justification of method. I'd like to turn to some of Nietzsche's specific ideas instead of his broad themes.

Fegataccio: Fire away, Apollonia, but we should remind ourselves that we should not present Nietzsche as the prophet of fixed truths or of definitive diagnoses of his culture. Instead, he reports, autobiographically, his own internal tensions and sense of possibility which are deeply representative of his time and cultural context. He speaks as one who challenges himself and us, not as a proclaimer of new "truths."[12]

Apollonia: I want to address Nietzsche's warrior rhetoric, his military imagery, and his willingness to sacrifice and exploit members of the herd in service of his precious aristocrats. This side of Nietzsche I find particularly repulsive: Its content is redolent with the stench of "might makes right"; its failure to understand the real human cost of such irresponsible talk strikes me as dangerous and juvenile; and coming from a man such as Nietzsche it reeks of fantasy, a fatuous overcompensation for his own sense of physical inadequacy. If I might borrow one of your pet phrases, Nietzsche strikes me as having "an alligator's mouth but only a hummingbird's ass."

But, first, let's open your Nietzsche "bible" and recall a few of these passages:

The essential characteristic of a good and healthy aristocracy, however, is that it experiences itself *not* as a function . . . but as their *meaning* and highest justification—that it therefore accepts with a good conscience the sacrifice of untold human beings who, *for its sake*, must be reduced and lowered to incomplete human beings, to slaves, to instruments. Their fundamental faith simply has to be that society must *not* exist for society's sake but only as the foundation and scaffolding on which a choice type of being is able to raise itself to its higher task and to a higher state of *being*. (*BGE* 258)

Life itself is *essentially* appropriation, injury, overpowering of what is alien and weaker; suppression, hardness, imposition of one's own forms, incorporation and at least, at its mildest, exploitation. (*BGE* 259)

The *goal of humanity* cannot lie in its end but only *in its highest exemplars.* (*UM,* "On the Uses and Disadvantages of History for Life," 9)

We count ourselves among conquerors; we think about the necessity for new orders, also for a new slavery—for every strengthening and enhancement of the human type also involves a new kind of enslavement. (*GS* 377)

I employed the word "state": it is obvious what is meant—some pack of blond beasts of prey, a conqueror and master race which, organized for war and with the ability to organize, unhesitatingly lays is terrible claws upon a populace perhaps tremendously superior in numbers but still formless and nomad. This is after all how the "state" began on earth. (*GM* II, 17)

Let us admit to ourselves, without trying to be considerate, how every higher culture on earth so far has *begun.* Human beings whose nature was still natural, barbarians in every terrible sense of the word, men of prey who were still in possession of unbroken strength of will and lust for power, hurled themselves upon weaker, more civilized, more peaceful races. (*BGE* 257)

I could go on but I think my point is made. While contemporary apologists for Nietzsche struggle mightily to make his work more palatable for intellectuals, the fact is that Nietzsche's "misinterpretation" by the Nazis is one plausible reading of his work.

The great advocate of multiplicity, the apostle of conflicting interpretations of great literary works, was hoist by his own petard!

Fegataccio: You are taking Nietzsche's rhetoric too seriously and too literally. A more refined interpretation would understand three aspects of the warrior imagery. First, the military metaphors pertain most directly to a person's internal struggles with conflicting impulses and multiple drives. To overcome one's self, to forge a unity and dramatic character out of inherent chaos, requires confrontation and conquest. But the most important parts of the process occur within a person and do not involve physically subduing others. Second, the confrontations and conquests are spiritual "wars" even when undertaken on a cultural level: They are battles over ideals and visions of the good life, they aren't military campaigns or true warfare. Third, we can't forget Nietzsche's stylistic preoccupations: to provoke, to gain attention, to stir controversy, to exaggerate self-consciously, and to provide vivid imagery. These stylistic aims are more easily fulfilled through warrior rhetoric than through unadorned prose.

In short, Nietzsche does not herald barbaric displays of dominance over others but, instead, cherishes sublimated passions that generate high cultures. The spiritualization of raging power, as illustrated by great artists and philosophers, is the culmination of Nietzsche's active nihilism. Although Nietzsche favorably mentions several military figures in his work, such as Napoleon and Caesar, he does so in recognition of their vigorous will to power, not because he considers them his model of cultural refinement. The process of personal and cultural deconstruction, reimagination, and re-creation is the journey toward excellence, while the pursuit of crude physical power over others demonstrates lack of creative imagination and immersion in facticity.

Take a closer look at some of your cited passages. In some of these, Nietzsche is only recounting how states and cultures arose historically. He isn't advocating a new age of "blond beasts." He stresses the barbaric aspects of the beginnings of the state to disarm the sentimentality of liberal ideologues who romanticize innate human goodness. And it is obvious that "blond beast" bears no particular racial connotation and probably refers to unrefined animal passion such as embodied by lions:[13]

> One cannot fail to see at the bottom of all these noble races the beast of prey, the splendid *blond beast* prowling about avidly in search of spoil and victory; this hidden core needs to erupt from time to time, the animal has to get out again and go back to the wilderness: the Roman, Arabian, Germanic, Japanese nobility, the Homeric heroes, the Scandinavian Vikings—they all shared this need. (*GM* I, 11)

Also, I must cite other passages in Nietzsche where my interpretation of his warrior rhetoric gains currency:

> The most spiritual men, as the *strongest*, find their happiness where others would find their destruction: in the labyrinth, in hardness against themselves and others, in experiments; their joy is self-conquest. . . . When the exceptional human being treats the mediocre more tenderly than himself and his peers, this is not mere politeness of heart—it is simply his *duty*. (*AC* 57)
> We should reconsider cruelty and open our eyes. . . . Almost everything we call "higher culture" is based on the spiritualization [sublimation] of *cruelty*, on its becoming more profound. (*BGE* 229)

> To "give style" to one's character—a great and rare art! It is practiced by those who survey all the strengths and weaknesses of their nature and then fit them into an artistic plan until every one of them appears as art and reason and even weaknesses delight the eye. . . . Here the ugly that could not be removed is concealed; there it has been reinterpreted and made sublime. . . . A human being should *attain* satisfaction with himself, whether it be by means of this or that poetry and art; only then is a human being at all tolerable to behold. Whoever is dissatisfied with himself is continually ready for revenge, and we others will be his victims. (*GS* 290)

Apollonia: I think you conveniently overlook Nietzsche's willingness to sacrifice, even enslave, the masses for the benefit of aristocratic notions of "higher culture" and the times when Nietzsche's warrior rhetoric cannot plausibly be taken as hyperbole. He talks about "universal military service with real wars" as a remedy of modernity (*WP* 126); about how military developments happily affirm the "barbarian and wild beast in each of us" (*WP* 127); and often about how war is necessary for the state, how a just war sanctifies any cause, how it trains men for freedom, and how it nurtures strength (see, e.g., *TI* and *Z*).

Fegataccio: But Nietzsche is never the apologist of the state. He opposes the major political forms with which he is familiar: democracy, communism, socialism, fascism. Historically, war and the state have joined together as naturally as pasta and olive oil. But when Nietzsche celebrates war he does so only because it vivifies will to power: struggle, passion, an antidote to the indolence of last men. Nietzsche uses warrior rhetoric in part because of his admiration of Homeric heroes and their unrefined will to power. But he is clear that barbaric struggle is not the goal of active nihilists. Nietzsche does not endorse war and cruelty as such. War, however, is better than the insipid peace of last men because war indicates vigorous will to power that, if refined, could animate cultural greatness; peace among the indolent indicates a muted will to power that ensures cultural mediocrity.

The goal, if there is one, is peace among the strong whose spiritualized will to power no longer requires war:

And perhaps the great day will come when a people, distinguished by wars and victories and by the highest development of a military order and intelligence, and accustomed to make the heaviest sacrifices for these things, will exclaim of its own free will, "We break the sword," and will smash its entire military establishment down to its lowest foundations. *Rendering oneself unarmed when one had been the best-armed,* out of a height of feeling—that is the means to real peace, which must always rest on a peace of mind. . . . Rather perish than hate and fear, and twice rather perish than make oneself hated and feared—this must someday become the highest maxim for every single commonwealth too. (*WS* 284)

Apollonia: My impression is that when you are backed against the wall, Fegataccio, you pull out a passage that domesticates Nietzsche in order to make him more digestible for us. My goodness, in the passage you cite, the master of multiplicity sounds like a liberal humanist. He even recognizes free will![14] But I can find other passages, just as the Nazis did, in which he sounds like an adolescent fool: glorifying Homeric militarists, wistfully imagining himself as a warrior, ignoring the horrible effects that wars produce. Don't, in deluded allegiance to Nietzsche, ignore the irresponsible rhetoric he employs.

Fegataccio: And don't you ignore Nietzsche's life as evidence for his considered views. He was not a thug. He embodied politeness, amicability, and even temperament. His work exemplifies his character: While he may have felt cruel impulses—toward others and himself—these were subordinated to higher passions. He spiritualized his will to power in the service of producing great literature and philosophy. Refined interpreters should look to his dominant instincts and his considered judgments, not to his experimental musings or expressions of unresolved inner conflict.

Apollonia: Maybe little Friedrich made a virtue out of necessity! Given his physical weakness, perhaps he merely wrote the good life he couldn't lead. Lacking the physical strength to be the thug or warrior he privately imagined himself to be, he vented his frustration through abusive ad hominem attacks on thinkers such as Kant and influential movements such as Christianity. Fantasizing himself as a neo-Homeric hero, he cloistered himself and his writings from precisely those competitions and struggles with others that he otherwise glorifies. He may well be nothing more than the effete academic philosopher toward whom he typically professed such disdain! And do you, Fegataccio, share his views on war? Do you see yourself as the Homeric warrior of the future?

Fegataccio: I am not a pacifist, Apollonia, but you already know that. I am also not an abject follower of Nietzsche. I try to interpret him charitably because I subscribe to many of his broad themes, but when we get to details he and I often part company. But we can talk more about that later. You ask me about war, so I must respond.

In times of war, the individual faces the intimate aspirations of family, the patriotic demands of country, and the more distant claims of the international order. War multiplies the tensions, exhilarations, fears, and hopes embodied by individuals and their communities.

Military conquest, especially when plausibly evaluated as the victory of the righteous over the irredeemably evil, vivifies a nation. It presents opportunities for expression of the deepest human emotions and, in fact, demands their revelation: unspeakable sadness and grief as loved ones perish; justified rage and vows of vengeance at the acts of the aggressor; undeniable experiences of making history as one participates courageously in a grand epic; intense spasms of self-esteem as precarious occasions to prove oneself to self and intimates are encountered and surpassed; and soul-searing intimacy as collective efforts at rebuilding national infrastructure transform the world, as in one's youth, into a forum of seemingly infinite possibilities.

Of course, military defeat produces our deepest feelings of shame: a lingering sense of historical impoverishment; convictions of inferiority, betrayal, and divine abandonment; and a profound understanding of failure. The world becomes, as in death, a place without hope, pity, or compassion.

No wonder that so many people who have encountered large-scale war describe that event as their defining moment, the period when they felt most alive. Much was at risk. Apathy and collective narcolepsy, the signature traits of last men, were impossible. The pathology of war, as the struggle for feeling writ large, is a pathetic reminder of our toxic historical condition.

In war, the price of humanness rises astronomically. We understand viscerally, not merely rationally, the radical indeterminacy of life: the dread of cosmic exile and the longing for infinite redemption.

Apollonia: You leave me temporarily speechless, Fegataccio. I did not know you fancied yourself a prose poet.

Fegataccio: I don't have the restraints Nietzsche imposed on himself: radical fluidity, recurrent conflict, no fixity, and an audience of a few.

Apollonia: I want to return to other Nietzschean moral themes I find repulsive: his rabid aristocratism, his willingness to sacrifice the masses for the few, and his espousal of new forms of valuation. Nietzsche's unsqueamish elitism, seasoned by erroneous appeals to origins as untransformable, is disgusting. His snobbish appeal to "high culture" is typically intellectual: music, art, literature, and philosophy as the epitome of sublimated will to power. The irony here, of course, is that the very "slave morality," based on Western religions, that he derides produced most of the great music, art, literature, and philosophy of the past twenty centuries! Also, on what basis can he sneer that the "justification" of human life resides in its "highest exemplars?" How do people such as Goethe and Nietzsche himself justify an otherwise meaningless human species undertaking an otherwise meaningless existence? And why are they the "highest exemplars?" Nietzsche's arrogance on these matters is beyond belief.

I suppose we could expand Nietzsche's favored examples of high culture to include explicitly scientific, technological, and other advances. But how do such achievements justify the enslavement of the less gifted? Yes, I know, that the history of the world and the great Mediterranean, Middle Eastern, Asian, and African cultures manifest how slavery has served cultural purposes. But we now assume that a refined moral understanding precludes the enslavement of some for the benefit of others; wars have been fought pursuant to that assumption. Harkening back to Homeric heroes is the worst form of retrospective falsification: looking back, wide-eyed and romantically, at the "beasts of prey" and their "innocent" exercises of instinctual power—oh, please!

Fegataccio: Again, I think you take Nietzsche too literally. He addresses the internal battles waged by artists and philosophers of excellence: their enslavement of some drives to others, their sublimation of cruelty, competition, and aggression for higher ends. He is not talking about the actual enslavement of some people for the benefit of others. As always, he looks to the spiritual conflicts raging within the human psyche. Granted, his metaphors are bold and vivid, but Nietzsche has stylistic reasons we have discussed for choosing them.

Apollonia: I am struck by another deep irony in Nietzsche's work: In order to be considered higher types and great facilitators of culture—to have the relevant self-image—the aristocracy needs the "herd" as a measure of comparison. All Nietzsche's key notions—order of rank, great culture, higher forms of life, exemplary creation—involve comparative judgments. Nietzsche's higher types need the herd both as a contrasting standard and as an audience!

Fegataccio: I don't agree that excellence requires any audience, much less an audience of mediocrities. People of excellence and creativity, to the extent they seek any affirmation of their work, seek it only from a select group: peers. There is a sense, I suppose, that the mediocrity of the herd serves as a point of departure for those of excellence, but I don't take that to be significant irony. By their very nature the masses will always be with us, the bulk of humans will always be common. It is not as if we have to nurture the herd to make sure mediocrity lives! Remember, they have the strength of numbers and a stronger instinct for self-preservation than do higher types. The greater danger, for Nietzsche, is that the strengths of the herd will germinate into the classless society of last men.

Apollonia: And what does Nietzsche advance to replace herd morality? A few boilerplate slogans. Go beyond good and evil, recognize the order of human rank, cultivate excellence, become who you are, create new values, sublimate your will to power, assess character not actions. This strikes me as evaluation by soundbite, a worthless series of platitudes.

Fegataccio: There are several approaches available. One is Nietzsche's inclination toward functional nonmoral codes of value, refined versions of the "good" and "bad" of master morality. Just as a good knife is one that performs its function well, so, too, good artists, philosophers, and warriors can be evaluated by functional criteria. To bypass herd morality, for those able to do so, does not eliminate evaluation. Again, Nietzsche does not celebrate unrefined cruelty, but, instead, distinguishes life-affirming modes of evaluation from life-denying modes. The former characterize active nihilisms, while the latter characterize passive nihilists.

A second approach is to devise codes of value that lack the general pernicious features of herd morality: dogmatic self-understanding; dubious origins; glorifying pity; downplaying earthly success and life; submitting to external authority and imposing a false equality; and embracing metaphysical presuppositions such as belief in a supernatural being, free will, independent moral choice, the transparency and assessibility of human motives and intentions, and the fixed opposition of good and evil. Stripped of these features, resulting "moralities" might well be acceptable to Nietzsche. Remember, he knows that only a fool would think that all current conventional evaluations were simply wrong.

A third approach is to focus on the individuals's cultivation of character: "to become what one is." Here we return to the rearrangement of passions and drives in service of the multiple soul, the creation of style that is not available to everyone, and the donning of masks to present the illusion of a unified self. Nietzsche underscores what you have failed to see, Apollonia: Higher human types luxuriate in the interior life; they often sing only to themselves. This effort to order the multiple soul, to give style to one's life, and to discharge one's creative energies in works and deeds is the process of becoming who one is.

Under any of these approaches, which are not mutually exclusive, the aspiration is not the creation of a code of specific principles and imperatives, but an entire system of power relations, psychological moods, and cultural institutions that reflect and sustain robust creation. Personal character is always at the core because it manifests the degree and intensity of one's will to power.

As such, Nietzsche does not have ten new commandments, and I have misled you somewhat by talking about the creation of new values. His major aim is to uncover the conditions that have artificially truncated human possibilities and invite the better of us to overcome ourselves and release our powers.

Apollonia: You struggle valiantly, Fegataccio, but I remain unsatisfied. The first approach dangerously conflates morality with certain functions within nonmoral roles. This approach would replace the "good person" with the "good banker," the "good custodian," even the "good murderer." To perform one's function well, to be a good role player, says nothing about the quality of the functions and roles themselves. Unless it is supplemented in some way, this approach disables us from anything higher than crude Homeric heroism.

The second approach seems, ironically, reactive. This approach cites the alleged deficiencies of herd moralities, counsels higher types to renounce them, and waits to see the results. Again, this is not even form without content, it is purely a *via negativa*.

The third approach reminds me of new-age sloganism: find your way, be an individual, learn to order your soul, take solace within your spirit. All that is missing is a twelve-step program, a videotape purchasable at $29.95, and a magic five-day diet plan! The entire character *uber alles* approach is, at best, a neo-Aristotelian call for virtue ethics. As such, it fails to help us decide what to do (as opposed to who to be), it cannot independently explain (as opposed to assume) substantively what makes a character good, and it fails to tell us, except in the vaguest way, why it is better to have trait X than trait not-X. Moreover—and once again we find precious irony—it does not resolve conflict of character-trait situations, where two seemingly positive character traits clash such that only one can be honored in a particular context.

Nietzsche also has no social practice upon which to build his new approaches, no contexts to nurture the revised self-understandings necessary for the veneration of character as such.[15] We cannot create new values abstractly or out of mere reaction to the "nihilistic moment" and the "death of God."

Fegataccio: But you have trivialized Nietzsche's call for self-realization and caricatured my responses on his behalf, Apollonia! More mean-spirited tricks of the analytic philosophy you have absorbed so well! We have yet to speak thoroughly of Nietzsche's notions of will to power, eternal recurrence, and *Übermensch*. These notions are the ballast of the general approaches I sketched. We have always invented moral codes and established social practices to sustain them, at least if Nietzsche is correct. We may have thought we were doing something else—peering into the order of nature, discovering the dictates of a supreme being, or whatever—but Nietzsche unmasks the origins of those beliefs. The question of values for Nietzsche is one of choosing ascending or descending modes of life, rich or effete expressions of the will to power, and self-affirmations or self-abnegations. He does not remove burdens for humans, he challenges those of higher rank to assume greater burdens in the service of self-realization. We must be hard on ourselves and overcome the "dwarf" within us. We must become conscious of the origins, contents, and effects of our dominant morality and resist the false comforts of futuristic last men.

You know full well that Nietzsche, under his own broad themes, cannot utter new specific codes that will satisfy your favored criteria of soundness and validity. To do so is dogmatic, the main malady of slave morality he diagnoses. While he must sound like a dogmatist at times because our language will not permit him to escape that rhetoric strategy, he cannot accept dogmatism as a second-order belief about values. You know all this, Apollonia, so why do you persist in your vicious language games?

Apollonia: I will tell you what I know, Fegataccio. Since your precious Nietzsche died in 1900, technological and ideological developments in this century have drastically increased the pressures of human choice. Many find themselves alienated from the comforting, if often illusory, certitudes of the past. Marx, Freud, and, yes, Nietzsche disaggregated the redeeming unassailability of religious meaning by pressing their suspicions that latent economic, psychological, and cultural motives underwrite, indeed create, religious conviction. Later, the rise of fascism, Nazism, and early stage socialism that aspired to communism amplified the risks inherent in state control of the individual and family.

The explosive hegemony of instrumental reason and abstract systems of control facilitated a crisis of the spirit as anxiety became addiction. Refined technology mocked itself by producing weapons that threaten a humanly inspired apocalypse. Lived experiences, especially of the body, are too often eclipsed by ersatz media-inspired substitutes: virtual realities, blatant commodifications, and mere images understood vicariously. The enormous increase in information finds no parallel in expanded wisdom. Too many of us seem unable to reconnect with or to re-create wholesome realities. The human search for meaning is caricatured by capitalist hucksterism, pop psychology, unspeakable violence, the sham transcendence of a drug culture, and craven flight from individual responsibility. Cynicism and thorough skepticism are falsely enshrined as insight. The citadel of the self is under siege.

So I turn to the "philosophers of the future" and I ask for guidance: What is the way? What is your way? What is a way? And how do they respond, Fegataccio? They recite the usual, lame litany: Analytic philosophy rests on unwarranted assumptions, outdated theoretical distinctions, and politically naïve understandings of power.

But where is their new world philosophy, where is their inspiring vision of the future, where is their seductive dance, their comforting song, their vivid painting? I look, I listen, I beseech, I touch, and I taste, but I discover only culturally lifeless, deconstructive rhetoric that mirrors and sustains the very social conditions it belittles.

We must now struggle for our own humanity in a technological fairyland that we created, we must win what was previously assumed: authentic, fully human experiences. The "nihilistic moment" has become a way of life! This is what I know, Fegataccio.

Fegataccio: I am not sure how I should respond to you, Apollonia (and then he blinked).

Feeling subdued and tired, Apollonia and Fegataccio departed for the mall's cinema. They felt their conversation was impinging on dangerous personal ground. Fegataccio sensed that Apollonia could peer right through his public face into his soul. Apollonia could not shake the feeling that Fegataccio was measuring her and finding her inadequate. They needed to relax and thought a movie would provide some respite.

Chapter 3

EAGLES, LIONS, AND TARANTULAS

Eternal Recurrence, Will to Power, and the Overman

Nietzsche writes that the "fundamental conception" of *Thus Spoke Zarathustra* is "the idea of the eternal recurrence, this highest formula of affirmation that is at all attainable" (*EH*, *"Thus Spoke Zarathustra,"* 1). Nietzsche also writes that "the great and small struggle always revolves around superiority, around growth and expansion, around power—in accordance with the will to power which is the will of life" (*GS* 349). In *Zarathustra* he says, "Behold, I teach you the overman [*Übermensch*]. The overman is the meaning of the earth. Let your will say: the overman *shall be* the meaning of the earth!" (Z I, "Zarathustra's Prologue," 3). Accordingly, interpreters of Nietzsche must confront the notions of eternal recurrence, will to power, and the *Übermensch*.

ETERNAL RECURRENCE

The eternal recurrence holds that events in the world comprise a cyclical eternity: Whatever is occurring will recur again and is a return of itself; it has all occurred before and will occur again, in exactly the same way each cycle, eternally. There is no beginning, no end, and no middle of the history of our world.

In another of his eloquent fables, Nietzsche describes the eternal recurrence:

What, if some day or night a demon were to steal after you into your loneliest loneliness and say to you: "This life as you now live it and have lived it, you will have to live once more and innumerable times more; and there will be nothing new in it, but every pain and every joy and every thought and sigh and everything unutterably small or great in your life will have to return to you, all in the same succession and sequence—even this spider and this moonlight between the trees, and even this moment and I myself. The eternal hourglass of existence is turned upside down again and again, and you with it, speck of dust!"

Would you not throw yourself down and gnash your teeth and curse the demon who spoke thus? Or have you once experienced a tremendous moment when you would have answered him: "You are a god and never have I heard anything more divine." . . . How well disposed would you have to become to yourself and to life to crave nothing more fervently than this ultimate eternal confirmation and seal? (*GS* 341)

It is unclear whether the eternal recurrence is a cosmological doctrine, a hypothesis, a moral imperative, a psychological test, a reaffirmation of the death of god, or an attempt at secular redemption from the nihilistic moment.

Cosmological Doctrine

In his *Nachlass*, Nietzsche, at least, toys with the eternal recurrence as a cosmological doctrine. He claimed that in the world there are a finite number of power quantities (aggregate energy) in a finite space and in an infinite time; no final state has been reached; energy has infinite duration and is conserved; change is eternal; every possible power combination must at some time be realized; and the same power configurations must recur eternally. He assumes there is no beginning of time and that power quantities must repeat themselves in the same configuration which recurs eternally.[1]

Taken as a cosmological doctrine, eternal recurrence is problematic. First, it is unverifiable because we cannot distinguish one cycle of power configurations from another which is a duplicate. Without the ability to distinguish cycles it is impossible to empirically verify the thesis of eternal recurrence, or even the belief that there are two cycles to compare. Second, from Nietzsche's premises it does not follow that that every event must recur in precisely the same sequence. Even if all particular events must recur, they need not recur in the same order eternally unless there is a necessary connection between the events in the sequence. In fact, there is no necessary connection between a finite amount of energy in the world and the number of possible arrangements of that energy. Moreover, the required necessary connections suggest cause-and-effect relationships that Nietzsche himself otherwise disparages (see, e.g., *BGE* 21; *GS* 112). Third, Nietzsche consistently, even fiercely, connects style of presentation with worth of content. Yet his "proofs" of the cosmological interpretation of eternal recurrence are written in what he otherwise takes to be the pedestrian form of deductive argument (see, e.g., *TI*, "The Problem of Socrates," 5; *HAH* 11; *GS* 111; *BGE* 4). This style of presentation, according to Nietzsche, seeks universal assent and undermines the order of human rank. Thus, it is doubtful, thankfully, that Nietzsche regarded the cosmological interpretation of eternal recurrence as paramount.

Moral Hypotheses and Imperatives

There are numerous ways that eternal recurrence can be formulated into a moral hypothesis or imperative. One way is to view eternal recurrence as a neo-Kantian imperative: Perform action X if and only if you can will that it becomes a universal act (in the sense of being performed by everyone under the same relevant circumstances) for eternity. But this is certainly not to what Nietzsche aspires. He denies the universality of moral judgments as misguided dogmatism that nurtures mediocrity. Moreover, to reformulate the imperative in a more localized way—perform act X if and only if you can will that you will perform X for eternity—confronts the obstacle that Nietzsche never ponders the moral quality of specific acts. While he is concerned with one's style, character, and manifestation of will to power, he never analyzes the inherent or even instrumental value of particular moral actions. In part this is due to his desire to distance himself from Platonic–Judeo–Christian morality and in part to his veneration of the order of human rank: One cannot assess the quality of specific actions, moral or otherwise, in the abstract, but only in relation to particular types of people at particular times.

Another way to view eternal recurrence as a moral imperative is to focus on an entire life rather than specific acts. Because any universalized formulation will run afoul of Nietzsche's insistence on rank order and specific evaluations, the most plausible rendering would be along these lines: Lead only that life that you can will you would live eternally. This rendering does not depend on a Kantian notion of willing in terms of logically consistent actions and choices, but, instead, on one's subjective acceptance of the magnitude (or insignificance) of leading this life an infinite number of times. As such, it retains a secular version of the Christian appeal to the eternal because it makes infinity a component of evaluation. Whereas Christians rely on the alleged imperatives of eternity in a transcendent world, this version of eternal recurrence relies on the alleged imperatives of eternity in this world.

One may well ask, "If this life lived once has value N, how does the prospect of this life lived an infinite number of times change N now?" While an advocate could argue that from the vantage point of eternity the value or disvalue of N is magnified infinitely, why should that necessarily affect evaluation from my vantage point now? Why should acting as if eternal recurrence were true have any significant impact on my decisions?

One might rejoin that the value of certain actions is dependent on the number of times they occur. For example, climbing Mt. Everest was a monumental event when it was first done, but if hundreds of thousands of people did it annually the significance of the climb would evaporate. But this rejoinder does not help. It could be used to show that no action would bear significance because of uniqueness from the vantage point of eternity because all actions, if eternal recurrence is true or we act as if it is true, would have infinite occurrences. Or it could be used to show that all actions bear the same significance within a cycle of power configurations as they would if eternal recurrence was false.

Moreover, if eternal recurrence is true as a cosmological doctrine—if everything that is occurring has and will occur again—how can I possibly not comply with the "imperatives" of the moral interpretation of eternal recurrence? The moral interpretation's imperatives would be illusory because whatever life I "choose" is what has come before and what will come later; or, more precisely, what is eternally.

In fact, it is probably a mistake to view eternal recurrence as a moral hypothesis or as issuing moral imperatives. Nietzsche was not concerned with moral evaluations as such. He directs his attention, instead, to Greek notions of goodness as personal excellence: achievement, intelligence, creative power, superior capacities, and deriving the merit of actions only from the actor's character. Clearly, one can embody this notion of personal excellence without exemplifying the goodness commanded by conventional morality. Furthermore, Nietzsche explicitly renounces the connection between moral rules and human action, even when that connection claims to be person specific: "But even when the moralist addresses himself only to the single human being and says to him, 'You ought to be such and such!' he does not cease to make himself ridiculous. . . . To say to him, 'Change yourself!' is to demand that everything be changed, even retroactively" (*TI*, "Morality as Anti-Nature," 6).

Psychological Test

Eternal recurrence is probably viewed best as a psychological test: One's reaction to the thought of eternal recurrence is evidence of one's place in the order of human rank. Eternal recurrence underscores the lack of inherent cosmic meaning and purpose and challenges us to respond positively: to accept our lives in their entireties and to fashion them in such a way that we luxuriate in our time on earth without the distractions of revenge and *ressentiment*. Nietzsche captures this response in his call for *amor fati* (love of fate):

I do not want in the least that anything should become different than it is; I myself do not want to become different. (*EH*, "Why I Am So Clever," 9). My formula for greatness in a human being is *amor fati*: that one wants nothing to be different, not forward, not backward, not in all eternity. Not merely bear what is necessary, still less conceal it—all idealism is mendaciousness in the face of what is necessary—but *love* it. (*EH*, "Why I Am So Clever," 9–10)

The acceptance of everything is paramount for Nietzsche, because he thinks that if my life were different in any way it would no longer be my life but the life of a different person. Moreover, he also thinks that events in the world are closely interrelated, such that to want things to be different is a denial of this world and one's self. Accordingly, eternal recurrence interpreted as a psychological test highlights several Nietzschean themes: Become who you are (by fully embracing all events in your life), celebrate this life and this world (by not deferring robust living in hopes of transcendent salvation), and avoid revenge and *ressentiment* (by affirming fate and understanding that the past is unalterable). Eternal recurrence eliminates the possibility of another life, either here or in a transcendent world. Although recognizing that we are in fact mortal, higher types can impress the form of eternity upon their lives by fashioning lives they can embrace joyfully in their entireties. To want nothing in one's life or in the world to be different in any way is the mark of higher human types.

For Nietzsche, the mark of lower human types is their need to edit out the pain, tragedy, and hardship in their lives. The desire for a life without struggle, suffering, distinction, and failure is the invariable sign of last men. Last men will "throw themselves down and gnash their teeth and curse the demon" who brings the message of eternal recurrence: their hopes for transcendent salvation have been dashed, their *ressentiment* of superior types has been rendered pointless, their (largely unconscious) transvaluation of master values has been devalued, and their irredeemable weakness and inadequacy have been unmasked.

Higher types, at first, will wince at the abysmal thought of the eternal return of the petty, the ugly, and the small. But upon fully understanding the interrelatedness of all events, the circularity of time, and the pointlessness of revenge, they will answer the demon: "You are a god and never have I heard anything more divine." At birth we all find ourselves in unchosen social contexts. Celebrants of *amor fati* will distinguish themselves by the quality of their performance: their confrontations with obstacles and suffering, their ability to forge a unified style out of their inherent multiplicity, their recurring self-creations and self-overcomings, their ability to luxuriate in the immediacy of life, and their understanding of life as a sequence of aesthetically self-fulfilling moments.

Unlike Eastern religions that seek detachment from the suffering of this world through minimizing desire and maximizing transcendence, and Western stoics who moderate passion as a means of coping with both the tragedies and triumphs of life, Nietzsche's eternal recurrence glorifies life in all its tragic dimensions. Moreover, eternal recurrence excludes every goal and purpose outside the eternal circularity of all things. Thus, one must affirm life without the invocation of linear goals. Keith Ansell-Pearson states the reconciliation with the tragic dimensions of life eloquently:

What one affirms in the eternal return is life as "self-overcoming," that is, life as an eternally self-creating and self-destroying force, and the "law" of life as a passing away, death, change, and destruction, and, as Nietzsche says, this must include: "saying Yes to opposition and war" [*EH*, "The Birth of Tragedy," 3]. This is a tragic view of life because it sees no redemption from the pain and suffering of life, and, moreover, wants none.[2]

The thought of eternal recurrence, however, invites numerous questions: Why and how are events in the world and within a life so closely interrelated that the slightest alteration has significant consequences? Why should the demon's message of eternal recurrence by itself cause any "gnashing of teeth" or proclamations of "divinity?" Could members of the lowly herd not sincerely shout, "*Amor fati!*" once they understand eternal recurrence metaphorically? How can Nietzsche, the acolyte of "Becoming," rely coherently on the notion of eternity, the paradigm of "Being," as the ballast for affirming life? Does Nietzsche's reliance on eternity betray the vestiges of herd morality within his soul? Would eternal recurrence not cultivate a passivity or resignation, responses antithetical to Nietzschean self-overcoming, in the hearts of believers?

THE WILL TO POWER

For Nietzsche, the fundamental drive of all living things is the will to power, the impulse to dominate one's environment and extend one's influence. In humans, the will to power sometimes manifests itself as brute force, but more frequently requires creativity, boldness, and innovation. Nietzsche claims that the typical catalog of human desires—for love, friendship, respect, procreation, biological nourishment, competitive glory, and so on—are all manifestations of the will to power. Accordingly, underlying the greatest altruistic and cultural values, such as justice, truth, beauty, self-sacrifice, and art, is the natural impulse to command and dominate.

Nietzsche expresses this most forcefully in his *Nachlass*:

My *Dionysian* world of the eternally self-creating, the eternally self-destroying, this mystery world of the twofold voluptuous delight, my "beyond good and evil," without goal, unless the joy of the circle is itself a goal; without will, unless a ring feels good will toward itself—do you want a *name* for this world? A *solution* for all its riddles? A *light* for you, too, you best-concealed, strongest, most intrepid, most midnightly men?—*This world is the will to power— and nothing besides*! And you yourselves are also this will to power—and nothing besides! (*WP* 1067; see also, Z I, "On the Thousand and One Goals"; Z II, "On Self-Overcoming"; Z II, "On Redemption"; *BGE* 259)

Clearly, the will to power does not depend on the presence of a free or any will. All living things possess a will to power, although many do not have "minds." Furthermore, even for humans the will to power is not grounded on the power of volitions to act as causes for various effects. The will to power is a "primitive" for Nietzsche: It is life, and life is a complex struggle within and outside the human psyche. The will to power is the name Nietzsche gives to the recurring struggle among closely interrelated entities in the world. Power does not mean anything when taken abstractly; instead, it requires the mutual resistance of linked living things. More subtly, will to power underwrites the struggles among the multiple drives we embody. These multiple drives, as well as the impulse for self-overcoming, are merely different manifestations of the same instinctual drive. Sublimation, self-perfection, and self-overcoming within the individual and influence, domination, and command over others and the world all fall under the rubric of will to power. Moreover, the will to power connotes a process, not a fixed entity, which has growth, expansion, and accumulation at its core.

The philosophical subtext of Nietzsche's invocation of will to power is clear: Our forms of knowledge, morality, truth, logic, and religion— all the alleged foundations of our institutions and theoretical enterprises—are the consequences of power struggles which themselves lack rational justification. While these alleged foundations present themselves as neutral exemplars of the persuasiveness of better rational arguments, undeniable metaphysical grounding, and glimpses of a natural order embedded in the universe, they are in fact nothing more than the effects of the will to power.

A crude reading associates the will to power with the drive for self-preservation, but Nietzsche claims that self-preservation is only one of the effects of the will to power, not its defining aim. Nietzsche calls higher types more fragile, and more likely to squander their abundant passions in acts of self-overcoming than herd members who are concerned narrowly with species survival. Expanding one's influence and discharging one's strength often jeopardize self-preservation.

Another crude reading concludes that Nietzsche wholeheartedly endorses all manifestations of the will to power. On a trivial level that may be true; his eternal recurrence and *amor fati* demand that higher types joyfully embrace all of life. But on a practical level Nietzsche distinguishes life-affirming from life-denying manifestations of the will to power, refined from decadent wills to power, and vital from effete quantities of will to power. The will to power manifests itself in philosophers' attempts to create the world in their own image; in every attempt of overcoming; in every valuation; in every vengeful and resentful act of the herd; in every physical confrontation, including war; in every artistic creation; in every attempt to control and command through religion, politics, and military force; in every invocation of love and friendship; in every act of charity and self-sacrifice; in every attempt to procreate; in every egalitarian reform; in every aristocratic reaction; and in every human act, including Nietzsche's own invocation of the will to power itself. Although all living things possess will to power, they differ in the quantity and quality of manifestations. Thus, acknowledgment of will to power, eternal recurrence, and *amor fati* does not preclude the continued evaluation that itself is part of the will to power. As the basic natural drive of life, the will to power embodies conflicting drives with self-destructive inclinations.[3]

Nietzsche's notion of will to power suggests several questions: If the will to power manifests itself in every human activity, does it retain any discrete meaning? Is Nietzsche wrongly reducing the activities of all living things to only one source, thereby reneging on the complexity of life? Does he yet again confront a self-referential paradox—his notion of "will to power," according to his own beliefs, emerges from his will to power? Is the use of "power" misleading? Does it slyly trade on the conventional meaning of "power" for its panache while distancing itself from that meaning once its stylized usages are unpacked?

THE *ÜBERMENSCH*

The *Übermensch* (overman) is the symbol of humans overcoming themselves to superior forms. Nietzsche does not give us a definite description, but the overman represents a superhuman exemplar that has not yet existed: "Never yet has there been an overman. Naked I saw both the greatest and the smallest man: they are still all-too-similar to each other. Verily, even the greatest I found all-too-human" (Z II, "On Priests"). *"I teach you the overman* Man is something that shall be overcome. What have you done to overcome him?" (Z I, "Zarathustra's Prologue," 3). "Man is a rope, tied between beast and overman—a rope over an abyss. . . . 'I am a herald of the lightning and a heavy drop from the cloud; but this lightning is called *overman'*" (Z I, "Zarathustra's Prologue," 4). *"Dead are all gods: now we want the overman to live"* (Z I, "On the Gift-Giving Virtue," 3). "Not 'mankind' but *overman* is the goal!" (*WP* 1001). "The Roman Caesar with Christ's soul" (*WP* 983).

Clearly, the overman would be joyous, in control of his instinctual will to power, able to forge an admirable unity and style out of his inherent multiplicity, severe with himself, in control of his desires, a sublimator and refiner of cruelty, an unrepentant bearer of great suffering, a pursuer of "truth" who is aware of the essential unity of truth and illusion, and a creator and imposer of values and meaning who experiences his existence as self-justifying. The overman will remain faithful to this earth and not defer gratification in hopes of transcendent salvation in another world, will possess great health and be able to experience the multiple passions he embodies, eschews the easy path of last men, understands the value he creates is simply what he embodies, celebrates a justified self-love, is free from resentment and revenge, wastes no time in self-pity, is grateful for the entirety of his life, understands and maintains a clear distance between himself and the herd, and exemplifies the rank order of life. The overman "shall be the meaning of the earth," in that the overman endows life with value and redeems the species's inherently meaningless tragic existence. In sum, the overman is a higher mode of being that approximates the human aspiration for transcendent greatness.

The overman represents the full process of Nietzschean becoming—recurrent deconstruction, reimagination, re-creation—the virtues of the active nihilist. To prepare to even approximate the joyful overman, we must pass through "three metamorphoses" of discipline, defiance, and creation. The spirit, like a camel, flees into the solitude of the desert to bear enormous burdens; the spirit, like a lion, must transform itself into a master, a conqueror who releases its own freedom by destroying the traditional "thou shalts." But it is not within the power of the lion to create new values so the spirit must transform itself into a child whose playful innocence, ability to forget, and capacity for creative games signals the spirit's willing its own will (Z I, "On the Three Metamorphoses").

The notion of overman as symbolic, dynamic, and indeterminate provides an ideal toward which to strive. It is as an (unattainable) ideal that the overman confers meaning and creates values.[4] The overman symbolizes a refashioning of our sensibilities and aspiration in service of an enhanced life. It points a direction rather than specifying a clear goal. Nietzsche warns readers not to view the overman as an evolutionary necessity or as an idealistic type of higher man:

The word "overman," as the designation of a type of supreme achievement, as opposed to "modern" men, to "good" men, to Christians and other nihilists . . . has been understood almost everywhere with the utmost innocence in the sense of those very values whose opposite Zarathustra was meant to represent—that is, as an "idealistic" type of a higher kind of man, half "saint," half "genius." Other scholarly oxen have suspected me of Darwinism on that account. Even the "hero worship" of that unconscious and involuntary counterfeiter, Carlyle, which I have repudiated so maliciously, has been read into it. (*EH*, "Why I Write Such Good Books," 1)

Nietzsche's *Übermensch* attracts several questions: Is the overman, despite Nietzsche's denials, a remnant of hero worship? Is it another vestige of the Judeo–Christian morality he repudiates? Is it consistent with his reliance on eternal recurrence? Does the fatalism of eternal recurrence coalesce uneasily with the recurrent striving and transcendent aspirations of the overman? Is the overman exemplified, or at least approximated, by the spiritualized will to power of philosophers and artists? Or is the warrior and conqueror of others a better, or at least a possible, approximation? Or is the overman nothing more than a signification of the process of destruction, reimagination, and re-creation that constitutes self-overcoming in a world of flux?

THE THIRD DIALOGUE

Neither Apollonia nor Fegataccio had enjoyed the movie. They had not paid much attention to the actors or the plot. The movie's only value was that it had permitted them to remain in each other's company while avoiding real engagement. Attendance had bestowed a comforting respite from their complicated and difficult encounters, yet it nurtured their mutual resolve to try again. They were glad they went. After the movie they went back to the mall's food court for a snack.

Apollonia: That was a good movie. I thought Robert De Niro and Al Pacino were terrific. Thanks for suggesting it.
Fegataccio: You're welcome. I am always ambivalent about those types of movies. Some of them are classics in the subtlety of their char-

acter studies, but their ethnic stereotypes disturb me. I wonder what messages such movies send to the herd.

Apollonia: Yes, we have to be careful of that nasty, witless "herd," don't we, Fegataccio? May I assume your reference signals your willingness to continue our discussions of Nietzsche?

Fegataccio: Yes.

Apollonia: Fine. I have always been puzzled by his eternal recurrence. Taken as a cosmological doctrine it is simply poor science and unsound reasoning. Taken as a moral doctrine it is vacuous. At least Kant tried to place his categorical imperative on a logical basis, what one can will with logical consistency; Nietzsche's eternal recurrence as a moral doctrine is nothing more than a reification of subjective whim. Taken as a psychological test, eternal recurrence is also vacuous. Why should the mere thought of eternal recurrence cause me to "gnash my teeth" or to rejoice? Why should it have any affect on what I do and how I act now? If I experience the same life an infinite number of times, then during each cycle I would be unaware of previous cycles, because if I were aware of upcoming or could recall previous cycles then some of the cycles would be different from others. Thus, being unaware of the past and unable to anticipate the future, I would feel no anxiety at upcoming events, could take no steps to avoid previous errors, nor foretell in any way my coming fate. The "eternality" of the events would have no bearing on me because I would experience myself as living the events only once. If Sisyphus knows that he is eternally doomed to push the boulder up the hill only to have it fall down that is much different from his being unaware that he is doomed to that fate for X years. In the former case, he can truly anticipate and experience the eternality of his fate, while in the latter case appeals to eternality are purely hypothetical. Taken as a psychological doctrine, eternal recurrence is a bogeyman, it raises a pseudoterrifying specter.

Fegataccio: I think eternal recurrence is best understood only as a psychological test. But I think your critical remarks interpret eternal recurrence as both a cosmological and a psychological doctrine.

Apollonia: I think we must view eternal recurrence as a combination of cosmological doctrine and psychological test if the doctrine is to embody any content.[5] If eternal recurrence is viewed merely as fable or myth, it amounts to a question in a parlor game: What if you were to live this life eternally? The answer could well be that nobody cares. Unless I can entertain that I (and not merely someone substantially similar to me) in fact will live this life eternally, the question of eternal recurrence lacks a point. Whatever answer I give to a "what if" question will be tainted by my understanding of the inquiry as purely hypothetical. What if I were seven feet tall, would I be a great basketball player? What if I were male instead of female, would I be recognized as a great artist? Such questions can be interesting and can elicit imaginative responses, but they suffer from their purely hypothetical natures; they neither engage our identities nor pose any significant practical problems. And that is why I think eternal recurrence must retain a cosmological flavor if it is to serve as a serious psychological test.

Fegataccio: It is true that for eternal recurrence to gain vivid hold we must entertain a vantage point outside of our current cycle and imagine it returning again and again. If that is what you mean by "retaining a cosmological flavor" I could agree.

But it isn't really a doctrine at all. It is merely a hypotheses which underscores some of Nietzsche's broad themes about life: the importance of the moment, the futility of revenge and resentment, the need to affirm life as a whole, the lack of inherent and ultimate cosmic meaning, the essential unity of joy and despair, and the need to embrace all events in your life because they constitute who you are. In fact, eternal recurrence isn't even a hypothesis, it is a metaphor for self-overcoming in the face of cosmic purposelessness, the pursuit of recurring transitory goals where there is no Goal, and the celebration of a graceful dance, raucous laughter, and stirring performance where there is no final End.

Apollonia: You make Nietzsche sound like a combination of Mussolini and Daffy Duck! But let me clarify my remarks. I am not—at least not yet—criticizing the broad themes you mentioned, but I am denying there is any connection between them and the eternal recurrence, whether you label it a doctrine, hypothesis, conditional statement, or metaphor. My critical remarks are aimed at the "sound and fury" of eternal recurrence which I take to signify nothing. Why not just state Nietzsche's broad themes and toss out the hocus-pocus of eternal recurrence?

Fegataccio: You are so much the literalist, Apollonia. A hint of poetry, a touch of vivid imagery, the seasoning of the ineffable, serve our spirits well. Remember, Nietzsche always connects literary style with content. He cannot state his message in prosaic terms because he sees the world as Becoming and all language as inherently indeterminate.

But let me give you an illustration of the connection between eternal recurrence and his broad themes. If we affirm the totality of life as it is, *amor fati*, then attitudes of revenge and *ressentiment* are futile and self-defeating. Those negative attitudes seek to right the perceived wrongs of the past, in effect to change the past. But eternal recurrence undermines such hopes because it suggests a circular, not linear, notion of time. The acceptance of eternal recurrence not only eliminates the possibility of the transcendent world of Being, but also manifests the poverty of Platonic–Judeo–Christian metaphysics: free will, immortal souls, infinite redemption, the justification of punishment, the will to equality, and so on.[6]

In eternal recurrence, the past and future meld together into an infinite moment. If everything recurs, then events of the future are merely events of a more distant past. Thus, the present is highlighted as every part of life is bound together in eternal flux.[7] Eternal recurrence contrasts with the linear trajectory of progressivism and evolution, it underscores the death of God, it affirms the creative unity of all things and events, and it invites higher types to overcome the lack of cosmic meaning by life-affirming destruction, reimagination, and re-creation.

Apollonia: Or does it nurture a fatalism and passivity, or perhaps a call to resignation in the face of eternal monotony? Why is Nietzsche's eternal recurrence any more than stoical acceptance of the status quo? If I cannot avoid it, why should I resist it?

Fegataccio: For lower types what you describe may well be the reaction. (I realize you are just presenting and not necessarily embracing the argument, Apollonia, so do not take me to be calling you a lower type.) Overcome by the spirit of gravity, lacking the exuberance to affirm life in the face of cosmic meaninglessness, and clinging to the shadows of gods and transcendent redemption, last men will wallow in comforting life-denying illusions and retard their own self-overcomings. Just as the burdens of Sisyphus would annihilate lower types, the thought of eternal recurrence can lead to passive nihilism at its worst. This is a Nietzschean way of speaking about fatalism and stoical acceptance.

Higher types, though, will see eternal recurrence as an opportunity to rebel and become who they are by creatively willing their fate; by embracing the entirety of life as self-overcoming in the world of Becoming. Remember, if Sisyphus has the desire to roll his boulder up the hill and then watch it roll back down eternally, his fate would not be meaningless. Such a desire creates meaning where none antecedently existed and Sisyphus would thereby become who he was. Fortunately, higher types are in a much better position than Sisyphus, even with his imagined desire: Higher types contemplating eternal recurrence can still revel in the process of self-overcoming which Sisyphus cannot.

Apollonia: That is much too facile. Nietzscheans use "self-overcoming" as a talismanic incantation that remedies all ills. Why is it anything more than a symptom of discontent, insecurity, and desperation? Isn't it only the wearing of different masks, the playing of different roles, the strained thespianism of those lacking a sense of self? Self-overcoming reminds me of reptiles who regularly shed their skins.

But back to fatalism—my point is that both lower and higher types could adopt fatalism in the face of eternal recurrence. The notions of fate, eternal cycles, and necessity lend themselves to fatalism, not spasmodic squeals of *amor fati*. There is a phony air to Nietzsche's entire "embrace the whole of life" creed. It depends on the zany idea that all things and events are interrelated so tightly that to want one small aspect of one's life to have been different is to try to will an entirely different world. Isn't he only trying to rationalize his own illnesses, isolation, and ineffectuality in the world? Aren't his efforts yet another lame attempt to convince himself of the worth of his labors in the face of a mountain of evidence to the contrary?

Fegataccio: I don't want to delve too deeply into self-overcoming right now. For Nietzsche, there is not one best kind of life for all humans. We must all discharge the burden of forging our own life. Nietzsche also denies the presence of a substantive self lingering beneath appearances. We are our "masks," so he thinks higher types should aspire to be the most interesting series of masks they can create. To accept a particular mask or role as definitive of who you are during a lifetime is to artificially truncate the multiplicity you embody and to accept the life-denying illusory world of being. To live beyond yourself in self-creation is to forge a complex subtle character that is worthy of "strutting its hour upon the stage" many times, even eternally.

Apollonia: The self-overcoming project and its thin explanation reflect only Nietzsche's aesthetic preferences, adolescent fantasies, lingering Christian aspirations for the eternal and infinite, and psychological discontent with the person he is. But I'll respect your desire to bracket discussion of self-overcoming for the moment. But what about fatalism? Have you forgotten my criticisms?

Fegataccio: Nietzsche's eternal recurrence and attitude of *amor fati* do not merely permit but demand active response. First, at the very least, humans have the freedom to order their interior life, their responses, to the thought of eternal recurrence. While lower types would adopt the passive nihilism you described earlier, higher types will embrace the entirety of life and view the lack of inherent cosmic meaning and infinite redemption as liberation from external authority. Even the Stoics recognized that nature could not control some things: humans' attitudes toward events in the world. Second, unlike the Stoics, Nietzsche glorifies the passions as robust manifestations of the will to power. To become who you are, to self-overcome, and to destroy, reimagine, and re-create require an active nihilism that elevates the present into a fated eternity. Embracing eternal recurrence rejoices in the return, not the abnegation, of our own wills.[8] Third, higher types will recognize that passive nihilism or fatalism rests on the life-denying illusion that the "individual" is separate from the world. On the contrary, the thought of eternal recurrence underscores the individual's complete immersion in the world of becoming. Cosmic fate is not external to us, it is us.[9]

Moreover, instead of inputing a crude determinism to the acceptance of eternal recurrence, we can view acceptance as a free act: the immediate moment, the present, affirming and characterizing its own return and that of every other moment. By visualizing the present moment in terms of eternity, Nietzsche challenges us to embrace the ceaseless world of Becoming in which eternity does not freeze our choices but, instead, fulfills the present with endless possibility.[10]

Thus, the eternal recurrence, in typical Nietzschean fashion, bears ambiguous tidings. For those clinging to the influences of religion and conventional morality which have historically sought to marginalize the self, the thought of eternal recurrence will lead to despair and self-abandonment. For those higher types who can will the return of even the small, ugly, and petty, the thought of eternal recurrence facilitates self-mastery.

Apollonia: If there is no substantial self then I don't know what there is to abandon or to master. I am sure you will respond with the mantra of "multiplicity, conflict, and self-overcoming," but those notions remain mysterious without a substantive self to underwrite the complex impulses you Nietzscheans sanctify. The rest of your reply reiterates your reformed Sisyphus: As long as we have the desire to be in a world lacking inherent meaning, then cosmic purposelessness loses its power to drain us of energy and we can confer our own meanings and purposes.

By the way, there are clear differences between rebelling against one's fate and gaining a desire to live that fate. To rebel against fate is to say and act, "I don't desire F (my fate) but I will resist F and all desire for F. My life will gain meaning by fighting for the impossible dream, the vanquishing of an unvanquishable F." To gain a desire to live fate is to say and act, "I will rejoice in my fate and desire nothing else. I will become my fate by willing nothing else. *Amor fati!*" Nietzscheans are not rebels, they are supplicant collaborators!

Furthermore, doesn't your suggestion turn Nietzsche into a snake-oil salesman or a master hypnotist? As long as he can mystify us into gushing "*amor fati!*" we suddenly become bearers of meaning. Why not just hire a master hypnotist to cast a spell on us such that we believe our greatest desire is to live with cosmic purposelessness? Once we awake from the spell we can all become Nietzscheans giddy with creativity and meaning!

Fegataccio: You're really getting sarcastic, Apollonia, and I was always taught that sarcasm is the weapon of the weak-minded. The will to power "underwrites" the complex impulses that constitute us. We'll have plenty of time to talk about it later. As for the hypnotist, you know full well that all a hypnotist can implant is ersatz desire and sham passion. The thought of eternal recurrence is not affirmed by those who are tricked or manipulated into saying "yes." Such compliance will eventually expose itself in feeble actions (or inactions) that fail to live the credo of *amor fati*. One must *have* the requisite desire, not merely think one has the desire. But, yes, in some sense Nietzsche is challenging higher types to search the spirits and to test their mettle to discover whether they can summon the desire, followed by actions, that can transform their sense of life.

In affirming eternal recurrence we are willing the flux of life and acknowledging the unity of opposites. What is eternal is the inherent flux and chaos of the world of Becoming. Affirmation leads to our willing creatively what we had previously muddled through unconsciously. We become who we are through this affirmation: By altering our attitude we take responsibility (although not in the Christian sense) for the people we are.[11]

Apollonia: You speak eloquently, Fegataccio, and perhaps my sarcasm betrays my own uneasiness with the thought of eternal recurrence. You must understand that for me Nietzsche's talk of eternity, willing the world, self-overcoming, and transcendence is redolent with the fragrance of secular redemption: religion for those who have lost their faith but retained their need. Furthermore, there is a witless "this is the best of all possible worlds" aura surrounding eternal recurrence interpreted as a psychological test. How can I, or anyone else, affirm the horrors of slavery, genocide, the subjugation of women, and intractable racial and ethnic strife?

Fegataccio: You may have a point there. In my heart of hearts I am not sure even I can affirm the existence of television quiz shows, the marriage of Sophia Loren to Carlo Ponti, the continuing popularity of Regis Philbin and Andy Rooney, or the worldwide failure to prohibit German cuisine!

Pardon my facetiousness, Apollonia, your remarks are too important to be obscured by my self-indulgence. In some ways, Nietzsche does offer a secular redemption, although it falls far short of the religious version. He admits as much himself:

I taught them all *my* creating and striving, to create and carry together into One what in man is fragment and riddle and dreadful accident. . . . I taught them to work on the future and to redeem with their creation all that *has been*. To redeem what is past in man and to re-create all "it was" until the will says, "Thus I willed it! Thus I shall will it"—this I called redemption and this alone I taught them to call redemption. (Z III, "On Old and New Tablets," 3)

When we take responsibility for ourselves by willing eternal recurrence and by becoming who we are, we are also willing and creating the world. Given Nietzsche's conviction that the world lacks inherent meaning, purpose, and order, we must become as gods, imposing order on chaos and creating meaning. This gigantic responsibility, along with the necessity of willing the return of the ugly, petty, and small and directly facing cosmic meaninglessness, creates the "great weight" that lies upon our actions (*GS* 341). The choices of active versus passive nihilism are transformed into human alternatives: to be finite gods or to self-annihilate. Moreover, because these alternatives form a unity (as do all "opposites") the choices are not as clear-cut as we have been imagining them.

But the texture and shadings of Nietzschean transcendence, eternality, and world creation are much different from religious versions. The focus is on this world, the premises are cosmic meaninglessness and a tragic view of life, the eternality is recurrent flux, and the transcendence is the process of destruction, reimagination, and re-creation. In sum, Nietzschean redemption is nothing more than a response to the lack of religious redemption, a message of affirmation to nudge away the nihilistic moment. There are no cosmic congratulations, but higher types, who embody the proper attitudes, do not need any.

As for this being the best of all possible worlds, Nietzsche understands suffering and the horrors you catalog. Remember, this is a man whose final moment of sanity was squandered trying to protect a horse who was being flogged. But given the unity of opposites and the interrelatedness of events and things in the world, we cannot edit life to fit our preconceptions. To affirm life is to affirm the entirety of the cosmos. To put it colloquially, we must accept "the sour with the sweet."

Apollonia: So much in Nietzsche depends on accepting the essential interrelatedness of the events and things in the world. But that belief is preposterous, not merely on the cosmic but also on the personal level. I can't edit my life and also affirm the thought of eternal recurrence. That means that if I wish I had chosen spumoni instead of vanilla ice cream yesterday I am denying eternal recurrence: Given the interrelatedness of events, to want myself to be different in any way is to want the entire world to be different. Worse, by wishing I had chosen spumoni I reveal my herd mentality and my unworthiness to enter the pantheon of higher types. I must, instead, giddily screech *amor fati*! as I recall the sour-tasting vanilla cone or the inadequately prepared fish I ate yesterday. Isn't it fanatical to assume that all my actions constitute who I am, that everything in the cosmos is so closely interrelated that to want any one event to be different changes the world, and that anyone who fails the test of accepting everything is therefore a lower type of human?

Fegataccio: Things aren't that bleak. As we both know, Nietzsche wasn't fond of making the clear distinctions and detailed qualifications so prized by analytic philosophers. But only a fool would claim that every action is equally constitutive of personal identity, that my choice of ice cream and, say, choice of spouse are equally important decisions for who I am. We must impute, in accordance with the principle of charitable interpretation, some understanding of proportionality: There are insignificant acts which, if altered, would not change who we are in any measurable way. To wish that you had chosen a different ice cream yesterday is not to want the world or yourself to be different in any measurable way. Of course, given the insignificance of the event, it isn't clear why you would be concerned with it now. In any case, it is clear that regretting your choice of ice cream, although a waste of time, does not relegate you to herd status. Probably no one can pass the strict test of eternal recurrence and affirm every event in their lives and in the world, but the measure of higher types is their capacity to affirm all, or virtually all, of the truly significant events, the ones that are constitutive of self and the history of the world.

Apollonia: I agree that, unhappily, Nietzsche lacked the rigor of clearer thinkers. But I am not so sure he could accept the principle of proportionality you enlist on his behalf. That principle domesticates Nietzsche and opens the door to elements of revenge and resentment as long as they are not directed to major past events in one's life. And if Nietzsche's quest is to eliminate in higher types the will to revenge and resentment, I don't see how he can allow even my yearning to have chosen a different flavor of ice cream to linger. Although the choice of ice cream seems insignificant, the motives that animate the urge to have chosen differently remain significant. Also, if I am unable to curb my desire to have chosen a different flavor of ice cream yesterday, will I be able to curb my attitudes of revenge and resentment on more significant issues? Doesn't permitting some resentment, on the basis of a principle of proportionality, invite the possibility of a slippery slope?

Fegataccio: We are running several different issues together. First, we have the question of whether all events are equally constitutive of self. The answer must be "no." Our choice of ice cream yesterday is not, unless extraordinary circumstances are present, a significant, life-molding event. Second, we have the question of whether your looking back and wishing you had chosen a different flavor is truly animated by revenge and resentment. The answer, I think, is "no." You may *regret* your choice as you look back today, but to call that resentment or revenge is too strong. Third, we have the question of whether allowing, as a practical matter, higher types to regret insignificant events in the past would lead them to resent significant events in the past. The answer is "not necessarily." The respective motives underlying the responses and the respective magnitude of the events are different. But you do raise a troubling issue.

Apollonia: Even if I agree that regret is not revenge or resentment, isn't the larger issue the way one regards time? To look back into the past and regret one's decision about ice cream reinstates a linear vision of time which reneges on one's commitment to eternal recurrence. Instead of luxuriating in the Being of the eternal Becoming, the person who regrets even an insignificant decision tacitly accepts the past–present–future model of time which characterizes the hapless herd. So while regretting an insignificant decision does not necessarily lead one directly down the slippery slope of resentment and revenge on significant matters, it may well indirectly seduce one into the conventional understanding of time which can lead to resentment and revenge. So Nietzsche cannot accept your principle of proportionality after all. He must maintain a hard line: no regrets, no apologies, no resentment, no revenge on matters small or large. *Quod erat demonstrandum!*

Fegataccio: You are insufferable when you think you are on a roll! We could consider insignificant events those with little or no measurable constitutive-making power. To reject the principle of proportionality is to claim that we should not regret any events in the past because those that were insignificant are unworthy of attention and those that were significant are constitutive of self. To accept myself, to will myself, and thus to become who I am, I must affirm all constitutive and, at least, forget all insignificant events. I am not sure how close my formulation is to Nietzsche's, but it should allow me to evade your harsher analyses.

Apollonia: I doubt whether "forgetting" is sufficient. One who truly practices *amor fati* cannot merely forget the relatively insignificant events of her past, she must joyfully embrace them. To be a higher type I must revel in my choice yesterday of sour-tasting vanilla ice cream. Not only can I not regret that choice, I must now esteem it.

Before you respond that my point is trivial, let me amplify. To be a higher type—to affirm myself and the world—I must not only tolerate the atrocities of the past, such as slavery, genocide, and large-scale gender, racial, and ethnic oppressions, I must joyfully affirm those events as constitutive of the history of the world. There are at least three problems with such an inhumane attitude: First, it depends on accepting Nietzsche's belief in the suffocatingly tight connections between events and between people. Second, it requires a callousness, even a sadistic glee, when evaluating the needless wronging of others. Third, it can translate to toothless deference to prevailing social conditions. I remain unconvinced that eternal recurrence is consistent with vigorous, progressive social action. To joyously embrace whatever one finds is the refuge of nitwits! Such an attitude neglects our duty to elevate, not merely affirm, our world.

Fegataccio: I do think your first point is trivial. The matter of yesterday's choice of ice cream is insignificant. You make it sound as if

Nietzsche must scream with delight at each reminiscence of his choice. You depict him as an inane simpleton who responds to every event with "that's nice." But look at his life and work. He was not trying to freeze the terms of social existence, but to "elevate" them. He constantly criticized the motives, the aimlessness, and the dogmatism that he took to be the dominant milieu of his time. He didn't walk around Italy and Switzerland humming "whatever will be will be." He suggested clearer attention to the rank order of humans, genealogical analysis of conventional morality, greater appreciation for the glories of this world, and a host of other things. There is no evidence that he took "sadistic glee" in the cruelties of the past. What he was doing was interpreting and explaining the nature of life. Your depiction, Apollonia, is a crude caricature.

Apollonia: Perhaps we find ourselves in another area of clever Nietzschean irony! The great affirmer of everything actually wishes to change the world. The joyous embracer of suffering and cruelty wishes to provide secular redemption. The pseudorebel decides to confer meaning by eliciting the requisite attitude toward cosmic meaninglessness. The contented liver-of-life burns for self-overcoming and transformation. Which is it, Fegataccio? Does Nietzsche joyously accept life or does he burn with his own resentment and revenge against it?

Fegataccio: I don't appreciate your tone, Apollonia. It is neither helpful nor necessary. But, as much as I hate to admit it, you do raise an important question: What is the connection between adopting the thought of eternal recurrence and vigorous personal and social action? We talked earlier of this issue, but more is needed. I think that embracing eternal recurrence focuses much on the present moment, rejoicing in who you are, recognizing that the person you are is the result of past events and interactions, and understanding inherent cosmic meaningless. But I don't think that eternal recurrence is simply circular time; it depends on reversions to linear time as well. This is especially true when we look at eternal recurrence's other side: a world of Becoming; the recommended personal process of self-overcoming; and the prescribed general practice of deconstruction, reimagination, and re-creation. Again, eternal recurrence is not a pedestrian affirmation of fate that precludes freedom and transformation; quite the contrary.

The question you pose can be stated in terms of the antinomies of Being and Becoming, or of necessity and freedom, or of the past and present. Eternal recurrence permits us to embrace the past—recognizing its unalterability which precludes resentment and revenge and understanding its role in constituting who we are now—yet remain active in the present through personal self-overcoming and the general process of deconstruction, reimagination, and re-creation. What you take to be the passivity of eternal recurrence is, at most, related to the unalterability of the past. What I venerate as the activity of eternal recurrence is related to Nietzsche's broad themes of contingency, imposition of meaning, and joyful creativity in the present and future.

I grant that my way of looking at eternal recurrence requires jumping from circular to linear time, but I think your criticism was also based on that leap.

Apollonia: I remain unconvinced that Nietzsche can claim all those things consistently. I think you are probably correct in thinking that Nietzsche was in some sense trying to fuse Becoming and Being. But I think his efforts are clumsy. Also, in my view too much about eternal recurrence hinges on his hugely unpersuasive belief that all events and all personal relations in the world are so closely connected that desiring alterations in past events or relations means one betrays the world and self.

Fegataccio: Eternal recurrence implies a pervasive principle of Becoming, yet retains an aura of Being as cycles return again and again. Nietzsche puts it this way:

To impose upon becoming the character of being—that is the supreme will to power. . . . That *everything recurs* is the closest *approximation of a world of becoming to a world of being.* . . . From the values attributed to being proceed the condemnation of and discontent with becoming, after such a world of being had first been invented. . . . Becoming as invention, willing, self-denial, overcoming of oneself: no subject but an action, a positing, creative, no "causes and effects." (*WP* 617)

Nietzsche's convictions about the interrelatedness of events and people flow from his disbelief in the substantive self: "The belief which regards the soul as something indestructible, eternal, indivisible, as a monad, as an *atomon*: this belief ought to be expelled from science!" (*BGE* 12). "In every act of the will there is a ruling thought—let us not imagine it possible to sever this thought from the 'willing,' as if any will would then remain over!" (*BGE* 19). "There is no such substratum [no neutral substratum behind the strong man which was free to express strength or not to do so]; there is no 'being' behind doing, effecting, becoming; 'the doer' is merely a fiction added to the deed—the deed is everything" (*GM* I, 13).

Once Nietzsche rejects the substantive self which lies beneath willing and doing and denies natural cosmic order and meaning, he is led to a Heraclitean world of Becoming and the interrelatedness of events. Power, good, evil, willing, and virtually everything else are the result of complex relationships or interactions within the multiplicity of drives that is the person or between different persons. Nietzsche's understanding of the "necessity" of events does not validate a flat-footed fatalism but is instead a description of the world's interrelatedness: To affirm my life is to affirm the world in its entirety. I cannot truly embrace some aspects of my life and edit out the disconcerting episodes: It is all or nothing! "All things are entangled, ensnared, enamored; and if ever you wanted one thing twice, if ever you said, 'You please me, happiness! Abide, moment!' then you wanted *all* back. All anew, all eternally, all entangled, ensnared, enamored—oh, then you *loved* the world!" (Z IV, "The Drunken Song," 10).

Apollonia: You've given your standard recitation of what Nietzsche believed, but you've given me no reason to accept it. I am still repelled by the crude—dare I say decadent—way Nietzsche renders all past events as essential to my identity now. Also, I think much is lost by any person who could affirm the past in all its horrors. That attitude strikes me as inhumane and, again, callous. Worse, under eternal recurrence I am willing the return of all those past horrors, in part because to refrain from doing so is to compromise on my acceptance of who I now am. Yet who I am now, whomever that might be, must be recurrently overcome.

Is there a surrealistic quality to all this or what? Nietzsche accepts all of the past as essential to what the world is and I am now. He claims that acceptance, indeed warm embrace, of the entirety of the world is essential to life-affirming types. Hence, Nietzscheans must sincerely howl *"amor fati!"* and will the eternal recurrence of everything, yet as wonderfully embraceable as my life up to now has been, my deeper quest is to overcome and transcend myself continually!

What is it that I am affirming? The wonderfulness of who I am now? The joy of the world of Becoming? The excitement of self-overcoming (which suggests dissatisfaction with who I am now)?

You have tried to finesse these problems through temporal indices: vacillating from circular to linear time, recitation of the Nietzschean mantra, and appeal to the mysterious interconnections and interrelatedness of people and events. You have failed, Fegataccio!

Fegataccio: Unless you are able to prove the existence of souls or substantial selves or some other metaphysical entity that exists above and beyond our relations and effects in the world, I think your criticisms of Nietzsche are vastly overstated. Furthermore, in accordance with Nietzsche's broad themes, there will always be times when it appears that Nietzsche's ideas depend on the very suppositions they aim at undermining. Given the "ensnarlment" of all things, the unity of opposites, the limitations of language, and our dominant rhetorical strategies, it could not be otherwise.

Apollonia: Fegataccio, you are on the defensive! I must press my case. The person who says, "I would not have done anything differently," when asked to assess her life is not a Nietzschean hero but a fool. If she continues by arguing that to respond anything else is to deny the self or the world, she is a fool twice.

Nietzsche takes kernels of truth, such as "suffering can often spur creative greatness," "the past is unalterable so don't dwell on it," "events often bear unforeseen, unintended consequences," "opposites are not separate substances," "we should be grateful for life," "we can create meaning in the face of cosmic purposefulness," and the like, and wrongly amplifies these bromides into the pseudosophisticated doctrine of eternal recurrence.

I'll describe and contrast three outlooks or attitudes on life. I'll call the first *general exuberance*: affirming the idea of life, recognizing fully the human condition, acknowledging mortality and inherent cosmic meaninglessness, but choosing vibrancy over despair. I'll call the second *specific exuberance*: affirming my particular life as a whole, but still harboring desires to edit out certain events that seem now to have been wrong, unnecessarily hurtful to others or self, without redeeming value, or prudentially disastrous. The third is Nietzsche's *eternal recurrence*: to affirm and to be grateful for every aspect, part, and moment of my particular life, to want to be who I am and all the moments connected thereto eternally, and to want nothing more deeply.

The problems with eternal recurrence are clear. To love each part of my life equally is to dull the very instincts of evaluation Nietzsche otherwise prizes. To want to be who I am eternally reneges on the commitment for recurrent self-overcoming. To love the world and self unconditionally is to demand *agape*: unwavering love that creates value in its object through the act of loving. *Agape* exists independently of the merits or demerits of the beloved, it overcomes all obstacles and endures all threats. Mistaken perceptions of value, defects in love's object, or the ingratitude of the beloved cannot erode the unshakeable certitude of the lover. But *agape* generates troubling paradoxes: If the beloved's actual properties are irrelevant, then it is unclear whether a person is truly the object of love. For stripped of all constitutive individuating attributes, what remains of personhood other than an abstraction called "humanity?" *Agape*, if wrongly amplified, offers much consolation but little growth. It is the love exhibited by innocents or gods, or maybe parents.

There are more problems with eternal recurrence. To rest affirmation of *amor fati* on feelings of gratitude is misguided. Lacking an antecedent notion of what, if anything, is genetically and culturally due to us from parents, formative environment, and the world, we can in every case fantasize about what we might have been and be resentful of being shortchanged and deprived, rather than grateful for who and what we are. If preoccupied by the gap between our real and fantasized selves, we are likely to blame the imagined discrepancy on others or the human condition itself. My point is that no matter who we are, we can always imagine a better life than the one we enjoy. Moreover, if Nietzscheans claim that to imagine a better or even different life is to imagine a different person, I think it is they who tacitly embrace a notion of substantive self. Unless one clings truculently to the absurd doctrine that all events equally constitute who I am, it is possible to affirm who I am and the world while desiring to edit out certain past events. Again, only a nit-wit or a Nietzschean says, "I wouldn't change a thing!"

Fegataccio: You insist on separating a life into discrete moments that can be evaluated independently, Apollonia. This is precisely what eternal recurrence denies. You cannot affirm some aspects of your life and edit out the discomforting episodes: All or nothing!

Apollonia: Your dance is repetitious; your song needs another verse, Fegataccio. Here is my larger point: General and specific exuberance can be readily affirmed. Notice neither attitude as I have described them relies on vestiges of gods, religion, or hope of transcendent salvation. Given the choice between life and death, or between life and eternal nonbeing, I choose life and I choose the world. Even without being able to edit out the worthless or destructive parts of my life and the world, I choose life and the world over nothingness. I can also eternally choose my life and the world rather than nothingness. My choice is hardly idiosyncratic; most people living in reasonably decent circumstances would agree. My choice does not distinguish me as a higher type, nor does it generate gnashing of teeth or squeals of divinity. *Amor proprio* (self-esteem) does not require "*amor fati!*"

Accordingly, if eternal recurrence required only attitudes of general and specific exuberance it would lack panache. But, as you correctly point out, it requires more: eternal validation of everything that constitutes life and "me" and the desire for nothing more. Beyond the criticisms I have already raised, I don't think that eternal recurrence is a human desire. It is an unconditional yearning in the context of a thoroughly conditional world, a vacillation between circular and linear time as convenience dictates, and a dangerous rationalization of the horrors of the past.

Fegataccio: As with every Nietzschean dialectic, there is a dark or tragic side to eternal recurrence. That is why it bears the "greatest weight." The world would, of course, be more cuddly if we imagined it without its past horrors and atrocities, but it would not be our world. In our world the will to power manifests itself in many ways, including cruelty and physical violence. Edit out the historical events that make us squeamish and you also eliminate the impulses that, when sublimated and refined, produce our greatest cultural achievements. I have been trying to tell you this: Given the unity of opposites and the impossibility of a world with only refined manifestations of the will to power, you either affirm this world with all its horrors or you imagine another world which edits out unfavored events. Aspiring to the latter is nothing more than secular Christianity and it is just as illusory.

Understanding this makes eternal recurrence vivid. To love this world and ourselves, we cannot flee to fictions or utopias. Instead, we must recognize our vulnerability to the tragedies of life. This doesn't mean we take sadistic glee in cruelty and violence. Instead, we should luxuriate in the immediacy of the moment by using the legacy of the past to create something valuable and meaningful. Although the past in unalterable, the ways we might respond to the past are numerous. By creating an interesting valuable self and by advancing culture now, we can elevate the past in the only available way: We can use the materials of the past to affirm life. Remember, we cannot view our lives or the history of the world as a series of discrete moments that can be judged independently of one another. To adopt *amor fati* one does not isolate and remember fondly the atrocities of the past; instead, one underscores the tragic nature of life but nevertheless joyfully embraces this world.[12]

Part of this quest is self-overcoming, which is not, as you suggest, animated by discontent or negativity. Instead, self-overcoming is part of and not distinct from the self. It does not presuppose a fixed substantial self, but rather recognizes the self's participation in the world of Becoming. To affirm eternal recurrence is not to renege on self-overcoming but to demand it. Once we understand and embrace this world, passive nihilism and abject fatalism cease to be viable options.

Apollonia: I must admit you gave measured reasonable answers to my concerns. It seems we have switched roles: You are becoming calmer and I am getting more impassioned. That is probably good for both of us.

But I am unpersuaded by your response for the usual reasons. It depends on the hocus-pocus of unity of opposites, tight interrelations of events, and a world of ceaseless Becoming. It may be better to move on to another Nietzschean "gem," self-overcoming in the context of will to power and the overman.

Nietzsche's notion of will to power troubles me for several reasons. First, he "defines" it so broadly that it loses clear meaning. Second, Nietzsche wrongly reduces the activities of all living things to only one source, thereby reneging on the complexity of life. Third, he once again is caught in self-referential paradox: His notion of will to power, according to his own beliefs, emerges from his will to power. Fourth, the will to power leads Nietzsche back to his male adolescent infatuation with warfare and physical conquest.

Fegataccio: Before I can tackle those questions I must talk about how the will to power honors instincts and passions—the "nonrational"—

yet retains a place for reason. Beyond revealing the egoistic instincts and passions that underlie all seemingly altruistic motives, Nietzsche shows the relationships of power underwriting our forms of knowledge and understandings of truth. Yet rationality, especially skeptical intellect, is itself an important form of will to power:

One should not be deceived: great spirits are skeptics. Zarathustra is a skeptic. Strength, *freedom* which is born of the strength and overstrength of the spirit, proves itself by skepticism. Men of conviction are not worthy of the least consideration in fundamental questions of value and disvalue. Convictions are prisons. Such men do not look far enough, they do not look *beneath* themselves: but to be permitted to join in the discussion of value and disvalue, one must see five hundred convictions *beneath* oneself—*behind* oneself. (*AC* 54)

Reason, then, is engaged in the process of revealing its own limitations and self-deceptions. A skeptical spirit such as Nietzsche's cannot take logic and argumentation as intellectual discoveries that stand above and beyond irrational impulses. Instead, all forms of conscious creativity, including logic and the universe itself, are products of the unconscious will to power: "And what you have called world, that shall be created only by you: your reason, your image, your will, your love shall thus be realized. . . . Creation—that is the great redemption from suffering, and life's growing light" (Z II, "Upon the Blessed Isles").

Nietzsche reinforces this idea of the intelligible character of the world as the creation of will to power:

Suppose nothing else were "given" as real except our world of desires and passions, and we could not get down, or up, to any other "reality" besides the reality of our drives—for thinking is merely a relation of these drives to each other. . . . Suppose, finally, we succeeded in explaining our entire instinctive life as the development and ramification of *one* basic form of the will—namely, of the will to power, as *my* proposition has it . . . then one would have gained the right to determine *all* efficient force univocally as—*will to power*. The world viewed from inside, the world defined and determined according to its "intelligible character"—it would be "will to power" and nothing else. (*BGE* 36)

Will to power, then, connotes a process of struggle and overcoming in internal and external relationships in a world of Becoming.

Apollonia: Thanks for the commercial and the exegesis. Will you now address my concerns?

Fegataccio: Fine. The "broadness" of the will to power, its lack of discrete meaning, is not an embarrassing consequence of Nietzsche's thought but, instead, is a methodological advantage, given his broad themes. Remember, will to power connotes a process, not a fixed metaphysical entity. And in a world of Becoming, the struggle to relate and create in the world is not susceptible to discrete descriptions. What you take to be a deficiency, from your vantage point of stable categories and meanings in a world of being, Nietzsche takes to be theoretical insight, from his vantage point of radical indeterminacy in a world of Becoming.

Apollonia: But that interpretation makes Nietzsche's will to power an inherently unverifiable, perhaps even metaphorical, postulate, a sort of hobgoblin writ large.

Fegataccio: The unverifiability and even the metaphorical nature of will to power do not concern Nietzscheans. We are neither positivists nor believers in literal fixed language. Once you understand that will to power does not denote a metaphysical entity, charges of unverifiability miss the mark. Once you understand that will to power is not expressed in literal language, charges of metaphorical nature miss the mark. Will to power represents the pervasiveness of unconscious instinctual impulses in recurring struggle in a world of Becoming. For Nietzsche, the key is not the existence of such impulses but the ways in which their struggle imposes order and meaning on an inherently formless world. Exercising power requires the resistance of other exercisers of power. Depending on the temporary outcomes of such power struggles, certain effects—institutions, self-understandings, ways of life—predominate rather than others.

Apollonia: You keep saying that will to power is not metaphysical, but as the ultimate reality—and it is ultimate, given that he says will to power actually defines the cosmos itself—it can't simply be metaphor. Unless he thinks metaphor itself is the ultimate reality, in which case Nietzsche is nuttier than even I thought!

Fegataccio: If one thinks, as Nietzsche did, that the world is flux, then the ultimate reality is that which gives form (and meaning) to flux. The will to power is not ultimate in any sense other than as form giver and meaning giver. Surely he doesn't mean that the will to power creates the matter of the cosmos, only that it gives form to that matter.

Apollonia: So he denies the commonsense view that most of the cosmos is not created by humans but only discovered by humans. He denies the limitations the cosmos places on interpretation, form giving, and power struggles.

Fegataccio: Clearly, there are human limitations, ones Nietzsche chronicles at length. Are these limitations the result of the cosmos or just part of the human condition? Nietzsche would not think it is the cosmos but our own psychological frailties that impose limits.

The will to power may seem broad and may seem to reduce complex phenomena to one cause, but these appearances lack substance. Once we understand that will to power has numerous manifestations because struggle, form giving, and meaning giving are pervasive, we also understand that will to power does not oversimplify. Charges of reductionism would bear currency only if Nietzsche was oversimplifying the phenomena. I don't think he is.

Apollonia: What about his self-referential paradox: the will to power must flow from Nietzsche's own will to power?

Fegataccio: Absolutely nothing new there; we have discussed self-referential paradoxes with regard to perspectivism, and raising that charge in the context of will to power adds nothing. Of course, he understands the paradoxical aspects of denying dogmatism, affirming skepticism, and advancing views (or, more precisely, metaphors). Remember our discussion of rhetorical strategies? That is about the only thing we seem to agree on.

The will to power itself bears the perplexing character of plurality, struggle, and overcoming. As the "ultimate reality," as you call it, it mirrors and sustains the ambiguities and mysteries of the world of becoming. There is no simple bivalent way to express or understand will to power or the cosmos itself. Jaspers puts it well: "A doctrine in which [Nietzsche] can entirely acquiesce never occurs to him, and he holds every view in check by opposing it to other views. The doctrine of the will to power is not his definitive metaphysics, but a thought-experiment performed within the more extensive whole of his investigation of being."[13]

Nietzsche understands well the limitations of our language and logic and the traps our intellects set for us. He rejects only those interpretations that deny multiplicity and indeterminacy. His reasons for rejecting them, however, have more to do with their second-order dogmatism than with their first-order content:[14]

How far the perspective character of existence extends or indeed whether existence has any other character than this; whether existence without interpretation, without "sense," does not become "nonsense": whether, on the other hand, all existence is not essentially actively engaged in *interpretation*—that cannot be decided even by the most industrious and most scrupulously conscientious analysis and self-examination of the intellect; for in the course of this analysis the human intellect cannot avoid seeing itself in its own perspectives, and *only* in these . . . the world [has] become "infinite" for us all over again, inasmuch as we cannot reject the possibility that *it may include infinite interpretations.* (GS 374)

Moreover, despite our efforts to impose a univocal meaning on Nietzsche's thought, he remains a complex thinker who self-consciously reverses perspectives to underscore his broad themes. To accept a world of Becoming is to undermine fixed cognitive categories and to resist discrete identities.[15]

Apollonia: I set you up for that advertisement, didn't I? You are correct about one thing: We aren't going to make any new headway on the self-referential paradox or on perspectivism. I remain unconvinced for the reasons I've already stated.

So I'll move on to Nietzsche's infatuation with war and conquest of others. Yes, I understand that one aspect of will to power is self-mastery and self-overcoming: forging a unity and giving a style to self. But you Nietzsche apologists act as if will to power has nothing to do with actual wars and actual conquest of others, despite Nietzsche's words to the contrary which place domination at the heart of freedom:

For what is freedom? That one has the will to assume responsibility for oneself. That one maintains the distance which separates us. That one becomes more indifferent to difficulties, hardships, privation, even to life itself. That one is prepared to sacrifice human beings for one's cause, not excluding oneself. Freedom means that the manly instincts which delight in war and victory dominate over other instincts, for example, over those of "pleasure." The human being who has *become free* . . . spits on the contemptible type of well-being dreamed of by shopkeepers, Christians, cows, females, Englishmen, and other democrats. The free man is a *warrior*. (*TI*, "Skirmishes of an Untimely Man," 38)

In one fell swoop, your hero Nietzsche celebrates war, exploitation, martyrdom, Spartanism, and aristocracy and defames women, merchants, Christians, WASPS, and egalitarians. As for cows, it isn't clear whether they are elevated or slandered by their inclusion with the other groups!

Fegataccio: I could just as easily cite passages in which Nietzsche depicts harming others as a deficiency of power (e.g., *GS* 13). But there are numerous admirable thoughts in the passage you selected: preferring a life of exertion and overcoming over a life of easy contentment; accepting self-discipline and suffering as the price of vigorous creation and self-overcoming; understanding that life as such is not the primary value; and embracing the warrior instincts as crucial for higher culture.

Apollonia: You are becoming quite the spinmaster, Fegataccio. The "warrior instincts" over which you gush have caused unspeakable horrors in the world, and accepting the sacrifice of others for one's cause has generated the worst gender, racial, religious, and ethnic oppressions in history!

Fegataccio: We have covered this before, Apollonia. For Nietzsche, the greatest cultural achievements and the greatest horrors flow from the same basic instincts and impulses. Nietzsche appreciates most deeply the spiritualized refined will to power of philosophers and artists. But he will not pretend that cruelties and atrocities can disappear or that robust will to power can only appear in sublimated higher forms.

Apollonia: Not good enough, Fegataccio. Nietzsche doesn't just regretfully accept the necessity of war and enslavement; at times he is absolutely giddy at their prospect. They affirm his adolescent swagger and yearning for the physical conquest unavailable to him.

Here is my test—call it the eternal reversal: Suppose an angel were to visit you and say, "None of the great musical, philosophical, and artistic creations of the world can exist without the cruel, sadistic wars and enslavements that spring from the same impulse. You are given the power of a god today, mere mortal! You can eliminate that impulse from humans for eternity, wiping away the horrors and the glories. What say you, speck of dust?"

As for me, you can take all the philosophical and artistic achievements the world has ever produced and if eliminating them would also wipe away the worst horrors and oppressions of history, I say, "So be it!"

Fegataccio: No, you would not! You are not a last man, Apollonia. To affirm eternal reversal is to eliminate humans and to will a new species into existence. This new species would lack robust ranges of emotions, passions, and actions. It would be a species of sheep or simpletons, a witless herd with plastic smiles and vacant eyes. The messenger of eternal reversal, Apollonia, is not an angel, it is *il Diavolo!*

Apollonia: Would it be so horrible, Fegataccio? Or are you so infatuated with intellectual artifacts and Nietzsche's fatuous squeals of *amor fati* that you are blind to other possibilities, ones that do not kneel in supplication before the gods of power and violence?

Fegataccio: Again, you wrongly amplify Nietzsche's embrace of wars, conquest of others, and physical assertion. Remember, for Nietzsche, power, rank, and value are not synonyms (if, indeed, metaphors can be synonyms). For example, although all living things exercise the will to power, not all power is of equal quality or value. The order of human rank is determined by the greatest quantity of high-quality power. As we have already learned, the herd has a significant quantity of low-quality, life-denying power. Thus, the greatest quantities of power as such do not necessarily produce the greatest value.

Life-denying power flows from ersatz character—lacking a unified center, drawn to moderation out of weakness and insufficient capacities, beset with feelings of resentment and revenge, dominated by unintegrated chaos, unable to resist stimuli and to transform suffering—in short, impoverished spirits who seek equality, harmony, and an insipid peace from motives of fear, envy, and repressed hostility.

Life-affirming power flows from psychological abundance. Having forged a unity out of multiplicity, the healthy will to power has the clear direction of self-overcoming: Moderation arises from joy in restraint, it transforms suffering and hardship into creative opportunities, it sublimates and spiritualizes cruel impulses into cultural advantages, and it finds joy in confronting the ambiguity of the world of Becoming. In short, abundantly healthy spirits are those who respect the order of rank and the importance of struggle and who deconstruct, reimagine, and re-create from motives of joy and love of life and without hope of transcendent salvation.

Apollonia: There are times when you switch on your didactic mode, and not even I can stand you, Fegataccio! Times when you chant the litany of Nietzsche as woodenly and disingenuously as the faithless preachers you so despise.

Nietzsche, in fact, was obsessed by fantasies of power. For him, power exists to increase its own accumulation. Where growth slows or ends, there is decline and muted power:

What is good? Everything that heightens the feeling of power in man, the will to power, power itself. What is bad? Everything that is born of weakness. What is happiness? The feeling that power is *growing*, that resistance is overcome. Not contentedness but more power; not peace but war; not virtue but fitness [Renaissance *virtu*, not moral virtue]. . . . Life itself is to my mind the instinct for growth, for durability, for an accumulation of forces, for *power*: where the will to power is lacking there is decline. (*AC* 2, 6)

Remember, Fegataccio, that Renaissance *virtu*, like ancient Greek *arete*, concerns only vitality, force, success, and achievement. As Nietzsche understands well, it is distinct from moral assessment. Accordingly, there is absolutely no reason why Nietzsche's higher types could not be moral monsters. And you can't have it both ways! You can't argue that Nietzsche derives his notions of goodness and greatest from the ancient Greeks and Romans, then add that his exemplars of greatness would also, coincidentally, be morally acceptable. That move doesn't work. You can't smuggle in concessions to "herd morality" to placate the masses, for if you do you compromise Nietzsche's understandings of power, goodness, and greatness. You confront a delicious dilemma: Either bite the bullet and accept that Nietzsche's "life-affirming" giants can be thoroughly evil, or make concessions to the herd that rob Nietzsche's thought of its panache.

Fegataccio: And I have a hard time putting up with you, Apollonia, when you switch into your dramatic mode! You announce a banal conclusion as if it were a grand discovery, as if you have wrestled Nietzsche, pinned him to the ground, and forced him to cry "uncle."

Of course, anyone who aspires to go beyond the evaluations of good and evil, such as Nietzsche, must accept that the qualities of life-affirming greatness can be embodied by those who will be judged "evil" by the criteria of herd morality. But so what! We have already talked about the suspicious origins and impoverished content of herd morality. Why should I "bite the bullet" squeamishly?

Apollonia: So Nietzsche has the Ty Cobb–Sonny Liston theory of greatness: As long as I hit for a high batting average or earn a high knockout percentage, I am good. Sure, I would be a good baseball player or prizefighter, but not necessarily a good person or even a possessor of good character. Thus, I could have a robust prizewinning will to power, given Nietzschean criteria, yet commit the worst sort of atrocities and horrors. It will not do, Fegataccio, to talk of sublimation, spiritualization, lack of resentment, and the like. Unless those processes ensure the impossibility of oppression of others—and they cannot unless you smuggle in moral criteria—the possibility of a Nietzschean ogre is strong.

Fegataccio: I can agree that the possibility must remain, but to point that out is no more devastating than if I pointed out to moralists that their belief in free will permits the possibility of a moral ogre. So what?

Apollonia: Terrible analogy, Fegataccio. The moralist rejoices in free will but regards the ogre as a moral failure. Nietzsche rejoices in will to power but must regard the ogre as a life-affirming good person (in the Greek and Roman sense).

Fegataccio: We are going around in circles again. To do justice to the instant inquiry we must explore Nietzsche's evaluations of character and understanding of perfectionism. But that will take us beyond eternal recurrence, will to power, and the *Übermensch*. Let's leave it for another time.

Instead, I want to summarize Nietzsche's understanding of the will to power. Remember, for Nietzsche the world as a whole is inaccessible to us because we are within it. When he speaks of will to power as that which underlies all living things, it may seem that he is resorting to a metaphysical linchpin that makes the world as a whole accessible. But, in fact, will to power underscores the world's inaccessibility: The world eludes our fixed cognitive categories because it is flux and becoming, and we impose contingent order and meaning through interpretation. Will to power names the essence of all living things, but that essence is not a fixed set of characteristics. Instead, it is the enigmatic process of struggle, assertion, resistance, submitting, and overcoming. The subtext of will to power is an attack on rigid distinctions, binary thinking, and dualistic oppositions. Thus, for Nietzsche the will to power is a primitive notion that resists specific definition.

Furthermore, will to power underscores Nietzsche's appreciation of deconstruction, reimagination, and re-creation. He is clear that "all great things bring about their own destruction through an act of self-overcoming; thus the law of life will have it, the law of the necessity of 'self-overcoming' in the nature of life" (*GM* III, 27).

Apollonia: I'm suspicious of "self-overcoming." It sounds too much like self-destruction which arises from psychological neurosis, grave insecurities, internal self-contempt, and repressed hostilities.

Fegataccio: For Nietzsche, self-overcoming is part of self-aggrandizement, not self-destruction as such. Life is lived at the expense of other lives (because power and identity are relational notions) and at our own expense. Nature and life are dialectical forces, and the value of the self lies primarily in its ability to transcend itself in tacit understanding of the contingency of the world of Becoming. Because the world is in a continuous state of flux, truculent adherence to a particular fixed self-understanding will interfere with the project of life.

I think of the will to power as a metaphor for life; the eternal recurrence as a psychological test of the value and vivacity of one's will to power; and the *Übermensch* as either the personification of the ideal will to power, merely a thought experiment Nietzsche discards, or another metaphor for self-overcoming and creative energy.[16]

Apollonia: The *Übermensch* has always struck me as the projection of Nietzsche's deepest fantasies, as the dream of the sickly, physically weak little boy who yearned for conquests that eluded him in life. The *Übermensch*, in my view, is the most pathetic of Nietzsche's notions because its origins lie in his weakness, alienation, and estrangement from life. Do you like the genealogical critique, Fegataccio? Have I revealed the suspicious origins and craven spirit that generate the *Übermensch*?

My evaluation shares company with some famous philosophers. Copleston says, "[*Übermensch*] is all that ailing, lonely, tormented, neglected Herr Professor Dr. Friedrich Nietzsche would like to be." Russell says, "There is a great deal in [Nietzsche] that must be dismissed as merely megalomaniac. . . . In his day-dreams he is a warrior, not a professor." Alasdair MacIntyre says, "The *Übermensch* [belongs] in the pages of a philosophical bestiary rather than in serious discussion. . . . [*Übermensch* is] at once [an] absurd and dangerous fantasy."[17]

Fegataccio: Stop! Otherwise I'll accuse you of an appeal to authority! Isn't that another one of your favorite logical fallacies? You and your trio of fellow travelers take the notion of overman too literally and too seriously. First, it isn't even clear to what the overman refers. Is overman just another name for philosophers of the future or nobles or free spirits or Dionysian masters? Or does it designate a being who stands above higher humanity? Or does overman confer quasi-divine status upon higher humanity?[18] Second, it isn't clear whether the overman is a suprahuman who has not yet appeared (see, e.g., Z II,

"On Priests"; Z I, "Zarathustra's Prologue"), or whether the overman has often appeared accidentally in the past as a glaring exception to the common run of men (see, e.g., *AC* 3–4).

Third, regardless of one's answers to the first two questions, the issue remains of whether the overman is intended to serve as an ideal, as a metaphor, or merely as a thought experiment that Nietzsche discards.[19]

Your trio of critics and I agree on one thing, although for different reasons: It is unwise to become preoccupied by the overman. Even by Nietzschean standards, analysis of the overman is problematic. Thus, a principle of charitable interpretation suggests that we shouldn't permit too much of our evaluation of Nietzsche's thought to turn on this notion.

Apollonia: You are not getting off that easy! If your description of the interpretive problems accompanying the overman is correct, I would take it to be a microcosm of all of Nietzsche's thought: Don't take it too seriously! Instead, relish Nietzsche as a master of self-parody, one who undermines even his own broad themes. Taken in this vein, we can enjoy Nietzsche as literary comedian and cunning stylist: someone who can make us laugh with his bombast, parodies, and rhetorical excesses; someone who can deconstruct our conceits but also demonstrate their necessity; and someone who laughs with us and at us (and himself) as he writes.

But, still, I must ask you to unravel some of the questions about the overman you have raised. We have come this far, we can't simply push the overman to the side.

Fegataccio: I'll give you my take on the overman. Although Nietzsche, characteristically, was loose in his use of overman, I do not equate overman with nobles or with higher humanity, nor do I take overman to confer quasi-divinity upon higher humanity. Instead, overman, to the extent it can be viewed nonmetaphorically, is a suprahuman ideal, someone who could fully affirm eternal recurrence and bellow to the sky, "*Amor fati!*" I don't think even great men could fully do that, at least not sincerely. As a suprahuman ideal of perfect affirmation of eternal recurrence and full commitment to self-overcoming, overman has never appeared on earth.

There is evidence that Nietzsche took overman merely as a thought experiment whose importance withered (see, e.g., Z II, "On Redemption"; Z II, "The Stillest Hour"), but I take overman as a metaphor for the process of deconstruction, reimagination, and re-creation. Taken as this metaphor, overman is perfectly compatible with eternal recurrence, and, indeed, is just another way of underscoring the themes of self-overcoming, life-affirmation, and creative energy.

Accordingly, I mix, perhaps dangerously, the ideal and metaphorical dimensions of overman. The ideal dimension permits a personified image toward which to strive but never reach, while the metaphorical dimension highlights Nietzsche's broad themes. Both dimensions are compatible with Nietzsche's commitments to dialectical transformation, the world of Becoming, and the need to become who you are.

Apollonia: What about the overman as redeemer? Check out this passage from Nietzsche:

The attainment of this goal would require a *different* kind of spirit from that likely to appear in this present age: spirits strengthened by war and victory, for whom conquest, adventure, danger, and even pain have become needs. . . . It would require even a kind of sublime wickedness, an ultimate, supremely self-confident mischievousness in knowledge that goes with great health. . . . Is this even possible today? But some day . . . he must yet come to us, the *redeeming* man of great love and contempt, the creative spirit whose compelling strength will not let him rest in any aloofness or any beyond, whose isolation . . . is only his absorption, immersion, penetration *into* reality, so that, when he one day emerges again into the light, he may bring home the *redemption* of this reality. . . . This man of the future . . . *he must come one day*. (GM II, 24)

If the overman is a redeemer, doesn't that betray Nietzsche's resentment of this world, his desire for revenge, his effacement of *amor fati*, and his secular transformation of God?

Fegataccio: It isn't clear whether that passage refers to the overman, to higher humanity, to a literary character such as Zarathustra, to prophets emerging during the death of God, or to something else.

I think of the redemption as movement toward accepting Nietzsche's broad themes, including their elements of self-undermining and self-parody. Moreover, redemption alludes to his understanding of greatness: self-integration and self-mastery, overabundance of energy, and a range and multiplicity that creates internal dialectical tension.[20] Approaching the overman requires recurrent self-creation, which does not necessarily require conquest over others. For Nietzsche, though, refraining from conquest over others is not necessarily *virtu*. It becomes so only if one has the power to dominate others but has made a decision from strength to refrain from doing so.

Higher types, those who approach the overman, create themselves without regard for social conventions and values. Higher types are great because they have not been leveled by the herd mentality, yet fragile because self-integration, overabundance of energy, and multiplicity form a combustible combination.

The redemption passage is dramatic and hyperbolic, but it doesn't necessarily manifest resentment, revenge, or renege on *amor fati*. We talked earlier about how affirming eternal recurrence was compatible with the constant self-creation and self-overcoming to which Nietzsche aspires, and how negative psychology need not underlie personal transformation. The same holds here.

As the son and grandson of ministers, it is unlikely that Nietzsche fully discarded his Christian background. I suppose if we take the overman literally and seriously we can view it as a secular surrogate for God. But that reading is obtuse. Even if we reject the thought-experiment interpretation of overman and accept a strong version of the overman-as-ideal interpretation, the overman falls far short of a god. Indeed, the overman's mortality, recurrent personal change in a world of becoming, and radical fragility embody antidivine themes. Nietzsche does not seek redemption from the human condition; instead, he suggests that higher types can renounce passive nihilism and embrace active nihilism.

Also, we should never lose sight of the personal nature of Nietzsche's thought: The eternal recurrence is *his* formula for greatness, the will to power is *his* interpretation of the cosmos, the overman is *his* personification of, or metaphor for, or thought experiment of greatness. Nietzsche fully lived the internal life and his writings were explicitly autobiographical. Thus, he chronicles his own struggles with the human condition and reveals his own devices for "giving style to one's character."

Apollonia: Let me levy a continuing concern. The three most commonly hashed and thrashed Nietzschean notions are eternal recurrence, will to power, and overman. But we can eliminate these notions from Nietzsche's work and retain the integrity of his thought. In other words, he didn't need all the hocus-pocus that too easily distracts critics from more important tasks. He could have stated his broad themes straightaway or used his preferred literary styles without resorting to these three notions. The three notions merely add yet another layer of mystification and obscurantism to an already daunting chore: interpreting Nietzsche in a fair and, hopefully, reasonably accurate fashion.

Fegataccio: You may have a point. That is why commentators, for example, can reasonably view the overman as a thought experiment that Nietzsche discards without otherwise disabling their interpretive or critical opportunities. But Nietzsche's literary styles are less vivid without eternal recurrence, will to power, and overman. They provide parables, visions, and images that animate his broad themes.

Apollonia: They also facilitate interpretive misunderstandings and invite misuses of his work. The "vision" of the overman, for example, turns into the nightmare of a Teutonic master race! The "image" of the will to power turns into a maelstrom of violence and oppression.

Fegataccio: Such misuses are part of the risks run by great works that challenge conventional thinking. We should, though, talk more about the connections between literary style and content.

Apollonia: But not tonight! When, as now, I am weary, I submit to your alternating vitriolic and seductive rhetoric too easily.

Darkness had fallen hours ago. Apollonia and Fegataccio were exhausted from their three discussions and their shopping. They desperately needed sleep. They checked into the motel adjoining the mall. It was the United States of America in the 1990s: There were few reasons to stray far from the mall.

Chapter 4

ARTISTS AND WARRIORS

Literary Style, Rhetoric, and Tragedy

In preceding chapters I have hinted at Nietzsche's understanding of the connections between literary style, philosophical content, and autobiography. In this chapter I discuss these issues more thoroughly and connect them with Nietzsche's tragic view of life and perceptions of teaching and learning.

FORM, CONTENT, AND PSYCHOLOGY

Nietzsche is unique among philosophers in inviting readers to examine his psychology and life while exploring his writings. Although he does not issue this invitation straightforwardly, it is surely a consequence of what he says about the connections between literary style, philosophical content, and autobiography.

First, he tells us that philosophical writings are intimately connected with personal confessions, even if involuntarily: "Every great philosophy [has been] the personal confession of its author and a kind of involuntary and unconscious memoir" (*BGE* 6), and "Most of the conscious thinking of a philosopher is secretly guided and forced into certain channels by his instincts" (*BGE* 3).

Second, Nietzsche cautions us about the self-deluded poses of objectivity and purely rational discovery that philosophers too often strike:

[Philosophers] all pose as if they had discovered and reached their opinions through the self-development of a cold, pure, divinely unconcerned dialectic

. . . while at bottom it is an assumption, a hunch, indeed a kind of "inspiration"—most often a desire of the heart that has been filtered and made abstract—that they defend with reasons they have sought after the fact. They
are all advocates who resent that name, and for the most part even wily spokes-
men for their prejudices which they baptize "truths." (*BGE* 5)

In the philosopher . . . there is nothing whatever that is impersonal; and above
all, his morality bears decided and decisive witness to *who he is*—that is, in
what order of rank the innermost drives of his nature stand in relation to each
other. (*BGE* 6)

The poses of objectivity and purely rational discovery also generate
methodological weaknesses. They obscure the order of rank in deference to a reassuring egalitarianism; they aspire to a universal human
as a common standard; they too easily degenerate into ahistoricism
and abstraction; and they disguise the underlying origins of one's
thought. Instead, readers should investigate the life influences on a
writer, the instincts, drives, passions, and experiences that constitute a
writer's psychological base.

Third, a writer's philosophical writings transfigure his internal condition into spiritual form. Intense suffering is especially useful for those
strong enough to channel it for artistic advantage:

A philosopher who has traversed many kinds of health, and keeps traversing
them, has passed through an equal number of philosophies; he simply *cannot*
keep from transposing his states every time into the most spiritual form and
distance: this art of transfiguration *is* philosophy. We philosophers are not
free to divide body from soul as the people do; we are even less free to divide
soul from spirit. . . . We have to give birth to our thoughts out of our pain and,
like mothers, endow them with all we have of blood, heart, fire, pleasure,
passion, agony, conscience, fate, and catastrophe. Life—that means for us constantly transforming all that we are into light and flame—also everything
that wounds us; we simply can do no other. (*GS* "Preface," 3)

Taken collectively, these three elements of Nietzsche's thought do
not merely invite readers to examine Nietzsche's own psychology, they
insist that readers who shun this task are misguided from the outset.
Nietzsche even gives us some hints about where to start:

My life is simply wonderful. For the task of a *revaluation of all values* more
capacities may have been needed than have ever dwelt together in a single
individual—above all, even contrary capacities that had to be kept from dis-
turbing, destroying one another. An order of rank among these capacities;
distance; the art of separating without setting against one another; to mix
nothing, to "reconcile" nothing; a tremendous variety that is nevertheless the

opposite of chaos—this was the precondition, the long, secret work and art-istry of my instinct. (*EH*, "Why I Am So Clever," 9)

He also recognizes, immodestly as usual, that he is at once a decadent, in the sense of declining life, and a beginning, in the sense of ascending life:

The good fortune of my existence, its uniqueness perhaps, lies in its fatality: I am, to express it in the form of a riddle, already dead as my father, while as my mother I am still living and becoming old. This dual descent, as it were, both from the highest and the lowest rung on the ladder of life, at the same time a *decadent* and a *beginning*—this, if anything, explains that neutrality, that freedom from all partiality in relation to the total problem of life, that perhaps distinguishes me. (*EH*, "Why I Am So Wise," 1)

Nietzsche even explains his solitude and celibacy. He must sublimate much of his sociable and sexual energy in service of artistic expression:

A philosopher may be recognized by the fact that he avoids three glittering and loud things: fame, princes, and women. . . . He is concerned with one thing alone, and assembles and saves up everything—time, energy, love, and interest—only for that one thing. . . . Every artist knows what a harmful effect intercourse has in states of great spiritual tension and preparation, those with the greatest power and the surest instincts [have] a "maternal" instinct [which] ruthlessly disposes of all other stores and accumulations of energy, of animal vigor, for the benefit of the evolving work: the greater energy then *uses up* the lesser. (*GM* III, 8)

For Nietzsche, then, the philosophical is the personal. His writings chronicle, often explicitly, his struggles with the human condition and mirror his interior life. He thus denies, contrary to the self-under-standings of most philosophers, any clear distinction between philo-sophically significant and merely autobiographical literature.

Those who accept Nietzsche's view on this matter will understand that robust philosophical critique cannot consist merely of systematic analysis of abstract propositions in terms of truth, logical implications, and soundness of argument. Indeed, if Nietzsche is correct, systematic analysis of this sort will obscure more than it reveals. To even under-stand a thinker's work concretely, an interpreter must attend to the psychological base, historical context, and internal struggles that de-fine the author. Moreover, we must regard carefully the tone, diction, voice, and language in which the author's thought is expressed.[1]

Accordingly, interpretation and critique become more complex and difficult. If readers have not shared an author's relevant experiences or historical context, or if they lack reliable access to an author's psychological base, they cannot fully understand and fairly critique that author's work. Such readers could perform only the arid dissections of systematic analysis or (mis)interpret the author's work in accord with their own psychological base, historical context, and internal struggles.

Nietzsche explicitly recognizes that reporting his spiritual struggles, creating art, and critiquing mainstream philosophy are merely pale images of his vivid, lived experiences:

Alas, what are you after all, my written and painted thoughts! It was not long ago that you were still so colorful, young, and malicious, full of thorns and secret spices—you made me sneeze and laugh—and now? You have already taken off your novelty, and some of you are ready, I fear, to become truths: they already look so immortal, so pathetically decent, so dull! And has it ever been different? What things do we copy . . . always only what is on the verge of withering and losing its fragrance! . . . We immortalize what cannot live and fly much longer . . . but nobody will guess from that how you looked in your morning, you sudden sparks and wonders of my solitude, you my old beloved—*wicked* thoughts! (*BGE* 296)

Although philosophical writing cannot capture the vivacity of lived experience, it can nevertheless serve multiple purposes: sharing the products of one's thoughts and experiences, even if in ersatz form; externalizing one's thoughts in order to open paths for new experiments and experiences; and creating literature as a form of personal therapy.[2]

STYLE AND RHETORIC

As I have already mentioned, Nietzsche embraces a variety of literary styles and a multiplicity of critical perspectives. Aphorisms, metaphors, poetry, calculated hyperboles, genealogical critiques, and personal invectives coalesce uneasily in his work. Some of the resulting literary tensions, which exacerbate the problems of clear interpretation, arise from Nietzsche's purposeful verbal equivocations or readers' failure to attend carefully to different contexts; others reflect Nietzsche's understanding of the complexity of reality which requires the use of multiple perspectives; others exemplify some of Nietzsche's broad themes, such as the inescapability of inner conflict, the connection between writing and life, the denial of absolutism, and the importance of self-overcoming in a world of flux.

It is clear, however, that Nietzsche's choices of style are not random. He employs literary styles as strategies: as ways, alternately, to provoke readers to examine their most settled convictions, to underscore the indeterminacy and tragedy of life, to highlight his aversion to dogmatism, to chronicle his spiritual struggles, to undermine his own convictions, and to glorify rank order. Although he could assert these ideas in the typical style of straightforward, didactic philosophical discourse, to do so would renege on his understanding of the connections between form, content, and personal psychology.[3]

Nietzsche's styles exemplify, rather than merely report, his philosophy by embodying the motifs closest to Nietzsche's soul. Thus, he writes in ways that resist univocal interpretation, that are not intended for a universal audience, that demonstrate the lack of fixed meaning in a world of Becoming, that sometimes indulge in self-congratulations only to later enjoy self-parody, and that present views in the strongest terms while simultaneously unmasking the pretensions of dogmatism.

He knowingly confronts and basks in a paradox of prose: To the extent we unconditionally accept Nietzsche's own conclusions we mock his anti-dogmatism, his call for self-overcoming, and his commitment to rank order. The world of Becoming and the differences among humans demand that Nietzsche's views cannot win universal absolute allegiance. Not that such allegiance was ever a real possibility.

Nietzsche, unlike mainstream philosophers, does not try to mask his partiality and partisanship. His views, including his notion of will to power, arise from his will to power. His perspectivism emerges from his perspective (or, more precisely, his multiple perspectives). His bluster and self-aggrandizing prose burst forth from his aristocratic understanding of humans. His reversals and self-parodies demonstrate self-overcoming in a world of flux. His (sometimes strained) attempts to self-justify his life manifest the attitude of *amor fati*. In sum, rarely does literary style track content as closely as it does in Nietzsche's work.

In that vein, Nietzsche relishes the oxymoronic character of his writings: Note his use of phrases such as "immoral morality," "illusory truth," "irrational rationality," "dogmatic nondogmatism," "irreligious religion," "ungodly gods," and the like. Under his broad themes, there cannot be one uniquely correct interpretation of Nietzsche's own work. There is no essence of Nietzsche to discover. Readers must creatively interpret Nietzsche from their perspectives, in accord with their wills to power, for their purposes, and in their contexts. If Nietzsche is correct, dominant conventional interpretations of his work will arise from victories won in social struggle. Institutional power—whether governmental, academic, literary, or from other media—will solidify interpretations that fulfill its purposes, but the work remains inherently contestable. There are no fixed renderings, no final serenities, no unshakeable discoveries. The good news is that we can rejoice in our freedom, search for our insights, and test Nietzsche's thought by our lives. The bad news is that attempts to present Nietzsche's work to others, including the instant effort, are doomed to trivialize, to (over)simplify, and to (mis)interpret. Readers must grapple with Nietzsche's thought directly, not learn of him through intermediaries. We must confront Nietzsche's modes of address and challenges of transformation on a personal and passionate, not merely abstract and rational, level.

TRAGIC VIEW OF LIFE

Nietzsche is concerned with the links between the conditions and fulfillment of culture and a tragic view of life. Nietzsche's tragic view of life was influenced significantly by Arthur Schopenhauer, who was in turn influenced significantly by Buddhist thought.

Schopenhauer's pessimistic outlook can be summarized as follows: Human life is beset with universal unavoidable suffering which precludes robust fulfillment of basic needs and wants. Life itself, not merely mortality and fear of death, is what renders human existence problematic. Although our world of appearance presents us the illusion of individuation, Reality, as thing-in-itself, is a primal unity without individual parts. Our notions of space, time, and causality are functions of the way the human mind actively shapes and organizes sensory material, they have no independent existence as substances of categories of Reality.

We are aware of ourselves as self-moving and active, as direct expressors of wills. Schopenhauer took this inner consciousness to be basic and irreducible. What we will and what we do are one phenomena viewed from the different vantage points of inner consciousness and body, respectively. He extended his notion of will, seeing it as definitive of the fundamental character of the universe, in order to undermine those who insisted on the underlying rationality and morality of the cosmos.[4]

Schopenhauer tries to reorient philosophy away from the dominant rationalism of his day to greater emphasis on unconscious biological forces. He "rejected such ideas as the inevitability of human progress and the perfectibility of man and replaced them with a picture of mankind in general as doomed to an eternal round of torment and misery."[5]

Striving is the basic nature of the will, but there is no finished project that can end striving. Because striving is incapable of final serenity, we oscillate between the lack of fulfillment we feel when not achieving temporary goals and the sense of letdown and boredom we feel when we attain them. Schopenhauer concludes, along with the Buddhists, that we minimize our attachments to and withdraw as much as possible from this life.

Although Nietzsche tries to distance himself from Schopenhauer, it is clear that his own views on suffering, the pervasiveness of will, the lack of final resolutions, the role of strife, and the contingency of individuation all owe much to Schopenhauer's work. The difference, however, between Nietzsche and Schopenhauer is the difference between active and passive nihilism.

I can illustrate this by placing both thinkers in the context of the myth of Sisyphus: Schopenhauer counsels Sisyphus to withdraw from his task of endlessly pushing the boulder up a hill, and, failing that possibility, to detach himself from the task as he performs it. Nietzsche advises Sisyphus to affirm his fate, to desire nothing more than to do what he is fated to do eternally, to luxuriate in the immediate texture of what he does, to confer—through attitude and will—meaning on an inherently meaningless task. Schopenhauer fails to see that value and meaning need not be permanent to be real, that process renders fulfillments independently of attaining goals, that the attainments of great effort and creation do not instantaneously transform to emptiness, and that suffering is not inherently negative but can be transfigured for creative advantage.

Whereas Schopenhauer tacitly accepts the criteria of hedonism and permanence, Nietzsche embraces the criterion of power: exertion, struggle, and suffering are at the core of overcoming obstacles, and it is only through overcoming obstacles that humans experience and truly feel their power. Higher human types joyfully embrace the values of power, while last men and utilitarian philosophers extol the values of hedonism: "Man does *not* strive for pleasure; only the Englishman does" (*TI*, "Maxims and Arrows," 12).

Nietzsche's tragic view of life fully understands the inevitability of human suffering, the flux that is the world, and the Sisyphus-like character of daily life. Yet it is in one's response to tragedy that one manifests either heroism or herd mentality. We cannot rationalize or justify the inherent meaningless of our suffering. We cannot transcend our vulnerability and journey to fixed security. We are contingent mortal beings and will remain so.

But we are free to create ourselves: We bear no antecedent duties to external authority, we are under the yoke of no preestablished goals. We need not recoil squeamishly from the horrors of existence; instead, we can rejoice in a passionate life of perpetual self-overcoming. And there is always art to validate our creativity and laughter, ease our pain, and soften our pretensions: "This crown of him who laughs, this rose-wreath crown: I myself have put on this crown, I myself have pronounced my laughter holy" (Z IV, "On the Higher Man," 18).

GOALS AND DISCIPLES

The meaning of life, for Nietzsche, focuses on stylistic movement—graceful dancing, joyful creation, negotiating the processes of a world of flux with panache and vigor—rather than goal achievement. Indeed, there is no ultimate reachable goal, only development through recurrent personal and institutional deconstruction, reimagination, and re-creation. Our exertion of our wills to power in the face of obstacles, with the knowledge of inherent cosmic meaningless and with profound immersion in the immediacy of life, reflects and sustains our psychological health.

Personal and institutional overcomings will permit us to become who we are: radically conditional beings deeply implicated in a world of flux. By affirming the question of eternal recurrence, we joyously embrace life for what it is and regard it (and ourselves) as part of a grand aesthetic epic: "We may assume that we are merely images and artistic projections for the true author, and that we have our highest dignity in our significance as works of art—for it is only as an *aesthetic phenomenon* that existence and the world are eternally *justified*" (*BT* 5; see also *BT* 24).

Having suggested all this, Nietzsche nevertheless returns to one of his broad themes: Readers cannot merely adopt his views and proclaim themselves his disciples. "When I imagine a perfect reader, he always turns into a monster of courage and curiosity; moreover, supple, cunning, cautious; a born adventurer and discoverer" (*EH*, "Why I Write Such Good Books," 3). To follow Nietzsche in his broad themes is to reject servile parroting of Nietzsche's specific conclusions: Compliant imitation honors neither teacher nor student. Instead, students must demonstrate their loyalty by overcoming, through joyous exertion of their wills to power, the teacher himself. Like all great instructors, Nietzsche understands that his most glorious task is to teach students how to teach themselves, thus making himself obsolete:

One repays a teacher badly if one always remains nothing but a pupil. . . . You are my believers—but what matter all believers? You had not yet sought yourselves: and you found me. Thus do all believers; therefore all faith amounts to so little. Now I bid you lose me and find yourselves; and only when you have all denied me will I return to you. (*Z* I, "On the Gift-Giving Virtue," 3; see also *EH*, "Preface," 4)

THE FOURTH DIALOGUE

Apollonia and Fegataccio awoke, refreshed and alert. They were "morning people" and enjoyed rising early, before the noise and distractions of the masses.

After running laps inside the mall, ten kilometers in all, they showered, then feasted on an exotic breakfast (by American standards): focaccia, bruschetta, and cardoona, washed down with generous portions of mango juice. They were both in expansive moods.

Apollonia: I feel great, Fegataccio! I'll say this for your hero Nietzsche: the man understood food! He had the eminent good taste to judge Italian cuisine superior to German and English cooking (*EH*, "Why I Am So Clever," 1).

Fegataccio: If I recall correctly, he extolled Northern Italian cuisine, not the Southern Italian fare we most enjoy. But on behalf of Nietzsche, thanks for the compliment. The comparison, though, is a no-brainer. If he had judged otherwise we would have conclusive evidence that he had gone insane prior to or during the writing of *Ecce Homo*!

Apollonia: Exactly right! It seems a shame to tread on this moment of agreement, but I must resume my critique of Nietzsche's life. Beyond his superb culinary sense, he led a shallow life. Writing a robust life is not living one. He gives credence to those who talk about ivory-tower intellectuals: In fact, he did not even rise to that level! He left academe to pursue even deeper solitude and refuge from the world. Let's count up the wins and losses of his life: no wives; chastity or near chastity; no children; a few friends who always seem to lurk in the distance; disappointments in his major emotional commitments (Wagner, Ree, Salome); ambiguous relations—mostly negative—with his mother, sister, and aunts; physical debilities throughout; every excursion away from his writing produced yet another physical humiliation; at a relatively early age he goes insane; later he is exploited by his own sister, including being occasionally dressed in white robes and put on display for gawkers; and his work is subsequently expropriated in service of Nazi propaganda. Not exactly a poster boy for lifestyles of the joyful and famous, is he, Fegataccio?

Fegataccio: You can't repress your sarcasm for long, can you Apollonia? We have covered this before but it is worth repeating. You are making a commonplace obtuse assumption: that intellectual activity, particularly writing, is not living life, it is only chronicling life. That assumption is stone-cold false. The major part of Nietzsche's life was his work. It wasn't separate from life, it was life.[6]

Nietzsche wages war in the life of the interior: He battles demons, overcomes illness, gives style to his life, creates himself as a literary figure, and records his triumphs in his writings. Granted, outsiders are denied direct access to his life of the interior—after all, it is his life—but we get images and indirect understanding from Nietzsche's work. Nietzsche squarely faces the human condition but renounces

Schopenhaurian pessimism and passive nihilism. He is a Sisyphus who refuses to go belly up. He joyfully embraces the world, he is grateful for his life, he lives his philosophy: self-overcoming, grand creation, cheerful demeanor, a courageous warrior waging battles that he knows resist final victories. For Nietzsche to enter the world of commerce, pursuit of worldly success, or profound heterosexual relationships would have been to retreat from his interior life. He needed to sublimate his sexual and competitive energies in the service of great art. He led a grand life, but it is simply not the typical life to which most of us aspire. In fact, most of us are incapable of replicating Nietzsche's life: We lack the self-knowledge, the strength of character, and the remarkable spirit needed to cast aside revenge and resentment. How many of us could attain Nietzsche's joy given his physical suffering? No, Apollonia, Nietzsche led a glorious life of the interior that, for him, far exceeded the models of existence you hold so dear.

Apollonia: Please stop, you sound like a greeting card! For someone who is so hard, so mentally tough, even downright hostile, you have swallowed a sappy bill of goods. You have been convinced by Nietzsche's rhetoric that he led an exemplary life. I think Nietzsche protests too much.

Allow me to interpret the matter differently. The "will to power" is Nietzsche's desperate attempt to understand his own impotence in the world; the affirmation of "eternal recurrence" with squeals of "*amor fati*" is a feeble effort to rationalize his illnesses and awkward personal relationships— what I cannot succeed in I will feign acceptance of; and the *Übermensch* is an adolescent fantasy which, even if a mere thought experiment, manifests Nietzsche's dissatisfaction with humans and the world.

Don't kid yourself, Fegataccio, Nietzsche craved worldly success deeply and resented it when it was not forthcoming. His disdain of masses as constitutive of herd mentality is nothing less than an indictment of those whom he believes have been too dense to honor him. He sees himself as a higher type who, like Zarathustra, is too wonderful to be appreciated by the dwarfs, oxen, spiders, and clowns who populate the earth.

He subconsciously blamed himself for his father's early death; he both feared and secretly needed women; he struck out, in writing, against all those he was too weak to strike out against physically. He retreated to "the life of the interior" because he was incapable of winning a high place in the world of everyday life. He battled with quill and paper, a warrior of the mind who waged bloodless skirmishes whose outcomes were fixed from the outset by their creator. Like many intellectuals, he vented his frustrations with words written in insolation instead of confronting his enemies directly. He used philosophy to act out the resentments, reconciliations, and emotions he could not express in person. He talked the talk but he couldn't walk the walk. And he knew this!

Nietzsche's final irony is that, despite his pitiless excoriation of the irrelevance of mainstream philosophers, he chose the abstractness of intellectual activity over the concreteness of robust interpersonal relations. Nietzsche's final tragedy is that in affirming life through philosophical legerdemain he denied himself life in its only meaningful form.

Fegataccio: Such an insufferable combination of shoot-from-the-hip psychology, trivializations, and (intentional?) oversimplifications. I am embarrassed for you, Apollonia! With your fancy education, polished intellectual demeanor, and self-assured rhetoric, you should know better!

You have missed the main point: Nietzsche's writings are not a *substitute* for life, they are his recordings *of* his life. True, his autobiographical reports are stale when compared to the experiences themselves, but they do nevertheless partially constitute his life. Where you and Nietzsche differ is on the value of literary creation. He believes that the spiritualization and sublimation of competitive and sexual passions in the service of great art is a worthy tradeoff, at least for him; you believe—if I interpret your diatribe charitably—that more commonplace pursuits, such as family and immersion in the daily activity of the external world, should not be ignored even if doing so decreases the prospects that one will create great art. Your judgment may well be sound, for you and for most others. But when you deny that Nietzsche's life was truly robust, you merely reveal your own pernicious dogmatism. Once we purge your attack of its rhetoric excess and vitriol, we are left with a simple disagreement about how to live. Nietzsche found his way, perhaps you have found yours. That the two ways are different does not threaten Nietzsche; why does it threaten you?

Nietzsche's internal struggles were neither contrived nor self-created. His struggles are our struggles: the search for meaning and value in an inherently meaningless and valueless cosmos. There is nothing abstract about these struggles and Nietzsche could not have made them abstract even if he had wanted to. These struggles define the core of the human condition; they are as concrete as life itself.

Remember, Nietzsche was not living his life through written words, he was purging himself of the stale thoughts that dimly or falsely chronicle his life experiences.

Apollonia: Wait a minute! Earlier you said that Nietzsche's intellectual activity was not merely chronicling life, but was living life, that the major part of Nietzsche's life was his work. Now you seem to be saying that his writing dimly reports his life experiences. The latter seems to separate Nietzsche's writing from his living, while the former insists on the identification of his writing with his living. Is this a clever Nietzschean "reversal" or a pedestrian self-contradiction?

Fegataccio: Neither. I'll put it more precisely, to satisfy your yen for "rigor" and "univocality." Nietzsche's writing was obviously a part of his life, it consumed so much of his time and thought that parts of his books are second-order writings about his writings. Clearly, I would not separate "life" from "writing." So I should, for precision's sake, talk about his nonwriting experiences and his writing experiences as constitutive of his life. His writing experiences often report on the nonwriting experiences of his life: his inner battles with fundamental intellectual and physical conflicts and his search for meaning and value. If you don't like the categories I have set out, it should at least be clear that I was not reversing my earlier remarks—I am not clever enough for that—and there is no self-contradiction.

Apollonia: It is precisely those nonwriting experiences I denigrate. They constitute, for the most part, a retreat from vigorous living. You can talk all you want about the life of the interior, but how is that life, when taken to the extremes Nietzsche took it, any different from a life of fantasy? Sure, we all have internal struggles generated by conflicting passions, but are those struggles going to occur in the context of engagement with the external world or are they going to occur in the context of isolation? Yes, I understand the joys of solitude and the need to retreat from daily routine, but if solitude and retreat are overemphasized they become estrangement and alienation.

Moreover, do we really thing that Nietzsche's writings constitute an honest sincere chronicle of his struggles? Sure, he sees himself as a doer of great deeds, a commander of high persuasion, but the deeds and the commands are entirely internal. Nietzsche is a grand solipsist who self-consciously reveals his inner battles behind masks, reversals, parodies, and abuse. It is no wonder that Heidegger could interpret Nietzsche as publishing only his masks and recording his more accurate self-renderings in his unpublished *Nachlass*. Although such an interpretation would be considered zany if it were imposed on other philosophers, when suggested of Nietzsche it is plausible. Even Jaspers, who expresses admiration for Nietzsche's work, understands the serious limitations of Nietzsche's style and method.[7]

Fegataccio: I understand that from the vantage point of one who is deeply engaged with numerous traditional life projects—family, profession, community groups, and the like—Nietzsche's life will seem shallow. But he was an artist of a certain sort, graced with high energy, astounding intellect, and a fragile mental and physical constitution. Neither his life nor his writing will appeal to everyone; in fact, they will appeal only to a few. And he understands this.

The Jaspers reference is important, but I read it differently from you. I see Jaspers as insightfully capturing several dimensions of Nietzsche's work. Even those of us who deeply appreciate Nietzsche do not do so simply or without qualification. Nietzsche's writings reflect, to the extent possible, the complexity and multivalence of life. While we may strive to joyfully embrace all the features of life, we should not deceive ourselves about the human condition: In the absence of ultimate meaning and value, human existence is inherently problematic. The "solutions," if any, that we adopt cannot purge themselves of the enigmas that are life. Nietzsche's writings explicitly retain their enigmatic flavor, both to celebrate his broad themes (e.g., radical contingency, flux, perspectivism) and to mirror the mysteries of life itself. Remember, for Nietzsche we *are* our masks, there is no clear separation between an authentic self and an apparent self. Indeed, for Nietzsche there is no substantive self at all. Heidegger's interpretation is less plausible than you suspect for that reason.

Instead of attacking Nietzsche's life, a more charitable approach is to appreciate his creations as we do with many great poets, artists, and philosophers. Emily Dickinson may not have been a poster lady for the fast life, but her poetry is evocative and enduring. And have you ever wondered why no one ever badmouths the lifestyles of Socrates or Kant? It is always Nietzsche who is abused for limited engagement. Does Kant strike you as a swashbuckler, one who luxuriated in the immediacy of life with panache? Does Socrates strike you as a good husband and father, one we should emulate in our daily lives?

Apollonia: You are straying from my point. My deeper concern is how Nietzsche's method connects with truth and criteria of value. I think it is important to seek a truth beyond ourselves, to conceive of the world as not simply of our making, and to search for deeper links between ourselves, others, and nature. You can talk about a world of Becoming all you want, but we don't experience the world as chaotic. Whether because of the categories of our mind, the inherent structure of the cosmos, or some combination, we experience regularity and pattern. There is no vantage point from which Nietzsche can justifiably proclaim that the world is flux, even if he is correct that I cannot independently establish that the world admits inherent design.

Nietzsche's approach is too autobiographical, both in its assumptions about the sources of truth and in literary style. Furthermore, I detect a disingenuity (dare I say mendacity) in the autobiography: An unhealthy dose of fantasy and wish fulfillment pervades Nietzsche's chronicles of his internal struggles.

Fegataccio: We don't know enough about Nietzsche to make some of judgments you have levied, Apollonia. Although we have outlines of his life, he died almost one-hundred years ago, much of the material we have is sketchy, and some has been transfigured in the service of his sister's or the Nazis' agenda. My view on this is simple: If there is a measure of fantasy and wish fulfillment, that just shows Nietzsche was human. Still, we can gain much from grappling with his work and asking the paramount questions about meaning, truth, value, motives, and origins he poses.

Nietzsche would agree with you that there is no neutral Archimedean point from which to assess truth claims. But remember, he is neither a subjectivist nor a cultural relativist regarding truth. In some sense, Nietzsche would agree with you about truth: All our truth seeking goes beyond ourselves in that we are not merely surveying our current internal state to determine what is "true" once and forever. Remember, for Nietzsche "truth" itself is in flux and our language is inadequate to resolve the paradoxes of our experiences. But we covered all this when we talked about perspectivism, I thought. Why do these issues keep reemerging?

Apollonia: They keep reemerging because we haven't resolved them and they infect all aspects of Nietzsche's work, including his self-image of what he is doing when he writes.

Fegataccio: Exactly! But he knows that, relishes the paradoxes, and is convinced they cannot be resolved, at least not in the sense you demand. There is no firmer ground we can access, no different light to use as background, no penetrating vision we can use to "resolve" these paradoxes in this or any other context. We are condemned to our cognitive and spiritual struggles.

Apollonia: But something is gained, even from Nietzsche's perspective, in raising the paradoxes in different contexts. Doing so, at least, highlights their pervasiveness, reminds us of the difficulties Nietzsche faces in engaging—not merely pontificating about—mainstream perspectives, and underscores methodological differences.

Fegataccio: Fair enough, but I want to address another of your remarks: autobiography as a literary style for philosophy. Your style of analytic philosophy has, from a Nietzschean perspective, masked its biases, prejudices, and descriptive and prescriptive worldviews by its manner of presentation. More specifically, particular authors advance their arguments and announce their conclusions in an ahistorical, effetely impartial fashion. They write and talk as if their investigations and findings flow from an impersonal vantage point. Even those who, if pressed, would deny we have access to a neutral Archimedean point nevertheless write as if their conclusions emerge from such a point.

Too often, you and your colleagues revert to the noble "we," implying that you speak authoritatively for all right-thinking scholars, all members of the moral community in good standing, or from the view from above. Give Nietzsche the credit he is due: He lays it on the line, admits his partiality, reveals many of his prejudices, and has the decency to laugh at himself. He admits, indeed goes out of his way, to exemplify ambivalences, dimly understood conflicts, and deepest personal commitments.

Apollonia: You might be surprised to discover that I agree with much of what you say. I agree that literary style is connected to philosophical content. Analytic philosophy presents itself impersonally because it is committed, in various ways, to objective methods and transcendent truths. Although robust strains of skepticism and relativism have historically flourished, or at least coalesced, within analytic philosophy, such positions have been presented within the dominant rhetorical strategies. Analytic philosophy tacitly assumes there is a truth beyond us and thus presents itself dispassionately and "scientifically." As you know, I am drawn to the demands for rigor and clear thinking. I am suspicious of Nietzschean "autobiography" because it too easily degenerates into narcissistic confession and banal subjectivism: To thine own self be true.

Fegataccio: Of course it can, and that is where laughter, self-parody, and reversal is so important: to catch oneself in the act and deflate one's own pomposity.

Apollonia: But remember that no discourse unsettles itself so consistently as analytic philosophy. Through self-examination of its own foundations, it undermines its own pretensions, and does so more effectively than external critiques. Of course, self-examination must cease, a truce must be called and some of the undermining must be temporarily forgotten if the enterprise is to continue. The limits of analytic philosophy are nothing more than the limits of humans.

Fegataccio: And so it is with Nietzsche. Self-parody must be a spice, not the main meal. What I object to in analytic philosophy is its self-conscious effort to disconnect philosophical reflection from daily experience. I am not just talking about excessive abstractness and ahistoricism, but also the concerted concealments of authors' identity. Authors write as if the experiences and life circumstances that molded their identities are irrelevant to their work. In fact, in most areas of philosophy one's life circumstances and definitive experiences greatly affect one's philosophical investigations and conclusions.

Apollonia: Perhaps in religious, moral, political, and legal philosophy what you say has force. But determining the logical validity of deductive arguments or the underlying foundations, if any, of language does not strike me as closely personal.

Fegataccio: We rarely stop at merely determining the validity of logical arguments, we also attend to soundness of arguments and that does implicate personality, in my view. Moreover, even the initial commitment to the structure of bivalent analysis requires personal commitment not based on "pure reason," whatever that is. Analytic philosophy structured itself as imitation of natural science and, as with most imitations, it falls far short of its own pretensions.

Apollonia: I am well aware of the limitations of all, not just analytic, philosophy. I am also well aware of contemporary philosophical attacks on natural science itself, which, by extension, are also critiques of analytic philosophy's self-understanding. But I resist the conclusion that the only viable alternative is Nietzschean bombast and obscurantism.

An analytic philosopher can assume that the proper use of bivalent reasoning will not necessarily result in unadulterated moral and political truths. She can perceive her task as illustrating both the powers and limitations of abstract reason, and conceive reason as setting the boundaries of plausibility.

Fegataccio: I can agree as long as invocation of abstract reason does not obscure the concrete circumstances and history that imbue our lives with meaning. Reason cannot by itself advance one worldview to which all humans must subscribe. There comes a point where reason runs out, where we must appeal to a self-evident principle, an unprovable assumption, or take a leap of faith. Thus, there may well be several conflicting world visions that do not violate general epistemological or political principles. Philosophy then becomes less of a deductive enterprise and more a project of wisely adjudicating ubiquitous normative puzzles.

Apollonia: I think analytic philosophy can accommodate all that and conceive of its valor as residing in its potential for stimulating participants to alternative ways of thinking and experiencing intellectual creativity as a redemption of spirit and flesh. This is a vision of philosophy as meaningful explanation and as a resource for an individual's arriving at solutions to his or her life struggles, instead of philosophy as exemplifying the demands of Reason itself and coercing participants to specific conclusions.

Now, to return to my deeper point: Our choices are not "either analytic philosophy conceived as pure science or Nietzsche." There is a lot of ground in between those equally disgusting (from my perspective) poles.

Fegataccio: I, of course, see Nietzsche as a salutary alternative, not an "equally disgusting pole." But at least we agree that autobiography is part of philosophy. I would go much farther than you in including the identity and personal experiences of authors in their work. I see narratives, fables, personal histories, and family stories as illustrations and embodiments of philosophical truths.

Apollonia: Whereas I accept that revealing a measure of personal background salutarily locates an author and her views in the wider world, I am wary of the sort of free-flowing confessions indulged in by Nietzsche, Kierkegaard, and Augustine. These tormented souls had an uncontrollable need to wallow in their existentialist angst and inflict equal suffering upon their readers: Why shouldn't the world participate in their narcissism and admire their martyrdom?

Fegataccio: That isn't really fair to any of the three thinkers. In all cases their autobiography was methodological: to point the way to deeper truths, to evoke vivid images, and to stimulate others to ponder the deepest questions of human existence.

Apollonia: I understand but do not fully accept your position. An ancillary problem of Nietzsche's tight linkage of literary style, content, and personal psychology is the threat of solipsism. Under his autobiographical method, interpretation and critique become even more complex and difficult than usual. Readers, happily, do not share Nietzsche's relevant experiences or historical context; they lack reliable access to his psychological base, so they cannot fully understand and fairly critique his work.

There is a cunningness to this aspect of Nietzsche that even I admire: Readers from the outset can't fully understand him so they can't fairly critique him. He is "misinterpreted," not because he was so far ahead of his time but because his metaliterary thinking precludes veridical interpretation straightaway. He doesn't present his critics a moving target, he presents them no target. He immunizes himself from successful attack at the start. Unfortunately, he also blockades readers from a crisp understanding of his work. What bothers me, though, is the way he sometimes whines about being misunderstood by "scholarly oxen" and the like. Of course he is misunderstood: If his metaliterary position is sound, the only person who could understand Nietzsche's writings is Nietzsche! And even that is problematic given what he says about our inability to know ourselves and our built-in self-deceptions! So Nietzsche is either a solipsist or, even worse, a fatuous irrationalist.

Fegataccio: You overstate the case, but you seem to do this repeatedly, adding more sarcasm and mockery as we talk. I don't know whether you are trying to irritate me, amuse yourself, or just purge yourself of vitriol. It is ironic that I am the one with a reputation for brashness. I think in the past you have hidden your insolence beneath the sham objectivity of analytic philosophy.

But I must address your attack. First, readers from radically different contexts from Nietzsche's may well misinterpret his work in accordance with their own psychological base, historical context, and internal struggles. All authors run that risk, especially those such as Nietzsche who push the envelope of style and language. Second, what you call his "metaliterary" position is not an independent theory, but merely an illustration of his general perception of the world: a cosmos in flux; languages that adopt conventional usages because they have to but which lack inherent stability; and philosophies that do not merely embody the abstract demands of reason and logic, but reflect and sustain selected modes of life. Books do constitute "texts" for Nietzsche, but the texts are inherently unstable. Third, admitting this does not relegate us to solipsism—writing only for oneself—or "fatuous irrationalism"—writing for no one. Nietzsche's metaliterary position can be understood properly as illustrating Nietzsche's broad themes, and, after all, these themes are the most important part of the work. His more specific experiments are inherently contestable, his more concrete proposals are typically reversed later on, and his vision for the future is intentionally vague. And he never loses sight of all this.

Apollonia: You always resort to Nietzsche's "broad themes" when you are pressed, don't you? The themes of which you speak, however, underwrite the irrationalism I rebel against. These themes are not foundations that can redeem his work from my critique; they are, instead, the underlying target of my critique.

Fegataccio: That's a good point. But once you make it we are back to the problem of rhetorical strategies and where we can go from here, how we can engage each other when speaking from incompatible horizons. If I embrace Nietzsche's broad themes and you accept the structures of bivalent logic, it isn't clear that we can proceed very far without begging the key questions against each other. Do you recall our discussion about rhetorical strategies?

Apollonia: Yes, and I think you are correct. We have an illustration of the main problems of the recurring struggle of those rhetorical strategies now. Perhaps this is where we should agree to disagree.

Fegataccio: In general, Nietzsche's styles distance him from the dominant form of analytic philosophy, underscore his perspectivism, trumpet his experimentalism, declare his partiality, and report his biases. Although Nietzsche understands that the limitations of our language and rhetorical strategies force him at times to sound like a dogmatist, his use of the specific literary forms you mention unsettles that dogmatic tone.

Specifically, each of the literary forms has its particular purposes.[8] Aphorisms are fragments that resist the type of fixed philosophical systems that repel Nietzsche. They exemplify Nietzsche's goal of reasking the enduring questions of human existence in full knowledge that these questions refuse final answers. Aphorisms generally contain no deductive arguments, and when joined together do not necessarily form a consistent whole. Thus, they celebrate, at least when Nietzsche employs them, discontinuity and liberation from fixed meaning.

Hyperbole attracts attention, reveals new connections, provokes response, and cultivates self-parody. Nehamas puts it this way:

Nietzsche's aphorisms, like most of the rest of his writing, are often hyperbolic. Hyperbole is in fact particularly well suited to the aphoristic style because it helps the aphorism attract attention and, in its startlingness, reveals quite unexpected connections. But the aphorism is an essentially isolated sentence or short text, and precisely because of its isolation it disarms the hyperbole as, at the very same time, it highlights it.[9]

Metaphors may illustrate Nietzsche's aristocratic commitments. He does not write for everyone and seemingly judges the rank of readers by their ability to discern the subtlety of his broad themes in his literary forms. Interpretation of metaphors can be a badge of membership: Aristocrats recognize each other by their similar interpretations, the masses are excluded by their dissimilar interpretations or abject puzzlement. Metaphors, like aphorisms, recognize their own conditionality and thus elude final univocal interpretations.

Genealogy, as we have seen, raises suspicions about the origins and partiality of dominant social practices and institutions. In so doing, genealogy forces us to confront the value-ladenness of our views and demands that we exit from the false shelter of abstract reasoning. Logical argument too often embodies an ahistoricism that permits us to forget the class interests and modes of life underwriting our institutions. Genealogy does not pretend to be a substitute for logical proof, but is, instead, an antidote for narrowness and blindness. Nietzsche's polemics, including ad hominem attacks, are self-consciously provocative.[10]

Apollonia: Of course, I can view these literary forms much differently: as the unsystematic ravings of a man degenerating to insanity; as the craven vituperations of a man who avoided direct confrontations; as the exaggerations of a frustrated thinker spoiling for greater attention and acclaim; as the disguised self-hate of the son and grandson of Lutheran ministers; as the self-aggrandizements of an unabashed aristocrat; and as the self-created sham wars of a physically decrepit man.

Fegataccio: I suppose you can, but that interpretation is obtuse. It ignores the vitality of Nietzsche's creations and the real challenges he poses to our thought and social practices. I wouldn't deny an element of truth in what you say—I don't even think Nietzsche would deny it—but the negativity plays a small role in the creation. I'll put it differently: Regardless of the mixed motives and psychology that animate

Nietzsche's writing, we are best served by accepting his challenge to grapple with the enduring questions of the human condition. Defaming Nietzsche, the biological person, does not contribute to our understanding of Nietzsche, the literary figure. More important, it does not contribute to our own quest to come to terms with our existence.

Apollonia: I disagree. I think it is folly to separate so neatly Nietzsche the person from Nietzsche the literary figure. It isn't even "Nietzschean" to do so! Nietzsche, the person or the literary figure, is the one who insists on the connection between literary form, content, and personal psychology. You do him an injustice by conceding me too much and then distancing yourself from Nietzsche's own metaliterary position.

But I won't press that now. We are beginning to spin our wheels and we have reached the point of diminishing returns on this conversation. There is a much more important topic to address: You remind both of us that Nietzsche's mission was not to gain approval for a particular set of abstract propositions, but to interrogate and evaluate different ways of life. In this we both agree with Nietzsche: Our struggles with the human condition are paramount. Our next and final conversation must confront the relevant issues and agonize over the enduring questions. Otherwise, we do injustice to Nietzsche and to ourselves.

With this, Apollonia and Fegataccio gained respite from their discussions. While at the mall, Apollonia always browsed through sporting-goods stores and health-food centers. Fegataccio was partial to bookstores and gambling opportunities. They realized that the tone of their discussions was changing. Their debates were now more like mock battles: They both played devil's advocate more than they had earlier, their intensity was more feigned than real, their conflict was more role playing than sincere. In fact, they both admired Nietzsche's literary styles because they had always felt constrained by the pseudoscientific writing style their profession had imposed on them. They both appreciated his intensity, sense of discipline and commitment, and ability to laugh at himself. He was no pasta asciutta *(dry macaroni). But they also realized that discussions on how best to live one's life were always charged with emotion because there was so much at stake. Their newly won harmony promised to be short-lived.*

Chapter 5

===============

DANCERS, DEMONS, AND DWARFS
Living Life

Nietzsche does not issue a series of concrete proposals for how to live, nor does he unveil ten new commandments for philosophers of the future. But his work is much different from the dreary logic-crunching of mainstream academic philosophy. He forces us to confront the paramount questions of human existence, invites us to live—and not merely contemplate—our answers, and challenges us to take responsibility for the persons we are becoming. In this chapter, I address Nietzsche's view of Dionysus and Apollo, his political reflections, and his notion of perfectionism.

DIONYSUS AND APOLLO

As noted earlier, Nietzsche was deeply appreciative of the Homeric Greeks capacity to affirm life while recognizing its tragic dimensions. In his early writings, Nietzsche celebrates aesthetic principles which he associates with two Greek gods, Dionysus and Apollo.

Dionysus symbolizes the stream of life, the overcoming of obstacles, and the crushing of barriers. As further expressed in lyric poetry, tragedy, and music, the Dionysian embraces life joyfully and irreverently. The Dionysian breaks down form, dissolves individuation, and strives for unification with the underlying primal unity. The Dionysian mocks the distinction between appearance and reality. "Under the charm of the Dionysian not only is the union between man and man reaffirmed, but nature which has become alienated, hostile, or subjugated, celebrates once more her reconciliation with her lost son, man. Freely, earth proffers her gifts, and peacefully the beasts of prey of the rocks and desert approach" (*BT* 1).

Apollo symbolizes light, measure, restraint, and beauty. As further expressed in sculpture, painting, epic, and myth, the Apollinian imposes order and form on the world of Becoming:

We might say of Apollo that in him the unshaken faith in this *principium* [*individuationis*] and the calm repose of the man wrapped up in it receive their most sublime expression; and we might call Apollo himself the glorious divine image of the *principium individuationis,* through whose gestures and eyes all the joy and wisdom of "illusion," together with its beauty, speak to us. (*BT* 1)

Through concepts and classifications, the Apollinian elevates the world of appearances into reality:

Apollo, the god of all plastic energies, is at the same time the soothsaying god. He . . . is the "shining one," the deity of light, is also ruler over the beautiful illusion of the inner world of fantasy. The higher truth, the perfection of these states in contrast to the incompletely intelligible everyday world, this deep consciousness of nature, healing and helping in sleep and dreams, is at the same time the symbolic analogue of the soothsaying faculty and of the arts generally, which make life possible and worth living. (*BT* 1)

The tensions between the Dionysian, as embodying tragic passion, and the Apollinian, as embodying Socratic reason, are a macrocosm of the antagonisms within humans. In his early writings, the two impulses appear as metaphysical principles of nature:

We have considered the Apollinian and its opposite, the Dionysian, as artistic energies which burst forth from nature herself, *without the mediation of the human artist*—energies in which nature's art impulses are satisfied in the most immediate and direct way—first in the image world of dreams, whose completeness is not dependent upon the intellectual attitude or the artistic culture of any single being; and then as intoxicated reality, which likewise does not heed the single unit, but even seeks to destroy the individual and redeem him by a mystic feeling of oneness. (*BT* 2)

The Apollinian can serve as the completion or the antithesis of the Dionysian. If Apollinian impulses predominate for too long, however, "rigidity and coldness" solidify: "Lest this Apollinian tendency congeal the form to Egyptian rigidity and coldness, lest the effort to prescribe to the individual wave its path and realm might annul the motion of the whole lake, the high tide of the Dionysian destroyed from time to time all those little circles in which the one-sidedly Apollinian 'will' had sought to confine the Hellenic spirit" (*BT* 9).

In Nietzsche's later work, the duality between Dionysus and Apollo as aesthetic principles disappears as Nietzsche more thoroughly disavows "metaphysical comforts" (*BT* 17–18) that make life bearable—including the synthesis of Apollinian and Dionysian impulses—and more clearly affirms eternal recurrence:

Saying Yes to life even in its strangest and hardest problems, the will to life rejoicing over its own inexhaustibility even in the very sacrifice of its highest types—that is what I called Dionysian, that is what I guessed to be the bridge to the psychology of the *tragic* poet. Not in order to be liberated from terror and pity, not in order to purge oneself of a dangerous affect by its vehement discharge . . . but in order to be *oneself* the eternal joy of becoming, beyond all terror and pity—that joy which included even joy in destroying. (*TI*, "What I Owe to the Ancients," 5)

The Dionysian hero in *The Birth of Tragedy* is the tragic artist as exemplified by Richard Wagner. There Nietzsche views Dionysian art—lyric poetry, tragedy, dance, and music—as a source of transcendent insight. In his later writings, however, Nietzsche abandons his overly sanguine view of the fine arts as a source of special insight and philosophers of the future assume the mantle of Dionysian genius. Just as Wagner's flagrant Christianity, anti-Semitism, and nationalism eventually repel Nietzsche, so, too, the metaphysical consolations of the tragic artist lose some of their appeal.

Dionysus, thus, remains in a transformed role: as symbolic of the indestructibility of life itself, as affirmer of eternal recurrence, as symbolic of the greatest human exemplars, and as the enhancer of life through creative strife.

Whether Dionysus transformed is a union of the Dionysus and Apollo impulses of *The Birth of Tragedy* is a matter of scholarly dispute. Walter Kaufmann, for example, argues that the Dionysus of the early writings was conceived as a "flood of passion to which the Apollinian principle of individuation might give form."[1] In Nietzsche's later writings, Kaufmann claims, he abrogates his metaphysical dualism and Dionysus represents sublimated passion, discipline, and self-integration:[2]

In his early work, Nietzsche tended toward a dualistic metaphysics. . . . In the "dithyrambs" of *Zarathustra* this opposition of the two gods was repudiated, and the will to power was proclaimed as the one and only basic force of the universe. This fundamental principle, which Nietzsche still called "Dionysian," is actually a union of Dionysus and Apollo: a creative striving that gives form to itself.[3]

Bruce Detwiler, however, emphasizes that in *The Birth of Tragedy* Nietzsche is under the influence of a cosmology he later repudiates:

The cosmology of *The Birth of Tragedy* invokes a distinction between the everyday world of mere appearance and a truer, more essential reality upon which mere appearance depends. Beneath the apparent world in which we all live . . . there lies a "truly existent primordial unity," also described as the "world will," which perpetually brings the world of appearance into being and then lets it pass away again.[4]

It is a mistake, Detwiler argues, to view Dionysus as merely a deity of formless frenzy: "On the metaphysical level Dionysus also appears to represent primal creativity."[5] By refusing to view Dionysus and Apollo as starkly opposed in Nietzsche's early writings, Detwiler draws the contrast between the early and late Dionysian heros differently from Kaufmann: "In the *Birth* Dionysian man joins his god by obliterating himself, whereas in the final period Dionysian man experiences his own divinity by obliterating self-consciousness and by going under, reuniting with the primal ground of his being."[6] Whereas Kaufmann celebrates the "rational self-mastery" of Dionysus transformed, Detwiler underscores "intoxication owing to increased strength":

In the Dionysian life affirmer the dominant creative drive is a kind of spiritualized sexual impulse to create the world in his own image. For the organism as a whole, to become more beautiful is to become more perfectly sublimated, to harmonize desire. The process is hardly one of rational self-mastery but one of Dionysian intoxication owing to increased strength, to "an infallibly perpendicular stress."[7]

The images of Dionysus and Apollo, in any event, prefigure numerous persistent Nietzschean themes: the mutual exclusivity between genuine creativity and conscious reflection; the human need to deconstruct, reimagine, and re-create; the inherent conflicting impulses within humans; the need to affirm life while embracing its tragic dimensions; and the value of self-overcoming.

POLITICS

Nietzsche is often viewed as hostile to politics, especially to the modern nation-state. He calls himself "the last anti-political German" (*EH*, "Why I Am So Wise," 3) and frequently derides the state as an enemy of high culture. Nietzsche sees the modern nation-state as the political extension of herd mentality and as an obstacle to human transformation:

Culture and the state—one should not deceive oneself about this—are antagonists. . . . One lives off the other, one thrives at the expense of the other. All great ages of culture are ages of political decline: what is great culturally has always been unpolitical, even *anti-political*. (*TI*, "What the Germans Lack," 4)

Liberal institutions cease to be liberal as soon as they are attained: later on, there are no worse and no more thorough injurers of freedom than liberal institutions. Their effects are known well enough: they undermine the will to power; they level mountain and valley, and call that morality; they make men small, cowardly, and hedonistic—every time it is the herd animal that triumphs with them. Liberalism: in other words, herd-animalization. (*TI*, "Skirmishes of an Untimely Man," 38)

The nation-state monopolizes "legal" coercion and demands an insipid conformity that is socially useful for the herd but anathema to potentially great individuals. Kaufmann summarizes Nietzsche's attitude: "Men are afraid of social retaliation and do not dare be their own unique selves. It is for this reason that the State becomes the devil of Nietzsche's ethics: it intimidates man into conformity and thus tempts and coerces him to betray his proper destiny."[8]

Those, such as Kaufmann, who conclude that Nietzsche is, as he says in his own words, "anti-political," point out that Nietzsche does not merely deride socialist and liberal regimes but also totalitarian idolators of the state:

State is the name of the coldest of all cold monsters. Coldly it tells lies, too; and this lie crawls out of its mouth: "I, the state, am the people." . . . Where there is still a people, it does not understand the state and hates it as the evil eye and the sin against customs and rights. . . . Everything about [the state] is false; it bites with stolen teeth, and bites easily. . . . State I call it where all drink poison, the good and the wicked; state, where all lose themselves, the good and the wicked; state, where the slow suicide of all is called "life." . . . Only where the state ends, there begins the human being who is not superfluous: there begins the song of necessity, the unique and inimitable tune. (Z I, "On the New Idol"; see also *UM*, "Schopenhauer as Educator," 4)

The picture that emerges is vivid: Nietzsche denounces the state in all its forms and extols "the antipolitical individual who seeks self-perfection far from the modern world."[9]

But remember, we are dealing with Nietzsche, and interpretations are never as straightforward as they might at first seem. The same writer who described himself as "the last anti-political German" also wrote that "the time for petty politics is over: the very next century will bring the fight for the dominion of the earth—the *compulsion* to large-scale politics" (*BGE* 208), and "What is *serious* for me, the 'European problem' as I understand it, [is] the cultivation of a new caste that will rule Europe" (*BGE* 251).

Thus, it may not be the state as such that Nietzsche denounces, but the deleterious effects that modern states typically produce: the state's disengagement from "a people," its destruction of creative possibilities, its conformist zeal which poisons true individuality, and its obsession with "leveling" that undermines high culture and great people.

Nietzsche appreciates the state's necessity for human creativity and its role in binding a people together through continuity of wider traditions. Where, as in ancient Greece and Renaissance Italy, state-born culture facilitates high culture and individual creativity, ensures the dominance of true nobility, and honors the natural hierarchy of men, Nietzsche lavishes praise.[10] Moreover, while castigating liberal democracies and "hybrids such as the 'German Reich'" as decadent and in decline, Nietzsche praises other states such as imperial Rome and nineteenth-century Russia:

In order that there may be institutions, there must be a kind of will, instinct, or imperative, which is anti-liberal to the point of malice: the will to tradition, to authority, to responsibility for centuries to come, to the solidarity of chains of generations, forward and backward *ad infinitum*. When this will is present, something like the *imperium Romanum* is founded; or like Russia, the *only* power today which has endurance, which can wait, which can still promise something. (*TI*, "Skirmishes of an Untimely Man," 39; see also *BGE* 201, 208, 251)

Moreover, Nietzsche sometimes extols political figures as paradigm cases of higher human types:

The highest type of free men should be sought where the highest resistance is constantly overcome: five steps from tyranny, close to the threshold of the danger of servitude. This is true psychologically if by "tyrants" are meant inexorable and fearful instincts that provoke the maximum of authority and discipline against themselves; most beautiful type: Julius Caesar. This is true politically too; one need only go through history. (*TI*, "Skirmishes of an Untimely Man," 38; see also *BGE* 199–200, where Napolean, Caesar, Alcibiades, and Frederick II are extolled, along with Leonardo da Vinci, as the "most beautiful expressions" of "victory and seduction.")

The key distinction is not between political activity within states and anti-political individualism, but rather between state forms which serve the interests of the herd by leveling men and state forms which celebrate the rank order of humans. While it is true that Nietzsche values culture over politics and internalizes politics in important respects— as the self struggles to form (temporary) unities among competing impulses and perspectives—he neither glorifies nor vilifies the state as such. Nietzsche, as always, evaluates states on the basis of their origins, purposes, and social effects.[11] As with much of the contemporary European culture and condition he observes, Nietzsche judges the prevalent modern forms of the state, whether they be democratic, liberal, socialist, or totalitarian, deficient on that basis.

If this understanding is correct, then what type of state does Nietzsche advocate? Certainly, it cannot be the liberal democracies with which Nietzsche is familiar:[12]

We do not need to plug up our ears against the sirens who in the market place sing of the future: their song about "equal rights," "a free society," "no more masters and no servants" has no allure for us. We simply do not consider it desirable that a realm of justice and concord should be established on earth. . . . We are delighted with all who love, as we do, danger, war, and adventure, who refuse to compromise, to be captured, reconciled, and castrated. (*GS* 377)

In broad terms, the state must be aristocratic. It must honor the rank order of humans, facilitate individualism, nurture culture, and bind a people together but not as a herd. Other than in his *Nachlass*, Nietzsche's clearest political pronouncements occur, as I noted earlier, in *The Antichrist*, where he talks, in terms reminiscent of Plato, about "the natural order" of aristocratic organization:

In every healthy society there are three types which condition each other and gravitate differently physiologically; each has its own hygiene, its own field of work, its own sense of perfection and mastery. Nature . . . distinguishes the pre-eminently spiritual ones, those who are pre-eminently strong in muscle and temperament, and those, the third type, who excel neither in one respect nor in the other, the mediocre ones—the last as the great majority, the first as the elite. . . . The order of castes, the *order of rank*, merely formulates the highest law of life; the separation of the three types is necessary for the preservation of society, to make possible the higher and the highest types. The *inequality* of rights is the first condition for the existence of any rights at all. . . . A high culture is a pyramid. (*AC* 57; see also *Z* II, "Upon the Blessed Isles"; *BGE* 203, 257, 259; *WP* 936, 978, 998)

Nietzsche also sometimes alludes to the political unity of Europe as the precursor to world government (see, for example, *BGE* 241–243, 256). But, as always, he does not posit unambiguous goals or indulge false senses of security: In the age when "God has died" and the nihilistic moment has descended, forms of politics, culture, and society are up for grabs and the future is uncertain. New conceptions of truth and transformed images of humans may emerge from social struggle vivified by creative genius. Nietzsche cannot unveil a concrete political theory because to do so would undermine his broad themes of contingency, inherent cosmic meaninglessness, and unremitting flux.[13] Nietzsche invigorates a political mood—animated by Dionysian philosopher-artists, directed at producing high culture and great individuals, and focused on luxuriating in the immediacy of life—rather than offering a specific vision of institutional structures.

Thus, the sense in which Nietzsche is "anti-political" is personal. He did not involve himself in the daily "petty politics" of his time:

It will probably be increasing the sign of spiritual superiority from now on if a man takes the state and his duties towards it lightly; for he who has [philosophical passion] within him will already no longer have time for [political passion] and will wisely refrain from reading the newspapers every day, let alone working for a political party: though he will not hesitate for a moment to be at his place when his fatherland experiences a real emergency. Every state in which anyone other than the statesman has to concern himself with politics is ill organized and deserves to perish by all those politicians. (*UM*, "Schopenhauer as Educator," 7; see also *GM* III, 7–8)

In sum, for Nietzsche political activity is neither necessary nor sufficient for personal greatness; depending on the type of state, the kind of politics, and the temperament and passion of the practitioner, such activity can sometimes hinder and sometimes facilitate the quest for self-mastery; and state politics is to be judged by familiar criteria—its origins, purposes, and social effects—underwritten by aristocratic values.

Those, such as Kaufmann, who interpret Nietzsche as "the anti-political individual who seeks self-perfection far from the modern world," conceive the will to power as directed solely toward self-mastery, spiritualization and sublimation of conflicting impulses, and cultural creation. Such interpreters view Nietzsche's warrior rhetoric and provocative aristocratic bombast as purely self-contained, and as describing internal psychological struggles and victories. Those who interpret Nietzsche as personally antipolitical for particular reasons see the will to power as directed inward but also externally. Such interpreters view Nietzsche's military imagery and aristocratic outpourings as partially self-contained but deeply problematic when applied to the external world.

PERFECTIONISM

Whether self-mastery and self-perfection are the sole focus of the will to power, they clearly are the prime concerns of Nietzsche's work. Neither state idolatry nor discredited supernatural images can provide humans with enduring consolation for their unresolvable existential crises. Instead, a new image of humans is necessary.

Nietzsche's desiderata for higher types includes the ability to marginalize but not eliminate negative and destructive impulses within oneself and to transfigure them into joyous affirmation of all aspects of life; to understand and celebrate the radical contingency, finitude, and fragility of ourselves, our institutions, and the cosmos itself; to regard life itself as fully and merely natural, as embodying no transcendent meaning or value; to harbor little or no resentment toward others or toward the human condition; to confront the world in immediacy and with a sense of vital connection; to refuse to avert one's gaze from a tragic worldview and, instead, to find value not in eventual happiness (as conceived by academic philosophers) but in the inherent activities and processes themselves; to refuse to supplicate oneself before great people of the past but, instead, to accept their implicit challenge to go beyond them; to give style to one's character by transforming our conflicting internal passions into a disciplined and dynamic unity; to facilitate high culture by sustaining a favorable environment for the rise of great individuals; to strive for excellence through self-overcoming that honors the recurrent flux of the cosmos by refusing to accept a "finished" self as dispositive of personal identity; and to recognize the Sisyphus-like dimension to human existence—release from the tasks described is found only in death. Given the human condition, high energy is more important than a final fixed goal. The mantra of "challenge, struggle, overcoming, and growth" animating and transfiguring perpetual internal conflict replaces prayers for redemption to supernatural powers.

The individualism Nietzsche suggests is neither the atomistic individualism of libertarianism nor the humanistic individualism of liberalism. Nietzsche, unlike atomistic individualism, does not see the individual as the fundamental unit of politics or the self as the embodiment of inviolable freedom; instead, he talks about the essential unity of the world of flux, the interrelationships that constitute existence, and the individual as a dynamic multiplicity. There is no stable self or single identity: The "individual's" uniqueness lies in the ordering of his or her internal impulses. Nietzsche, unlike humanistic individualism, does not see human life as inherently sacred or as embodying intrinsic dignity and value; nor does he subscribe to a regime of moral equality or equal consideration.

Nietzsche promotes the individualism of the highest human types while understanding that values are initially established by peoples. The "individuals" of libertarianism and liberalism are themselves a creation of a people, not a metaphysical fact (see, for example, Z, "Prologue," 9; Z I, "On the New Idol"). Lacking intrinsic value, humans create the value they embody by living experimentally and by nurturing an environment that propagates great humans and high culture. It is still "as aesthetic phenomenon that existence and the world are justified" in the sense that the highest artistic creations are great humans themselves.

To understand, even vaguely, the new human image Nietzsche celebrates, it is important to sketch the roles of laughter, love, pity, and suffering. Laughter is an appropriate response to the inherent absurdity of human existence. It reminds us that we do not inhabit a special place in the universe, that our inclination to take ourselves too seriously is misplaced, that our quest for certitude is futile, that the cosmos is indifferent to our standards and aspirations, that despair is the refuge of passive nihilists, and that when allied with wisdom it offers us possibilities for the robust active nihilism that constitutes high culture. A tragic worldview should be accompanied by appreciative comedy. To laugh at oneself spices one's affirmation of life:

To laugh at oneself as one would have to laugh in order to laugh *out of the whole truth*—to do that even the best so far lacked sufficient sense for the truth, and the most gifted has too little genius for that. Even laughter may yet have a future. I mean, when the proposition "the species is everything, *one* is always none" has become part of humanity, and this ultimate liberation and irresponsibility has become accessible to all at all times. Perhaps laughter will then have formed an alliance with wisdom. (*GS* 1; see also *GS* 107, 327, 383; *BGE* 223; Z IV, "On the Higher Man," 16–20)

"*Life as a means to knowledge*"—with this principle in one's heart one can live not only boldly but even gaily, and laugh gaily, too. And who knows how to laugh anyway and live well if he does not first know a good deal about war and victory? (*GS* 324)

Love is an essential part of passing the test of eternal recurrence. Nietzsche tells us that "the spiritualization of sensuality is called *love*" (*TI*, "Morality as Anti-Nature," 3). To love is to affirm, to affirm is to value, to value is to find meaning. First, one must learn to love oneself: "One must learn to love oneself—thus I teach—with a wholesome and healthy love, so that one can bear to be with oneself" (Z III, "On the Spirit of Gravity," 2). Second, one must love the earth: "There are many good inventions on earth, some useful, some pleasing: for their sake, the earth is to be loved" (Z III, "On Old and New Tablets," 17). Third, one must love life itself: "I fear you [life] near, I love you far; your flight lures me, your seeking cures me: I suffer, but what would I not gladly suffer for you? . . . Who would not love you, you innocent, impatient, wind-swift, child-eyed sinner? (Z III, "The Other Dancing Song," 1). Fourth, one must love eternity: "Never yet have I found the woman from whom I wanted children, unless it be this woman whom I love: for I love you, O eternity. *For I love you, O eternity!*" (Z III, "The Seven Seals," 1–7). Fifth, one must love others, particularly friends. While Nietzsche disparages the purity of such love—for where there is love there is always self-interest and the will to power, and there is sometimes inadequate self-creation—he appreciates that love can nurture the lovers' quest for perfection: "I teach you not the neighbor, but the friend. . . . One must learn to be a sponge if one wants to be loved by hearts that overflow. I teach you the friend in whom the world stands completed. . . . In your friend you shall love the overman as your cause" (Z I, "On Love of the Neighbor"), and "all great love . . . wants to create the beloved" (Z II, "On the Pitying").

Nietzsche warns of the dangers of sexual love, reiterates his appreciation of friendship, and underscores his view of salutary love as a yearning and struggle for perfection:

Sexual love betrays itself most clearly as a lust for possession: the lover desires itself most clearly as lust for possession: the lover desires unconditional and sole possession of the person for whom he longs; he desires equally unconditional power over the soul and over the body of the beloved; he alone wants to be loved and desires to live and rule in the other soul as supreme and supremely desirable. . . . One comes to feel genuine amazement that this wild avarice and injustice of sexual love has been glorified and deified so much in all ages. . . . Here and there on earth we may encounter a kind of continuation of love in which this possessive craving of two people for each other gives way to a new desire and lust for possession—a *shared* thirst for an ideal above them. But who knows such love? Who has experienced it? Its right name is *friendship*. (GS 14; see also GS 334, 363)

Pity is the enemy of salutary love. The decadence of pity is the elevation of the sharing of suffering and the marginalization of striving for mutual self-perfection:

Having seen the sufferer suffer, I was ashamed for the sake of his shame; and when I helped him, I transgressed grievously against his pride. Great indebtedness does not make men grateful, but vengeful; and if a little charity is not forgotten, it turns into a gnawing worm. . . . Where in the world has there been more folly among the pitying? And what in the world has caused more suffering than the folly of pitying? Woe to all who love without having a height that is above their pity! . . . All great love is even above all its pity. (Z II, "On the Pitying"; see also BGE 171, 201, 222, 260, 293; GS 118, 271, 338)

Salutary love requires hardness and exertion because it focuses on the recurring struggles of mutual self-perfection and self-overcoming. Pity reneges on the affirmation of eternal recurrence and *amor fati*: It desires that things were otherwise, refuses to transfigure suffering into spiritual advantage, devalues life, and indulges weakness. Beyond its general complicity in the herd mentality, pity masks its motives and its grounding in feelings of superiority, negative evaluation of its object, and disguised resentments (see, for example, GM III, 14; BGE 225; D 133–134; GS 13; AC 7).

Nietzsche understands that greatness necessarily involves suffering and the overcoming of grave obstacles (see, for example, *BGE* 225, 228). He evaluates peoples, individuals, and cultures by their ability to transform suffering and tragedy to spiritual advantage. We cannot eliminate suffering, but we can use it creatively. Suffering and resistance can stimulate and nourish the will to power. By changing our attitude toward suffering from pity to affirmation, we open ourselves to greatness. For Nietzsche, joy and strength trump the "happiness" of the herd:

Every art, every philosophy may be viewed as a remedy and an aid in the service of growing and struggling life; they always presuppose suffering and sufferers. But there are two kinds of sufferers: first, those who suffer from the *over-fullness* of life—they want a Dionysian art and likewise a tragic view of life, a tragic insight—and then those who suffer from the *impoverishment of life* and seek rest, stillness, calm seas, redemption from themselves through art and knowledge, or intoxication, convulsions, anaesthesia, and madness. (*GS* 370; see also *BGE* 225, 229, 270; *Z* II, "Upon the Blessed Isles"; *Z* II, "On Self-Overcoming")

Clearly, Nietzsche's new image of humans is not projected for or achievable by all. It is an explicitly aristocratic ideal that is pitched only to the few capable of approximating it. Greatness and genius are fragile and vulnerable: They bring about their own destruction but arise stronger than ever. In the end, however, the only way to evaluate Nietzsche's new image is to live it: "The only critique of a philosophy that is possible and that proves something, namely trying to see whether one can live in accordance with it, has never been taught at universities; all that has ever been taught is a critique of words by means of other words" (*UM*, "Schopenhauer as Educator," 8).

Accordingly, Nietzsche is not looking for disciples who will examine his work for a specific formula for discovering meaning and value, or those who will contemplate and analyze his thoughts abstractly. Instead, he is seducing and persuading those few humans who combine a Nietzschean attitude with the potential for transvaluing values through creative action: "One has to compel men to take [philosophy] seriously, that is to say to let it inspire them to action, and I consider every word behind which there does not stand such a challenge to action to have been written in vain" (*UM*, "Schopenhauer as Educator," 8).

THE FINAL DIALOGUE

Apollonia and Fegataccio returned more quickly than they had imagined. Neither had purchased anything. As with most of their shopping forays, this venture was little more than distraction. The numbers five, six, eight, and ten were rushing through Fegataccio's mind; they reminded him of greatness and of family. He was filled with exuberance and enjoyed the sense of physicality his dedicated exercise program had produced. He strutted more than walked through the mall. Apollonia was pensive and wary. She suspected that she and Fegataccio would differ strongly on how best to live life. They were drawing closer but understood how fragile their union might be. They knew this was to be their final discussion about Nietzsche, at least for now.

Apollonia: We can agree, I think, that our earlier discussions about Nietzsche were merely preliminary. His perspectivism, eternal recurrence, genealogical inquiries, notion of will to power, and literary style bear little currency unless they generate lessons for life. The paramount question must be, "How should I live my life?"

Fegataccio: Agreed. But remember, Nietzsche does not offer us a specific menu for living life. In accordance with his broad themes, he can only advance general thoughts for certain types of humans, those with the potential for greatness and true individuality.

Apollonia: We must dissect this "true individuality" later. For now, I am interested in his fascination with suffering. Clearly, part of this fascination stems from his need to rationalize his own physical debilities. For someone such as Nietzsche, who feels complete affirmation of life is essential and who insists on the inherent meaninglessness of the cosmos, suffering takes on heroic proportions. So he defines health idiosyncratically as the overcoming, not the absence, of great suffering. He tries desperately and pathetically to show that he is among the healthiest of humans despite his decrepit physical condition. His subsequent insanity underscores his failures in this regard: He was neither healthy nor heroic.

Fegataccio: I think he was enormously heroic. He didn't whimper or whine about his illness. Instead, he uses it for theoretical and practical advantage. Think of all he accomplished despite his physical ailments. He was among the healthiest humans in that he transformed self-pity and misfortune into joyous affirmation and high creativity.

Apollonia: I am suspicious about the "joyous affirmation." Was he using written words to mask his own internal discontent? Was the great advocater of masks and multiplicity throwing us off the track with his overstated cheerfulness?

Fegataccio: I don't think any of those are important questions. The issue is not Nietzsche himself or the life he led or the sincerity with which he wrote. The key is whether what he wrote can help us find our way in the world.

Apollonia: That move is too easy. Remember, it is Nietzsche who insists on the autobiographical nature of great philosophy. He is the one who demands genealogical inquiries, who casts suspicion based on ad hominem attack, who gleefully ladles out sarcasm. Why do you now seek to protect him from the same sort of interrogation?

Fegataccio: Partly because our interrogation of such matters is overly speculative. We lack sufficient reliable information to thoroughly examine such questions. Also, you are forgetting two of Nietzsche's prized suggestions. First, "All great things bring about their own destruction through an act of self-overcoming" (*GM* III, 27). Second, health is not defined by the absences of illness but by the presence of creative transformations. The last men are "healthy" and "happy" in a certain banal sense, but they are decidedly mediocre and unworthy of emulation; they are ill in a more important sense.

The insight Nietzsche shares relates to the connection between suffering, greatness, and fragility. I remember reading an article on the great football coach of the Green Bay Packers, Vince Lombardi. The writer described the Lombardi era at Green Bay as "a comet burned out by the heat of its own brilliance."[14] That is a beautifully apt way of portraying Nietzsche. Even his insanity verifies his broad themes of the fragility of greatness, the self-overcoming and self-destruction of greatness, and health defined by creativity instead of by absence of maladies.

Apollonia: There is something obscene about connecting Nietzsche with Vince Lombardi. Next you'll be comparing him to Janis Joplin, Billy Martin, and Lenny Bruce! Greatness and high creativity need not be self-destructive. I can name dozens of great philosophers who never went insane, hundreds of wonderful musicians who never died from an overdose of drugs, numerous football coaches who consistently win, and so on. What Nietzsche sensed, correctly, was his own fragility and his approaching self-destruction. Then, in decidedly un-Nietzschean fashion, he universalized his condition as definitive of greatness. What unabashed ego!

Fegataccio: Self-overcoming and self-destruction, in a fully negative sense, are different. Self-overcoming connotes the tearing down in order to reimagine and re-create. Self-destruction connotes, in its fully negative sense, tearing down from deep irredeemable dissatisfaction. Self-overcoming is done in service of affirming life, while self-destruction is often done to escape from life.

But Nietzsche, Lombardi, Joplin, Martin, and Bruce did share at least one trait: searing intensity. Nietzsche and Lombardi employed that trait positively as self-overcoming. Joplin, Martin, and Bruce were highly creative but ended up self-destructing. It may not be accidental that all five died relatively young: In one way or another they were "burned out by the heat of their own brilliance." Typically, we can draw a Nietzschean lesson about searing intensity: It has a decadent form, self-destruction, and an affirmative form, self-overcoming. In any event, I don't think Nietzsche meant to universalize his condition as a definition of greatness, at least not in the sense you imply.

Apollonia: This talk about suffering is beginning to illustrate its subject. I want to move on to pity. Nietzsche's reductionist tendencies—his inclination to assume one set of motivations for our passions—are most obvious when he discusses pity. He sees it as stemming, apparently necessarily, from a disguised sense of superiority and a decadent attempt at amplifying self-esteem. In truth, pity does *sometimes* stem from such motives, but at other times pity is merely our recognition of misfortune, our support of another human who endures suffering. Pity does not necessarily reinforce weakness or prevent the other from transforming suffering into creative possibilities. Indeed, knowing that others are moved by our suffering may strengthen our resolve to overcome it. Of course, it is important to share joy, as Nietzsche is so fond of reminding us, but sharing grief is also an essential requirement of humanity.[15]

Imagine a world in which my response to the grave suffering of another is this: "That bozo should stop whimpering and realize that suffering bears transformative possibilities. So he has lost his wife and children to the brutality of an axe murderer; so he has lost his uninsured home to a major flood; so he has just been diagnosed as HIV-positive—his rank will be determined by his response. He'll receive no pity from me."

Granted, ultimately the sufferer's response will be crucial but it is inhuman to expect him to immediately jump for joy and scream *"amor fati!"* as he endures a parade of horribles. Surely our common rituals of bereavement and exchanges of condolences are not simply manifestations of the weakness of herd morality. Although the expression "I feel your pain" can be a disguise for feelings of superiority or a hackneyed political strategy, it can also speak to our basic humanity without which life is not worth living.

Fegataccio: What Nietzsche abhors in pity is its connection with *ressentiment.* For Nietzsche, resentment may lead the strong to undermine their own values by altering their judgments of themselves and the suffering weak:[16] "If they [the resentful] succeeded in *poisoning the consciences* of the fortunate with their own misery, with all misery, so that one day the fortunate began to be ashamed of their good fortune and perhaps said to one another: 'it is disgraceful to be fortunate: *there is too much misery!*'" (*GM* III, 14).

Nietzsche himself was capable of great empathy for others (see, for example, *D* 119; *GS* 338). Although he counseled hardness, he was not the cold-hearted brute caricatured in your remarks. It was precisely the decadent forms of pity that he disparaged. He does not condemn all fellow-feeling.

Apollonia: There isn't much ambiguity when Nietzsche says, "Pity is the most agreeable feeling among those who have little pride and no prospects of great conquests; for them easy prey—and that is what all who suffer are—is enchanting. Pity is praised as the virtue of prostitutes" (*GS* 13).

Your response is typical of Nietzsche apologists. By qualifying his statements with "sometimes" and "certain" you make his work more palatable, but you also steal his panache and uniqueness. If Nietzsche is merely saying some forms of pity can be self-defeating and lead to more suffering, his statement is true but trivial. If Nietzsche is saying pity as such emerges from inferior motives and produces pernicious effects, his statement is interesting but false and inhumane. Which is it, Fegataccio?

Fegataccio: Neither. You pose a phony dilemma. Nietzsche derides the pity that undermines self-mastery and self-overcoming (see, for example, *D* 135; *GS* 338; *BGE* 225). Suffering is necessary for greatness and true fellow-feeling should not degrade, condescend, or exhibit contempt. Instead, mastery of our impulses demands that we concentrate our efforts internally: "My humanity does *not* consist in feeling with men how they are, but in *enduring* that I feel with them. My humanity is a constant self-overcoming" (*EH*, "Why I Am So Wise," 8). For Nietzsche, pity takes on a specific, technical, negative meaning.

Apollonia: Another transparent move! Now, Nietzsche isn't talking about pity as you and I talk about it; but, instead, he builds into the term a necessarily negative connotation. If so, his work is certainly trivial; he merely brandishes and embellishes upon definitional truths. This move gives Nietzsche a pedestrian, flat-footed, Kantian flavor. I am sure he would appreciate that irony!

Moreover, once we impose some content into his notion of pity we discover a "self-mastery" accomplished and exercised in seclusion, without communal interaction! It just doesn't work. Humane forms of pity, I would argue, are essential to self-perfection once we understand the self as embodying both individual and communal dimensions. These dimensions, themselves, are part of the cherished multiplicity that constitutes the human condition. Is Nietzsche sometimes guilty of trying to suppress the communal pole, as opposed to dealing fully with the conflicts it presents to individualism? Doesn't this carryover to his truncated view of love?

Fegataccio: Your talk of seclusion and immunizing oneself from community is too extreme. Other than for temporary respites, that isn't Nietzsche. But it will serve our purposes to talk of love because love is directly connected to pity.

Love's decadent form is pity, which both suspends and jeopardizes judgment. When the sufferer is pitied (in the Nietzschean sense of the term), the instincts for greatness of the pitier lose vitality. Instead, the pitier suspends his healthy contempt for weakness and the herd mentality, focusing instead solely on his inclinations to sympathize. But, as I noted earlier, pity also jeopardizes judgment because the pitier, if a higher type, may come to undermine his own values and be drawn into the herd mentality. For Nietzsche, love's affirmative form includes judgment, especially continued contempt for the base instincts that hinder striving for self-perfection. He venerates friendship because he views it as love based on ideals, on what is noblest within humans.[17]

Apollonia: Earlier you said pity involves the disguised disdain of a superior to an inferior. If so, there is a judgment. Now you say that pity involves a suspension of judgment, a refusal to view the sufferer's weakness and mediocrity with contempt. Which is it?

Also, if Nietzsche holds that love is based on the unrealized ideal embodied by the other, it isn't clear that love's object is a concrete person. Isn't it unintentionally ironic that Nietzsche, who otherwise disdains abstractness, advances a notion of love based on abstraction: love of an unrealized ideal instead of an actual person?

Fegataccio: Good point. I must make myself clearer. Among members of the herd, pity is often of the first kind: disdain masked mendaciously as fellow-feeling. When the pitier is a higher type and the pitied is a member of the herd, pity is often of the second kind: a dangerous suspension of negative judgment toward baser instincts.

For Nietzsche, love must elevate, it must transform the lovers into life-affirmers and self-overcomers. At its best, it strives for the particular unrealized ideals embodied by specific people. It is not, as you intimate, love of an abstract, disembodied, and universalizable ideal. Instead, love recognizes the particular unrealized ideal of the beloved. The aim of love, then, is mutual nurturing of each lover's specific ideal possibilities, nurturing which requires hardness, toughness, and clear focus on love's purpose.[18] Remember, transforming suffering, struggling with multiplicity, and overcoming satisfaction are at the core of self-mastery. Healthy love cannot degenerate into the banal contentments of last men.

Apollonia: There is something disgustingly calculating and cold about love so conceived. Your description could just as easily be applied to weightlifters who are training partners. Also, if I were you I wouldn't be so quick to portray Nietzschean love as the mutual elicitation of unrealized ideals. It isn't that simple. Even Nietzsche reminds us, *"What do you love in others?—My hopes"* (*GS* 272). I remain unconvinced that his version of love involves concrete people. If the beloved is transformed into an idealized image of *my* aspirations, then what is love's object? My fantasies of the overman? My projections of what I can be? My speculations of what the other can be molded to be?

Fegataccio: Once one holds, as Nietzsche did, that the self is neither substantive nor fixed, love must assume the form of self-overcoming, a striving for self-mastery and self-perfection which requires deconstruction, reimagination, and re-creation. Lovers should facilitate their beloved's quest for self-overcoming. Love should not idealize, in the sense of seeing what cannot be or glorifying the beloved's character of the moment. Thus, the lover is not and cannot, for Nietzsche, be fixated on the beloved's static self-understanding, but, instead, promotes the beloved's particular unrealized ideals. What you continually insist is a "concrete particular person" is, for Nietzsche, an illusion. For him, struggle, affirmation of becoming, and creative reconstruction remain paramount.

Apollonia: I am still not persuaded, seduced, or moved. There remains a coldness and a remoteness to Nietzschean love. I understand why he focuses on self-love and friendship, and speaks sparingly (and usually derogatorily) of sexual love. For Nietzsche, the lover is a helpmate, perhaps even a co-creator, but always from a distance. His version of love fails to implicate our souls. At best, it vivifies our mutual creativity and quest for individual greatness.

Fegataccio: But yours is an utterly romantic view of love: two hearts beating as one, candlelight, flowers, soulful glances, an artificial and temporary world of illusion. Romantic love is a flight from our world, a temporary escape from suffering, and as dangerous a narcotic as heroin. Nietzsche understands the self-delusions of romantic love, how it is grounded in possession and power and how it mendaciously conceals its aims behind the conventional pieties of herd morality.

Apollonia: Stop your tired litany right now! I know you don't believe the venom you spew. You switch to your default "defend Nietzsche" mode to evade an uncomfortable subject that hits too closely to home. Sometimes I think the only thing Nietzsche knew about love was that he enjoyed precious little of it!

Love is neither Nietzsche's cynical mutual use for individual greatness nor the romantic moment you caricature. Love must involve an expansion of subjectivity: opening access to oneself and yielding a measure of privacy; intimacy and sharing; common activities and mutual benefit; and, most of all, establishing a common good and forging an identity. What Nietzsche fails to understand is how love binds parties to a new identity, not merely a renewed quest for individual greatness. When I love another, I do not merely seek my self-perfection and the other's self-perfection, I seek *our* perfection.

There is pure safety only in the womb, in the grave, maybe in sleep. Love demands grave risk and full commitment. The lovers announce, "This is where I stake my faith, my being." Love is unsafe. While it promises salutary union and transformation and pledges to mediate the alienation of the human condition, it also threatens to suffocate, to overprotect, and to force dependency. Love ignites the spark of divinity and the image of the ideal, but it also magnifies the tensions between unrealized ideals and real persons.

Love is a process, not a fixed condition. It begins in lack and is grounded in power. But the grandeur of love is that it is not a commodity; it can't be bought or sold, yet it isn't costless. Love struggles to overcome its internal paradoxes of consolation and growth, dependency and freedom. The uniqueness and specialness of the lovers, not in terms of their facility in guiding the mutual quest for individual perfection, forms the core of love. Love is a mysterious mixture of choice and discovery that changes our perception of the world without actually changing the world. Love is transformative but not redemptive. But, mostly, it is an acknowledgment of bonds not fully chosen.

Love cannot be an arm's-length, mutual-aid exercise in individualism. Lovers cannot be creators *in lontananza* (in the distance). No, love widens our subjectivity and creates a new identity that immediately embodies its own unrealized ideals. And the unrealized ideal possibilities of lovers bound are never merely the sum of the unrealized ideal possibilities embodied by the two individual lovers. This is what I think I know about love, Fegataccio, and why I find Nietzsche so dull on this issue!

Fegataccio: You and Nietzsche have much common ground: love as grounded in power, as transformative, as process, as possessive, as dangerous, as perception of the other's ideal possibilities, and as based on common activities and mutual benefit.

Apollonia: But Nietzsche's lovers are always at a distance; they avoid the intimacy and soul-searing experiences that bind individuals into a wider subjectivity. He offers us friendship, love of the cosmos, love of self, love of eternity, love of the earth, but what does he know about deeper, more intimate love? Sure, he can nitpick about the common motives and frailties of lovers and how sexual love often ends in frustration and mutual destruction, but that gives only the dangerous, not the salutary, side of love. Nietzsche's depiction is calculatedly one-sided because he lacked the personal experiences to complete the picture.

Fegataccio: Nietzsche does complete the picture, but apparently not in the way you would prefer. He recognizes a decadent form and a life-affirming form of love, just as he generally recognizes decadent and life-affirming forms of other emotions. One's motives, as always, are important for distinguishing the two forms. Moreover, he doesn't fall prey to a pedestrian dualism because, first, he views decadence and life-affirmation as matters of degree that admit numerous intermediary forms and, second, he understands that we all embody elements of decadence and life-affirmation. Part of our life struggle is to confront and overcome the last man within each of us. In the case of life-affirming love, Nietzsche celebrates the mutual pursuit of self-perfection, while you prefer to focus on the lovers' amplified identity.

Apollonia: My misgivings about Nietzsche's understanding of love have general implications. He consistently exaggerates the human need, even among "higher types," for individual fulfillment, while he seriously underplays the human need for intimate communal attachments.

Throughout history, writers have argued that existential tension is at the heart of human experience: Our yearning for intimate connection with others and the recognition that others are necessary for our identity and freedom coalesces uneasily with the fear and anxiety we experience as others approach. We simultaneously long for emotional attachment yet are horrified that our individuality may evaporate once we achieve it. This disharmony may never be fully reconciled; we instead find ourselves making uneasy compromises and adjustments as we oscillate between "radical individuality" and "thorough immersion in community." This existential tension replicates itself at numerous levels: The individual confronts family, the family confronts village, villages confront wider society, and society confronts the state.

The individual confronts other people at many different levels. When we meet others at institutional levels, the stakes rise in some respects. Our need to retain individual freedom and resist coercion intensifies when our relations are impersonal, where we experience less direct control over our destiny, and when entrenched bureaucracies seem ready and able to usurp our autonomy. Circumscribed by socioeconomic reality, the relentless socializing of the established order, and the inherent inertia of the masses, our sense of possibility resists extinction and thereby honors the human craving for transcendence. Moreover, the individual confronts several different, often conflicting communities. One faces the intimate aspirations of family; the often conflicting ultimatums of ethnicity, gender, and race; the stirring, history-laden, patriotic implorations of country; and the more distant claims of the international order. Clearly, the individual–community continuum expands in several dimensions. In fact, only in the simplest cases is it ever merely one-dimensional. As such, contexts such as family, ethnicity, gender, politics, and war multiply the tensions, exhilarations, fears, and hopes invariably embodied by the continuum.[19]

My general objection to Nietzsche is that he fails to capture the subtlety of the antinomies generated by the individual–community continuum. When he does address them, he presses his dreary diatribe against the herd, the community, as the leveler of potentially great creators.

Fegataccio: I think you have misunderstood his notion of individualism. I suspect you may have been unduly influenced by Alasdair MacIntyre's distorted portrayal of Nietzschean individualism as socially isolated and self-absorbed.[20] MacIntyre's caricature to the contrary notwithstanding, the Nietzschean philosopher of the future concentrates on self-perfection and great cultural creation. The pursuit of greatness is a goal all individuals can partake of and stimulate one another toward (see, for example, Z I, "On the Friend"; Z I, "On Child and Marriage"). The activity and self-overcoming of the Dionysian philosopher–artist connect the individual's paramount quest to a more general project which involves others.

Nietzsche is in fact implicitly recognizing the individual–community continuum and trying to moderate its force. By recognizing the life-affirming aspects of community, especially its possibilities for nurturing the pursuit of excellence, we will be more aware of the decadent aspects of community, especially its possibilities for leveling humans to a common standard and for glorifying mediocrity.

Nietzsche is acutely aware that humans necessarily find themselves within a social context which includes a thick set of traditions, practices, and dominant worldviews. But he highlights the fact that human flourishing requires creativity, which demands that the individual distance himself from those practices and traditions. While we cannot escape social context, there is no particular social context which timelessly commands our allegiance. Indeed, the deconstruction of social contexts is one step toward self-overcoming. But deconstruction, as always, must be followed by reimagination and re-creation.

For Nietzsche, the well-being of the highest human exemplars is more valuable than the survival of any particular society, although societies (and polities) can be ranked by how well they nurture their great individuals. But one thing remains clear: Individuals and communities and societies and individuals are necessarily linked, for better or worse.

Apollonia: First, I don't subscribe to MacIntyre's understanding of Nietzsche's individualism. Although I agree with him that such individualism is impossible, I don't think it is fair to saddle Nietzsche with the view. But I don't agree with your portrayal of Nietzsche as a moderator of the tensions of the individual–community continuum. Clearly, for Nietzsche, societies and polities lack inherent value. Their only value is providing necessary temporary contexts for individuals. At best, they nurture individual greatness. Just as friends and lovers are instrumental goods—tools by which people of excellence can be nurtured—societies also bear instrumental value. Nietzsche fails to appreciate the psychological need people have for intimate, not merely instrumental, attachments.

Again, Nietzsche's own alienation and estrangement color his writing. He requires a philosophical justification, or should I say rationalization, for his loneliness and lack of intimacy. So with typical bluster he tries to convince himself that isolation brings redemption: "We [philosophers of the future] are born, sworn, jealous friends of *solitude*, of our own most profound, most midnightly, most middaily solitude" (*BGE* 44).

Fegataccio: You are running together several disparate experiences: alienation, estrangement, loneliness, solitude, isolation. Remember, Zarathustra often requires solitude to recharge his energies and reassess his thinking, but he always returns to the world. Solitude is not the enemy but a prerequisite of intimacy.

For Nietzsche there are no intrinsic goods, so it is unsurprising that he fails to regard societies, communities, and states as more than instrumentally valuable. Because humans must create value and meaning where none antecedently exists, he posits great cultural creators and joyous self-overcomers as the highest values.

Again, your quarrel with Nietzsche is that you seem to value intimacy as such, while he harbors grave suspicions about the origins and motives underwriting both the view and the phenomenon. Intimacy has value in its life-affirming form for reasons we have already discussed; it lacks value in its decadent forms of pity and human leveling.

Apollonia: In what way, if any, do you see Nietzsche as appreciative of society beyond its possible instrumental value in facilitating an individual's quest for greatness?

Fegataccio: Nietzsche understands full well that he is not free from his past socialization or from his present social context. Neither he nor anyone else can ascend to a vantage point purified of social context. Humans are judging, evaluating beings. Indeed, meaning and value would be impossible if we were otherwise. Thus, we should not, really cannot, remain in a particular fixed social context: we cannot freeze our judgments and evaluations because to do so undermines our humanity. Moreover, our most important judgments and evaluations do not occur in a social vacuum (see, for example, *BGE* 200, 262). As long as we keep in mind the human need to transcend our present context in service of self-overcoming and societal-overcoming and the life-affirming and decadent forms of societal interaction, Nietzsche celebrates the social dimension of self-perfection and cultural re-creation.

Apollonia: We must separate two types of criticisms of Nietzsche's individualism. The first, which is not mine, takes him to be a radical individual counseling withdrawal from society while denying the effects of his past socialization. This line of attack, as you correctly point out, must fail. If Nietzsche holds the we are dynamic multiplicities of impulses which are ordered and maintained only through power relationships, then he could not simply counsel withdrawal from society. Such withdrawal would threaten to annihilate us. Nietzsche cannot accept a thick description of human nature, but must, instead, concentrate on our ability to transcend our particular context even though we cannot escape altogether from our past, our need to judge and evaluate as a prerequisite for value and meaning, our inability to achieve a perfect permanent unity out of our multiple impulses, our opportunity to strive for greatness through self-overcoming, and the huge range of ranks and orders among individuals and peoples. All the while he must also stress his favored descriptions of "decadent" and "life-affirming."

The second type of criticism of Nietzsche's individualism, which is mine, concerns his limited understanding of the human need for community. Again, he stresses only the instrumental value of community for the individual's quest for self-perfection. That reminds me of a religious theme: how the family is valuable because it can aid one's personal salvation and eternal reward. Both rationales are chilling. I see the human need for intimacy as more essential. I don't have to use the language of inherent or intrinsic value, for I know that Nietzscheans break out in hives in the presence of such talk. I can argue that my notion rests on a different kind of instrumental value from Nietzsche's. My notion sees intimate connection as necessary for psychological health, as required for self-worth, and as essential to meaning and value. For me, judging and evaluating are necessary but not sufficient for meaning and value. Humans require a purpose beyond creating and self-overcoming as such. That purpose is connected to intimacy in ways that go beyond the mutual quest for individual self-perfection. One cannot simply self-overcome in a salutary way without intimate attachment.

What would Nietzsche say about the following mind experiment? Suppose a person knew in advance that intimate relations with another person would neither hinder nor aid the quest for self-perfection. Let's say this could be antecedently demonstrated to a practical certainty. Suppose further that the person is attracted to the other. Would there be value in pursuing this relationship?

Fegataccio: Your example is devious. You build in a host of values under the surface—such as the fulfillment of desire and the prior attraction—that suggest the relationship would bear value. But then you claim, without specifying any negatives, that on the whole there is no effect on the lover's quest for self-perfection. I don't think you can legitimately do that. While it is true that you and Nietzsche have different views on the value of intimacy, although I don't think you are as far apart as you think, those differences cannot be settled by addressing your hypothetical.

I understand that love need not result in self-perfection. Even despicable people, in the sense of the mediocre, can truly share a type of love. But Nietzsche, I suspect, would not be concerned much with that.

Apollonia: Speaking of despicable people, such specimens could pass Nietzsche's test of striving toward self-perfection, couldn't they? If so, he offers us a flawed model of giving style to one's character.

Fegataccio: I see the trap and I'm not going to play the game. If I say "yes" then you attack Nietzsche for not adequately discouraging his misappropriation by the Nazis and for offering a "morally" bankrupt model that right-thinking people will find indigestible. If I say "no" then you attack me for domesticating Nietzsche, for robbing him of his panache, and for rendering him as yet another bourgeois liberal moralist. You've run this game before!

In fact, the answer is not clear. Nietzsche cannot offer us specific imperatives, only a series of broad themes. The dynamism of his thought, the experimentalism of his life, and the fluidity of his prose yield no definite answer. And that itself is dearly Nietzschean.

Apollonia: You can't sidestep that easily. At least you must talk more about the philosophers of the future and their cultural creativity.

Fegataccio: I think Nietzsche's philosophers of the future labor at several related tasks. First, they must recognize, utilize, and integrate multiple cognitive perspectives. They must see with many "different eyes" (see, for example, *GM* III, 12; *BGE* 4, 43). Second, while recognizing their debts to the past and their inability to escape fully from the present, they must serve as social critics and prophets (see, for example, *BGE* 63, 203, 207, 211). Third, philosophers of the future must concentrate on self-overcoming in the quest for self-perfection (see, for example, *BGE* 205, 292; *GS* 270, 380). Fourth, they may serve as teachers to those few disciples who are themselves capable of becoming philosophers of the future and who understand well that "one repays a teacher badly if one always remains nothing but a pupil" (*EH*, "Preface," 4; *Z* I, "On the Gift-Giving Virtue," 3; *UM*, "Schopenhauer as Educator," 3; *BGE* 295).[21]

These tasks embody Nietzsche's familial broad themes: recurring deconstruction, reimagination, and re-creation; recognizing that social context is inevitable but no particular thick context deserves enduring privileged status; striving for an individualism within a cultural setting; affirming the tragic dimensions of life; using one's multiplicity of impulses and perspectives for emotional and cognitive advantage; refusing to seek validation from the masses; honoring the rank order of humans; avoiding dogmatism while recognizing the kernels of insight in many perspectives; luxuriating in the world of Becoming; and loving the earth, the cosmos, life, self, and others.

Philosophers of the future must embody proper attitudes: joy, laughter, courage, hardness, experimentalism, honesty, cleanliness, and integrity (see, for example, *BGE* 207, 212, 213, 227, 294). They must overcome "the last men" within them. Most of all, their philosophy must be lived (see, for example, *UM*, "Schopenhauer as Educator," 3).

Apollonia: If your description is correct, there is much to admire in Nietzsche's philosophers of the future. I am interested, however, in hearing more about living one's philosophy.

Fegataccio: Nietzsche is at his best, I think, when he contrasts his vision with that of mainstream academic philosophers. The latter too often assume that the proper use of abstract reason will result in pure moral and political truths. Nietzsche, instead, illustrates both the necessity and limitations of abstract reason. Appeals to abstract reason can obscure the concrete circumstances and history that animate our lives with meaning. Moreover, reason cannot by itself advance one worldview to which all humans must subscribe. There comes a point where reason runs out, where we must appeal to a self-evident principle, an unprovable assumption, or take a leap of faith. While reason is necessary to set the boundaries of plausibility, there may well be several conflicting world visions that do not violate general principles or biological requirements. Philosophy then becomes less of a deductive enterprise and more a project of wisely adjudicating normative puzzles.

As such, the valor of philosophy may reside in its potential for stimulating participants to alternative ways of thinking and experiencing; intellectual creativity as a redemption of spirit and flesh. This is a vision of philosophy as meaningful explanation and as a resource for an individual's arriving at temporary solutions to his or her life struggles, instead of philosophy as exemplifying the demands of reason itself and coercing participants to specific conclusions.

Apollonia: We are both trained analytic philosophers. Although I remain closer to that tradition than you, I have always detested the writing style philosophy demanded of me: ahistorical, aridly impersonal, effetely impartial. Philosophy, fashioning itself as a quasiscience, demands that I hide who I am, that I avoid rhetorical flair, that I pretend to speak from the view from above. It encourages use of the noble "we," implying that I speak authoritatively for all right-thinking scholars or all members of the moral community in good standing or all rational people. We were trained well in the rigors and pretensions of analytic philosophy, Fegataccio.

Fegataccio: Nietzsche, on the other hand, gleefully includes personal narratives that help to mark the prejudices, biases, and descriptive and prescriptive worldviews that necessarily color his work. His writing mirrors his own ambivalences, dimly understood conflicts, and deepest personal commitments.

Apollonia: But he, unmercifully, too often burdens readers with unexpurgated autobiography and the uncensored revelations of his self-obsessions.

Fegataccio: In your view, maybe. I prefer to focus on the insightful way psychological, historical, sociological, and political descriptions and speculations intrude freely into his work. I am firmly convinced that scholars should underscore the fallowness and counterproductiveness of rigid disciplinary boundaries. Such academic distinctions emerge from particular historical, personal, and contingent circumstances soon forgotten by most.

But the real key to Nietzsche's contrast with academic philosophy is how he lives his view, how philosophy helps him find his way. Most academic philosophers remain detached, manipulate concepts, teach how to fight certain words with other words, narrate tediously the history of philosophy, and fight desperately to drain the personal out of the philosophical. This is philosophy patterned after chess: games of enormous intellectual stimulation and challenge which demand high skill but are absolutely irrelevant to life. Moreover, philosophers, unlike chess masters, tend to deaden their students' curiosity and intellectual spirit by their dismal logic crunching and remoteness. Philosophy so conceived conceals its own genealogy and encourages the creation of permanent idols and authorities, thereby crushing the very creativity it pretends to prize.

In contrast, Nietzsche tells us that philosophy is only worthy if it can be lived. The recurring test for Nietzsche's philosophers of the future is whether they can vivify life, celebrate greatness, and transform culture. Thinkers must exemplify, not merely solemnly recite, their philosophy.

Apollonia: Although I have much sympathy for what you say, I think you exaggerate the maladies of mainstream philosophy. There have always been philosophers of the type you seem to admire. And while some philosophers are crushingly banal and paralyzingly dull, that doesn't necessarily describe the majority. Also, there is delicious irony in what Nietzsche proposes: Judged by his own standards, did he "vivify life, celebrate greatness, and transform culture," or did he lead a desperate, banal, isolated life that he tried to redeem through writing and fantasy?

Fegataccio: We covered this earlier. Given his tremendous influence, I think he has met his own standard, at least posthumously. It is more difficult to make a confident determination about his life itself. He did, after all, go insane, which hinders a fair assessment. However, his interior life seems rich, full, and vibrant, at least to me.

Apollonia: All of which says to me that he led a reclusive painful life with minimal intimacy. And that is why he will never be my hero. His final defeat is that he, too, talked a bigger game than he could live. In talking about philosophers of the future, you have also glossed over Nietzsche's elitism, his willingness to judge a society by its production of high human exemplars and to submerge the interests of the masses in deference to his self-styled "nobles."

Fegataccio: I'll call the crux of Nietzschean aristocratism the principle of nobility:

Mankind must work continually at the production of individual great men—that and nothing else is its task. . . . Its only concern is the individual higher exemplar, the more uncommon, more powerful, more complex, more fruitful. . . . Mankind ought to seek out and create the favourable conditions under which those great redemptive men come into existence. . . . How can your life, the individual life, receive the highest value, the deepest significance? How can it be least squandered? Certainly only by your living for the good of the rarest and most valuable exemplars, and not for the good of the majority, that is to say those who, taken individually, are the least valuable exemplars. (*UM*, "Schopenhauer as Educator," 6; see also *BGE* 126, 199, 258, 265; *GS* 23)

The principle of nobility is Nietzsche's ballast for an averaging approach to perfectionism which prefers the greatest average perfection per year (or even per day) of a person, with the overall goal being the greatest average lifetime value in history.[22] An individual's value—what is to be averaged—is determined by his or her approximation to the highest human exemplars or by his or her contribution to the production of the highest human exemplars. Nietzsche recognizes that insofar as all humans embody the will to power, and power is the standard of excellence, all humans have some value.[23] Even the most decadent negative nihilists exhibit power and value in muted form and meager degree. But the principle of nobility grades the quantity and quality of value by aristocratic criteria.

Apollonia: Some principle: The masses have value insofar as they serve a few "great" people who in turn care about the masses only insofar as the masses can serve them. Even if you weaken the force of the principle of nobility by adding intermediate principles that recognize a hierarchy of graded degrees of excellence, the principle is still noxious. The intermediate principles would give more reason to care for the "nongreat" to the degree, however slight, to which they approach greatness, but would still not satisfy basic egalitarian inclinations. The principle of nobility abstracts accomplishments and creative greatness from the lives which sustain them. Nietzsche, again, ignores concrete human beings and wrongly amplifies artistic, philosophical, musical, scientific, and military creation in the abstract. He would willingly sacrifice human lives for great works. The principle of nobility thereby obscures the suffering of numerous humans by glorifying the cultural artifacts generated by a few.

Fegataccio: There is no question that egalitarians, utilitarians, Kantians, traditional natural-law theorists, and social-contract theorists will not accept Nietzsche's views. He didn't accept their views either. In fact, his unsparing criticisms of their views was the point of departure for his own philosophy.

Apollonia: Nietzsche's fatuous aristocratism and reptilian indifference to the lives of the masses are the low point of his work. All humans, mediocre or potentially great, need a deep sense of purpose in their lives. Nietzsche would have us believe that such purpose should center on becoming great or serving those who can become great, where "greatness" translates to the creation of cultural artifacts and a vague type of self-mastery. I still believe Nietzsche focuses excessively on the self to the exclusion of real intimacy and community. We must find meaning, I think, outside the self and beyond cultural creations. We need communal involvements in causes greater than nurturing cultural superstars. Would Nietzsche have us believe that Mother Teresa's life, at least the part spent ministering to the poor and diseased, was in vain? Is she only the queen of the herd? Does she merely waste time resuscitating the replaceable?

Nietzsche too easily identifies the masses with fungibility, as if all the nongreat are sparrows whose lives are indistinguishable. But, contrary to Nietzsche, greatness is not found only in art, philosophy, music, and science. Greatness is often embodied by those whose lives are among the simplest and who lack public renown. Such greatness is not focused on Nietzschean creativity or trendy donning and discarding of personal masks. Instead, it is centered on love, caring, making the world a better place by deeply influencing those around you in uniquely positive ways, and speaking to our higher instincts rather than obsessing about power and domination. Our choices are not simply herd conformity or Nietzschean greatness.

Of course, Nietzsche could sneer and claim that I have described only another manifestation of power. And given the broadness of his use of the term, Nietzsche could make a case. But even under his own background assumptions there are different forms of power embodying different values. I would still insist that the "power" I describe is psychologically and, yes, morally preferable to other manifestations.

Fegataccio: I fear you take Nietzsche too literally, Apollonia. He could celebrate self-mastery and the quest for self-perfection among whomever it appeared and in whatever form.

Apollonia: If everything is a "metaphor," then nothing is a metaphor. But I have a more important point to make.

Remember when we were young, Fegataccio? We sought heroes, among sports figures mainly. We pursued a derivative sense of greatness through identification with superstars such as Joe DiMaggio, Rocky Marciano, Phil Rizzuto, Yogi Berra, Charlie Trippi, and Willie Pep. They were a child's metaphor for winning a place in the world, for gaining external recognition, and for self-acceptance. For every mindless loudmouth who expressed his unrecognized self-hate to us with taunts of "wop," "dago," and "guinea," there was a DiMaggio home run, a Marciano knockout, and a Trippi touchdown to ease our pain and energize our hopes. Our heroes reminded us that we belonged here too. And we vowed, only to ourselves, to someday show them all, friends and foes alike, who we were and what we could achieve. Do you remember, Fegataccio?

When we grew, I came to realize that there were heroes all around us. Men and women of strength, honor, and courage who were capable of stunning self-sacrifice because they perceived themselves as part of a wider subjectivity, as a link in a generational chain that stretched from Sicily to America. They were the giants upon whose shoulders you and I stood. I learned that heroes don't always get their names in the newspapers.

No cultural artifact, whether created by Mozart, daVinci, Caesar, Kant, or Curie, is worth as much as one of those people. While Nietzsche rants and raves about the herd and self-servingly positions himself above it, I retain my faith in the immediacy of flesh and blood and in redeeming intimacy.

Fegataccio: You take an unfair approach. You seduce and beguile me by conjuring my history, my debts, my emotions, my very identity. Surely you recognize your lack of scruples.

Apollonia: I advance what you Nietzscheans must accept: The philosophical is personal, a philosophy must be lived to be worthy, and concrete understandings trump abstract theorizing.

Fegataccio: But this is *too* personal!

Apollonia: Philosophy can't be too personal for a Nietzschean. I want you to defend Nietzsche's aristocratism and gleeful elitism while retaining your sense of self, Fegataccio. Or perhaps I should put it this way: retaining your sense of Becoming as you strive for self-perfection.

Fegataccio: Not all humans are equal. Only a few can invent their own lives. The vast majority simply follow established societal teachings and habits. The few are better humans than the many. The best human exemplars are indifferent to the valuations of the masses. The many are last men: They aspire to material comfort and indolence; they do not even "strut and fret their hour upon the stage," but, instead, somnambulate through life leaving no mark other than promulgating more of their kind.

As you well know, Nietzsche measures people by nonmoral criteria: by their excellences, personal achievements, intelligence, and creative powers. He centers human uniqueness on creativity. The greatest humans relish the immediacy of life, neither dwelling on the past nor overly anticipating the future. For Nietzsche, vengeance and resentment cannot issue from robust self-love and love of life. Only insecurity, self-doubt, and the repressed hostility of inferiors for superiors generate vengeance and resentment.

Apollonia: You can't even mount a vigorous lawyerly defense for Nietzsche's elitism. Unless you fall back on the too facile—"Nietzsche's elitism is only a metaphor for ordering our internal lives"—you are left with nothing other than tired repetition of litany. Excellences, personal achievements, intelligence, and creative powers can all be exemplified by common people. We aren't all either herd animals or cultural geniuses. Nietzsche identifies, as do most philosophers, excellence too closely with intellectual activity. Apart from his adolescent worship of military battle, he sees genius only in art, music, philosophy, and science. He also oscillates between valuing creativity as such and valuing creativity in terms of its social effects. The former values creativity independently of effects on others; for example, under this view *Thus Spoke Zarathrustra* is a wonderful creation regardless of whether anyone reads it other than its author. The latter values the book because of its cultural impact and, hopefully, its role in nurturing highly creative people.

While I do not disparage the life of the interior, it is woefully insufficient for engaging the world. Private fulfillment is less purposeful than public involvement that requires passionate identification with particular communities. Such activity, horror of horrors, means mingling with the herd.

Fegataccio: I hope you aren't reverting to a picture of Nietzsche as radical individualist that we agreed earlier was hopelessly flawed.

Apollonia: No, but I do want to indulge in some amateur psychology, an indulgence which is certainly in the Nietzschean tradition.

Humans have a need for belonging, and much fear, insecurity, selfishness, and anxiety arise from the unfulfillment of that need. This need does not flow from a herd instinct, at least not in a pejorative sense, but is a prerequisite for a highly textured and meaningful life. Moreover, the lack of belonging undermines the self.

It may be no accident that Nietzsche was afflicted with numerous physical ills. Could these maladies have arisen from underlying emotional factors? Many scientists recognize the connection between physical pain and emotional distress.[24] Was Nietzsche ridden with anxiety, fear, and repressed anger that stemmed from his alienation from others and that translated into his strident aristocratism?

Physicians understand that insecurity, a relentless striving for achievement, chronic impatience, intense competitiveness, and deep hostility increase bodily stress and their presence is the best predictor of several diseases.[25] These characteristics are much more likely to be embodied by people alienated from others than people intimated connected to others. The path to health, wisdom, and joy is reached by broadening one's boundaries and widening one's subjectivity. The moral of the story is that one's inner deconstructions, reimaginations, and re-creations must ultimately invigorate the quality of one's participation in the external world. Otherwise, internal explorations are merely exercises in abstraction and narcissism.

Fegataccio: What you say has little force against Nietzsche. Not all physical ills emanate from emotional distress. Moreover, Nietzsche's life shows little or no sign of the hostility and intense aggression you decry. In fact, it sounds as if you are projecting your own psychological symptoms upon Nietzsche. I thought we had agreed to curtail speculation on Nietzsche's psychology based on insufficient biographical data.

Apollonia: My point has less to do with Nietzsche's illnesses—although I do relish and think he deserves a few cheap shots—and more to do with human psychology. I think Nietzsche misunderstands the human need to belong and the effects of its lack of fulfillment. While I have no more appreciation of last men than he does, that description does not accurately characterize most members of the "herd."

Fegataccio: Your armchair psychological musings are too thin to be convincing. I could just as easily bring in Freudian psychology to aid Nietzsche's case. The id is a bundle of instincts: endlessly demanding, impulsive, irrational, asocial, and pleasure seeking. The id refuses to recognize contradictions or accept limitations. In the id, sex and aggression combine to dominate the personality. The superego is irrational but less powerful than the id. It sets high standards of perfection, acting as the personality's harsh parent. The superego, unlike the id which is instinctive, is developed through socialization. It has two parts, the conscience and the ego ideal. The former punishes us when we fall below perfection, while the latter, which internalizes the standard of perfection, rewards us for striving to meet its impossible expectations. The ego is our cautious rational voice of common sense that tries to moderate the demands of the id and superego. The ego embodies a reality principle, which contrasts with the pleasure principle of the id and the perfection principle of the superego. The ego is the weakest of the three parts of our personality. The ego tries to moderate the id's demands for sexual gratification and total domination but is less powerful than the id. When the ego seeks help from the superego it is usually punished.

Thus, humans, for Freud, are inherently beings of psychic conflict. We want to hurt others and we get pleasure from doing so, but the less powerful aspects of our personality (ego, superego) usually ensure that our pleasure is ambiguous. Humans employ numerous coping mechanisms to lighten our internal conflict and our interpersonal suffering: drugs, isolating ourselves to atrophy our instincts, and forms of sublimation (e.g., sports, love, work, and absorption in media).[26]

This crude and overly brief picture of Freudian psychology can be used to illustrate many of Nietzsche's favored contentions.

Apollonia: And that is probably why Freudian psychology has been superseded by more convincing forms! Nietzsche's radical aristocratism still leaves me cold. I have nothing against perfectionism as such, but resist versions that are insufficiently communal, that misunderstand the fundamental need for intimacy, and that overly intellectualize character.

Fegataccio: You must remember that one can greatly appreciate Nietzsche's broad themes without subscribing to all of his more specific psychology or political experiments. Take the structure of politics, for example. Contemporary philosopher Roberto Unger is greatly influenced by Nietzsche.[27] He has zeal for transcending existing social contexts, has an attraction to heroic and romantic action, participates in prophetic social visions, and values culture over the state. But he combines these with decidedly un-Nietzschean themes that you may accept: distrust of political hierarchy and social division and concern for economic equality. He calls his view "superliberalism." His work shows one way to combine communally based, highly intimate notions of politics and society with Nietzsche's broad themes of transcending existing social contexts, engaging in heroic action, striving for self-mastery, and valuing culture over the state.

My subtext should be clear: to show you, Apollonia, how retaining your distrust of political hierarchy and social division, appreciation for relative economic equality, and commitment to community can be compatible with some of Nietzsche's broad themes. Even if Nietzsche did not talk, in your judgment, about perfectionism and politics satisfactorily, you need not reject his views as a whole. I know, Apollonia, you agree with several of his broad themes, despite the fervor with which you resist many of Nietzsche's specific pronouncements.

Apollonia: At least Unger understands that the problem of transition—how we get from our present context to what we desire politically and socially—is paramount. Nietzsche seems to think that centuries of socialization can be overcome by a coterie of amoral aristocrats. By separating morality from natural life he may undermine rather than facilitate the conditions of cultural greatness. His contempt of the masses, in my mind, harbors vengeance and resentment that he otherwise warns against. His juvenile use of "scary" warrior rhetoric systematically aspires to impress, but remains unimpressive.

Nietzsche's self-serving celebration of hierarchy and division is merely his psychological defense against loneliness, isolation, and alienation. His obsession with genealogy leads him to beliefs bordering on predestination, genetic determination, and overly simple categorization of humans. The master of multiplicity is too often seduced by pedestrian reductionism. His self-obsession, psychological defense mechanisms, and embarrassing self-promotions reveal the university professor, the mere academic, never overcame his origins. Nietzsche's irritating misogynism, while perhaps explainable by his upbringing, underscores his emotional separateness. That he wrote a stirring life while living a sad one highlights the desperation of his cry, *"amor fati!"* His quest for protean transcendence masks his personal dissatisfaction and lingering need for redemption. The strident proclaimer of the death of God still needed idols, despite his vitriol to the contrary. His constant screams for attention, compulsive need to provoke, and adolescent daydreams of glory betrayed a life and a person that were easily ignored. Nietzsche's recurrent illnesses, eventual insanity, and shameful expropriation by his sister and the Nazis were a tragic and ironic metaphor of his view of life.

Fegataccio: I feel badly that you choose to caricature and misrepresent. My Nietzsche celebrates life despite suffering and obstacles that would destroy lesser men. He vivifies our imagination and demands that philosophy relate to life. Reading Nietzsche is a refreshing change from being students of those who teach philosophy as an academic discipline and not as a way to live.[28]

Nietzsche insists that we fully understand the tragic dimensions of life and accept the challenges of active nihilism. He unmasks the self-conceits and disguises of dominant society, and forces us to confront the "truth." He casts suspicion where smug assurance had reigned, and reminds us that striving toward worthwhile goals is accompanied by meaningful and valuable hardship. Nietzsche counsels love, laughter, and joy where resentment, mendacity, and suffering had prevailed. He seeks disciples among the strong, hard, courageous, and creative, and then he implores them to go beyond his teaching. He insists that the cosmic is inherently meaningless, but emphasizes that the imposition of value and meaning on our world is part of the human quest.

My Nietzsche shares insights on the most important human themes: the inescapability of inner conflict; the perspectival nature of truth; the links between psychological types of humans and their embrace of different truth claims; the need to perceive reality from multiple perspectives; the connection between writing and life; the inability of language to capture life's complexities and fluidity; the denial of absolutism; the need to impose order and meaning on the world of Becoming; the salutary rhythms of deconstruction, reimagination, and re-creation; the need to recognize and welcome the tragedy and contingency that constitute life; replacing the task of objectively disproving truth claims with the project of casting suspicion upon their origins and the psychology of those who embrace them; the importance of self-overcoming, which includes subjecting one's own theoretical and practical commitments to the strictest scrutiny; and the call to luxuriate in the immediacy of life.

Apollonia: We seem to have completed our inquiry on Nietzsche's work with many of our familiar impasses intact, Fegataccio.

Fegataccio: We have not completed anything, Apollonia. Our journey has barely started. Do not confuse temporary exhaustion with resolution.

Apollonia: Let me guess: There is serenity only in the womb and, perhaps, in sleep; there is final serenity only in the tomb. It appears, Fegataccio, that I am stuck with you for the rest of life.

Fegataccio: As I am stuck with you, Apollonia.

Vertiginoso had struggled for almost two days sorting out his conflicting impulses and passions regarding the work of Friedrich Nietzsche. It was time to leave the mall and begin, again, to live.

NOTES

NIETZSCHE'S TEXTS AND THEIR ABBREVIATIONS

As is the common practice in Nietzsche scholarship, where I have cited from Nietzsche's writings the references in all cases have been given immediately in the text and not in the notes. All references are to sections, not page numbers, unless stated otherwise. I have used the following abbreviations:

AC *The Anti-Christ* (1895), in *The Portable Nietzsche*, trans. Walter Kaufmann (New York: Viking Press, 1954).

BGE *Beyond Good and Evil* (1886), trans. Walter Kaufmann (New York: Random House, 1966).

BT *The Birth of Tragedy* (1872), trans. Walter Kaufmann (New York: Random House, 1967).

D *The Dawn* (1881), trans. Walter Kaufmann (New York: Random House, 1968).

EH *Ecce Homo* (1908), trans. Walter Kaufmann and R. J. Hollingdale (New York: Random House, 1967).

GM *On the Genealogy of Morals* (1887), trans. Walter Kaufmann (New York: Random House, 1967).

GS *The Gay Science* (1882), trans. Walter Kaufmann (New York: Random House, 1967).

HAH *Human, All-Too-Human* (1878), in *The Portable Nietzsche*, trans. Walter Kaufmann (New York: Viking Press, 1954).

TI *Twilight of the Idols* (1889), in *The Portable Nietzsche*, trans. Walter Kaufmann (New York: Viking Press, 1954).

UM *Untimely Meditations* (1873–1876), trans. R. J. Hollingdale (Cambridge: Cambridge University Press, 1983).

WP *The Will to Power* (from unpublished notebooks, 1883–1888), ed. Walter
Kaufmann, trans. Walter Kaufmann and R. J. Hollingdale (New York:
Random House, 1967).
WS *The Wanderer and His Shadow* (1880), in *The Portable Nietzsche*, trans.
Walter Kaufmann (New York: Viking Press, 1954).
  Z *Thus Spoke Zarathustra* (1883–1885), in *The Portable Nietzsche*, trans.
Walter Kaufmann (New York: Viking Press, 1954).

In the text, I also referred once to "On Truth and Lie in an Extra-Moral
Sense," a fragment published posthumously in *The Portable Nietzsche*, trans.
Walter Kaufmann (New York: Viking Press, 1954).

INTRODUCTION

1. My sketch of Nietzsche's life borrows freely from Karl Jaspers, *Nietzsche:
An Introduction to the Understanding of His Philosophical Activity*, trans. Charles
F. Wallraff and Frederick J. Schmitz (Tucson: University of Arizona Press, 1965),
27–115; and Walter Kaufmann, *Nietzsche: Philosopher, Psychologist, Antichrist*,
4th ed. (Princeton: Princeton University Press, 1974), 21–71.

CHAPTER 1

1. Karl Jaspers, *Nietzsche: An Introduction to the Understanding of His Philosophical Activity*, trans. Charles F. Wallraff and Frederick J. Schmitz (Tucson:
University of Arizona Press, 1965), 10.
2. Hereafter I refer to these as Nietzsche's "broad themes," although on
occasion I use "fundamental themes" or "general themes."
3. See, for example, Steven D. Hales and Robert C. Welshon, "Truth, Paradox, and Nietzschean Perspectivism," *History of Philosophy Quarterly* 11 (1994):
101, 106–107. There is persuasive textual evidence to support this interpretation of Nietzsche (see *AC* 23, 52–55; *WP* 377, 483; *BGE* 4, 25; *HAH* 54, 483; *GM*
III, 8, 12).
4. Hales and Welshon, "Truth, Paradox, and Perspectivism," 107.
5. Robin Roth, "Nietzsche's Metaperspectivism," *International Studies in
Philosophy* 22 (1990): 66, 70. See also Paul Redding, "Nietzschean Perspectivism
and the Logic of Practical Reason," *The Philosophical Forum* 22 (1990): 72, 78.
6. John T. Wilcox, *Truth and Value in Nietzsche* (Washington, D.C.: University Press of America, 1982), 17–21.
7. Ibid., 38.
8. Ibid., 158.
9. Ibid., 158–159.
10. "Which are the truths which are of this perspectival nature? . . . First,
epistemological truths . . . truths about truth itself. . . . Second, cosmological
[truths]: these are large-scale interpretations of the whole [such as] there is no
free will . . . there is no God . . . what our culture calls good and evil are not causes
. . . man is an animal among animals . . . and the doctrine of eternal recurrence. . .

.. Third, truths about the details of life . . . about the history of the church, the motivation of slave morality, the effects of pity, the role of cruelty in life, the relation of Kant to the ascetic ideal, and so forth." Ibid., 156–157.

11. See, for example, Arthur C. Danto, *Nietzsche as Philosopher* (New York: Columbia University Press, 1965), 72; Frederick Copleston, *A History of Philosophy*, vol. 7, pt. 2 (Garden City, N.Y.: Doubleday, 1946–1965), 395.

12. Walter Kaufmann, *Nietzsche: Philosopher, Psychologist, Antichrist*, 4th ed. (Princeton: Princeton University Press, 1974), 204–205.

13. Copleston, *History of Philosophy*, 410, 418–419.

14. Ken Gemes, "Nietzsche's Critique of Truth," *Philosophy and Phenomenological Research* 52 (1992): 47, 51.

15. Ibid., 54.

16. Ibid., 55.

17. Ibid., 61.

18. For a sampling of Nietzsche's views of binary logic, see *TI*, "'Reason' in Philosophy," 3; *GS* 111–112, 354; *BGE* 3–4; *HAH* 9, 11, 19; *WP* 507, 512, 521.

19. Charles Altieri, "Ecce Homo," in *Why Nietzsche Now?* ed. Daniel T. O'Hara (Bloomington: Indiana University Press, 1985), 394.

20. See, for example, Richard Rorty, *Consequences of Pragmatism* (Minneapolis: University of Minnesota Press, 1982), 160–175.

21. Alexander Nehamas, *Nietzsche: Life as Literature* (Cambridge: Harvard University Press, 1985), 68.

22. Ibid., 65–68.

23. Bart Kosko, *Fuzzy Thinking: The New Science of Fuzzy Logic* (New York: Hyperion, 1993), 101.

24. Ibid., 6, 102–103.

25. Ibid., 102; Stanley Rosen, *The Limits of Analysis* (New York: Basic Books, 1980), 200.

26. Altieri, "Ecce Homo," 395.

27. Hales and Welshon, "Truth, Paradox, and Perspectivism," 111–116. The authors refer to *WP* 522. See also *BGE* 4 and *OTL*. In the dialogue of the text, Fegataccio asserts only the possibility of certain across-perspectives truths: perspectivism's own truth, Nietzsche's broad themes, and the presuppositions required to assert his broad themes. Are the laws of binary logic one of those presuppositions? Not necessarily, although some rules of inference do seem to be presuppositions.

28. Hales and Welshon, "Truth, Paradox, and Perspectivism," 113.

29. See, for example, Alexander Nehamas, "Who Are 'The Philosophers of the Future?'" in *Reading Nietzsche*, ed. Robert Solomon and Kathleen Higgins (New York: Oxford, 1988), 62–63, 65.

30. Jaspers, *Nietzsche*, 184–185.

31. Ibid., 190.

32. Ibid., 220.

33. Leslie Paul Thiele, *Friedrich Nietzsche and the Politics of the Soul* (Princeton: Princeton University Press, 1990), 58.

34. The inspiration for this analysis is Pierre Schlag, "Missing Pieces: A Cognitive Approach to Law," *Texas Law Review* 67 (1989): 1195. See also

Raymond Angelo Belliotti, *Justifying Law* (Philadelphia: Temple University Press, 1992), 211–220. My analysis of rhetorical strategies can be viewed reflexively as predominantly analytic (the quest for classification and logical analysis), with significant pragmatic (appreciation for flux, pluralism, fallibilism, and a community of inquirers), intuitive (faith in progress of discourse and commitment to standard method of analysis), and substructural elements (the quest for an underlying substructure of discourse which can account for superstructural ideological phenomena).

35. See, for example, Thiele, *Nietzsche*, 208–209; *UM* 111.

CHAPTER 2

1. Karl Jaspers, *Nietzsche: An Introduction to the Understanding of His Philosophical Activity*, trans. Charles F. Wallraff and Frederick J. Schmitz (Tucson: University of Arizona Press, 1965), 141.

2. Brian Leiter, "Morality in the Pejorative Sense: On the Logic of Nietzsche's Critique of Morality," *The British Journal of the History of Philosophy* 3 (1995): 112, 119–121.

3. Paul S. Loeb, "Is There a Genetic Fallacy in Nietzsche's Genealogy of Morals?" *International Studies in Philosophy* 27 (1995): 124, 128.

4. Raymond Geuss, "Nietzsche and Genealogy," *European Journal of Philosophy* 2 (1994): 274, 276.

5. S. Kemal, "Some Problems of Genealogy," *Nietzsche-Studien* 19 (1990): 30, 35.

6. Ibid., 41–42.

7. Buddhism is based on four noble truths: This life is suffering; desire and attachment are the sources of suffering; suffering can be overcome; and the eightfold path of right understanding, thought, speech, action, livelihood, effort, mindfulness, and concentration is the way to attain release from suffering. The eightfold path requires ethical conduct, mental discipline, and wisdom. It emphasizes detachment from the ego, meditation, and self-purification through transcendence. The doctrine of *karma* holds that we reap what we sow: We will receive our just punishment, if not in this life, then in our next life. Our souls or karmic effects can become attached to successive physical bodies and hence be reincarnated over and over again. The eightfold path is the way of purification which leads to escape from the endless cycle of rebirth and suffering, and to *nirvana*. *Nirvana* is the release from the suffering of this world through fusion with the Absolute.

Shakespeare's *MacBeth*, Act 5, Scene 5, contains one of the clearest and most eloquent expressions of the sense of cosmic purposelessness:

> Tomorrow, and tomorrow, and tomorrow
> Creeps in this petty pace from day to day
> To the last syllable of recorded time,
> And all our yesterdays have lighted fools
> The way to dusty death. Out, out, brief candle!
> Life's but a walking shadow, a poor player
> That struts and frets his hour upon the stage

> And then is heard no more. It is a tale
> Told by an idiot, full of sound and fury,
> Signifying nothing.

8. See, for example, Albert Camus, *The Rebel* (New York: Vantage Books, 1956). Camus illustrates this type of existential nihilism. In his *The Myth of Sisyphus* (1942), he adapts a Greek myth: Sisyphus, a mortal who would not submit to the authority of the gods, is condemned to push a huge boulder up a hill only to see it roll down again. This endless repetition is his eternal fate. Sisyphus's seemingly meaningless life is a metaphor for human life. But in recognizing our condition, in accepting our fate only to defy it, we can give meaning to existence. Sisyphus knows the boulder will roll down once he reaches the top of the hill, but he refuses to despair. He does not hope for release from his fate, he faces the absurd with strength: revolt, freedom, and passion. Many of these themes are prefigured in Nietzsche's eternal recurrence and attitude of *amor fati*. Camus's rebellion, however, has strong liberal–humanistic aspects which Nietzsche would suspect flow from herd morality.

9. Keith Ansell-Pearson, *An Introduction to Nietzsche as Political Thinker* (Cambridge: Cambridge University Press, 1994), 39.

10. Ibid., 200–201.

11. The call for "human solidarity" would be seen by Nietzsche as obscuring the rank order of humans, thus ensuring that mediocrity prevails. Thus, the spiritual development of higher types would be impaired by appeals for general human solidarity. See also Leslie Paul Thiele, *Friedrich Nietzsche and the Politics of the Soul* (Princeton: Princeton University Press, 1990), 56–61.

12. Jaspers, *Nietzsche*, 246–247.

13. "The 'blond beast' is not a racial concept and does not refer to the 'Nordic race' of which the Nazis later made so much. Nietzsche specifically refers to Arabs and Japanese, Romans and Greeks, no less than ancient Teutonic tribes when he first introduces this term (*GM* I, 11)—and the 'blondness' obviously refers to the beast, the lion, rather than the kind of man." Walter Kaufmann, *Nietzsche: Philosopher, Psychologist, Antichrist*, 4th ed. (Princeton: Princeton University Press, 1974), 225.

14. Nietzsche's denial of free will yet frequent calls for freedom pose a problem for interpreters. See, for example, Theodore R. Schatzki, "Ancient and Naturalistic Themes in Nietzsche's Ethics," *Nietzsche-Studien* 23 (1994): 146, 163.

15. Robert C. Solomon, *From Hegel to Existentialism* (New York: Oxford University Press, 1987), 110, 117.

CHAPTER 3

1. See, for example, Jerry H. Combee, "Nietzsche as Cosmologist," *Interpretation* 4 (1974): 38, 45–46; Arthur C. Danto, *Nietzsche as Philosopher* (New York: Columbia University Press, 1965), 206–208; Laurence Lampert, *Nietzsche's Teaching* (New Haven: Yale University Press, 1986), 258–259. See also *WP* 1062–1064, 1066–1067.

2. Keith Ansell-Pearson, *An Introduction to Nietzsche as Political Thinker* (Cambridge: Cambridge University Press, 1994), 52.

3. Walter Kaufmann, *Nietzsche: Philosopher, Psychologist, Antichrist*, 4th ed. (Princeton: Princeton University Press, 1974), 242, 246–247.

4. Karl Jaspers, *Nietzsche: An Introduction to the Understanding of His Philosophical Activity*, trans. Charles F. Wallraff and Frederick J. Schmitz (Tucson: University of Arizona Press, 1965), 166–168.

5. Ibid., 363–364.

6. See, for example, Lester H. Hunt, "The Eternal Recurrence and Nietzsche's Ethic of Virtue," *International Studies in Philosophy* 25 (1993): 3, 6.

7. See, for example, Kathleen Higgins, *Nietzsche's Zarathustra* (Philadelphia: Temple University Press, 1987), 175; Martin Heidegger, "Tragedy, Satyr-Play, and Telling Silence in Nietzsche's Thought of Eternal Recurrence," trans. David Krell, in *Why Nietzsche Now?* ed. Daniel T. O'Hara (Bloomington: Indiana University Press, 1985), 35.

8. See, for example, Richard White, "Zarathustra and the Progress of Sovereignty," *International Studies in Philosophy* 26 (1994): 107, 110–111.

9. Ibid., 113–114.

10. See, for example, Robin Small, "Three Interpretations of Eternal Recurrence," *Dialogue* 22 (1983): 91, 108–109; Ansell, *Nietzsche as Political Thinker*, 113.

11. See, for example, Ansell-Pearson, *Nietzsche as Political Thinker*, 111, 112.

12. See, for example, Hunt, "Eternal Recurrence," 9.

13. Jaspers, *Nietzsche*, 294–295, 318.

14. See, for example, Robin Roth, "Nietzsche's Metaperspectivism," *International Studies in Philosophy* 22 (1990): 67, 75; Danto, *Nietzsche*, 230.

15. See, for example, Peter Heller, "Nietzsche's 'Will to Power' *Nachlass*," *International Studies in Philosophy* 22 (1990): 35, 42–43.

16. The first place Nietzsche mentions the *Übermensch* is GS 143. After *Z*, the *Übermensch* is mentioned in *GM* I, 6; *TI*, "Skirmishes of an Untimely Man," 37; and three times in *EH* ("Why I Write Such Good Books," 1; "*Thus Spoke Zarathustra*," 6; "Why I am a Destiny," 5) when Nietzsche refers back to *Z*. The *Übermensch* usually appears in the singular. It appears in the plural in *GS* 143 and twice in *Z* II, "On Poets."

17. Frederick Copleston, *A History of Philosophy*, vol. 7, pt. 2 (Garden City, N.Y.: Doubleday, 1946–1965), 414. Bertrand Russell, *A History of Western Philosophy* (New York: Simon & Schuster, 1945), 767. Alasdair MacIntyre, *After Virtue*, 2d ed. (Notre Dame: University of Notre Dame Press, 1984), 22, 113.

18. See, for example, Daniel W. Conway, "Overcoming the *Übermensch*: Nietzsche's Revaluation of Values," *Journal of the British Society for Phenomenology* 20 (1989): 211–212.

19. Here are a few of the conflicting interpretations of the overman. Laurence Lampert writes,

One of the greatest single causes of the misinterpretation of Nietzsche's teaching is the failure to see that the clearly provisional teaching on the superman is rendered obsolete by the clearly definitive teaching on eternal return. That there is no call for a superman in the books after *Zarathustra* is no accident, but rather an implicit acknowledgment that the philosopher of the future has already come in the one who teaches that the weight of things resides in things and not in some future to which they may or may not contribute. . . . The superman, if the word can still be used, is the one who has brought the teaching of eternal return. Lampert, *Nietzsche's Teaching*, 258.

Daniel Conway writes, "The *Übermensch* ideal is not Nietzsche's but Zarathustra's. . . . We must therefore beware of precipitately attributing to Nietzsche the provisional teachings of Zarathustra. . . . It is crucial to our understanding of Nietzsche's ideal that Zarathustra abandons his initial teaching of the *Übermensch* and moves on." Conway, "Overcoming *Übermensch*," 215–216.

Leslie Thiele writes,

The overman is proposed as the hero of a nihilistic age. Like his forerunners, he bears his own standards of morality and reason and attempts to vanquish the hitherto reigning traditions and values. . . . He bears a "spiritualized enmity" toward himself, a soul "rich in contradictions" that "does not relax, does not long for peace." Strife is not merely tolerated, it is welcomed. . . . The overman should not be projected as one of Nietzsche's heroic incarnations or personae, for he contains none of the contradictions that prove to be the driving force behind the philosopher, artist, saint, educator, and solitary. He is their deification. His presence is felt at the victorious culmination of a battle, as a temporary release from struggle. Leslie Paul Thiele, *Friedrich Nietzsche and the Politics of the Soul* (Princeton: Princeton University Press, 1990), 12, 185–186.

Alan Schrift writes,

Many of the interpretive paradoxes concerning the *Übermensch* can be avoided if one refrains from interpreting *Übermensch* as Nietzsche's model of the ideal subject or perfect human being. . . . [It] is, rather the name given to a certain idealized conglomeration of forces, what Nietzsche calls . . . "a type of supreme achievement." . . . We can only speak of the becoming-*Übermensch* of human beings, of the process of accumulating strength and exerting mastery outside the limits of external authoritarian impositions. Nietzsche called this process of becoming-*Übermensch* "life-enhancement," and he indicated by this a process of self-overcoming and increasing of will to power rather than an ideal form of subjectivity. . . . This approach will emphasize not a way of Being but the affirmation of self-overcoming and transvaluation that makes possible the infinite processes of becoming that I am here suggesting we call becoming-*Übermensch*. Alan Schrift, "Putting Nietzsche to Work," in *Nietzsche: A Critical Reader*, ed. Peter R. Sedgwick (Cambridge, Mass.: Blackwell, 1995), 262–264.

Richard Schacht writes,

The *Übermensch* may be regarded as an image introduced and employed to provide the (re-) education of our aspirations and our thinking about the enhancement of life with a kind of compass, enabling us to gain a sense of direction even if not a clear description of our goal (which would be impossible). Its upshot for our lives is the notion of attained and attainable "higher humanity." Richard Schacht, "Zarathustra/ Zarathustra as Educator," in Sedgwick, *Nietzsche*, 237.

Keith Ansell-Pearson writes,

The notion of the overman is inseparable from the experience of *Untergang* contained in the eternal return since it is the thought-experiment of return which discloses the kind of *experience* of time . . . out of which *Menschen* are to become those that they are—the *Übermenschen*. Properly thought, therefore, the notion of the overman is not to be construed as an ideal at all for this would turn it into something unattainable by mere mortals—the superman of legend. . . . [The overman should be construed] in terms of the existential constitution of time (time's timeliness) in which "we" *become* those who "we are": to go beyond or across is also to go "back," to go "after" is to go "before," and so on—repetition as original creation. Keith Ansel-Pearson, "Toward the *Ubermensch*," *Nietzsche-Studien* 23 (1994): 123, 125–126.

Kathleen Higgins writes,

The overman represents something that in principle is unattainable by the merely human. . . . The overman's mode of being is continuously creative . . . the erotic mode of being *par excellence*, and while it surpasses human capacity for resilient self-transcendence, it establishes a project for human beings by serving as this capacity's ideal. . . . It is significant that the overman is by definition a goal that human beings will always fail to achieve. . . . The overman is an emblem for the goal of human development toward greatness, and as such it is an essentially abstract and formal concept. The concept is necessarily abstract because it is not instantiated, and also because various lives that aspire toward it might have only general characteristics in common. Higgins, *Nietzsche's Zarathustra*, 81, 125.

Walter Kaufmann writes,

The *Übermensch* at any rate cannot be dissociated from the conception . . . of overcoming. . . . The man who overcomes himself, sublimating his impulses, consecrating his passions, and giving style to his character, becomes truly human or—as Zarathustra would say, enraptured by the word *über*—superhuman. . . . The overman does not have instrumental value for the maintenance of society: he is valuable in himself because he embodies the state of being that has the only ultimate value there is. . . . He has overcome his animal nature, organized the chaos of his passions, sublimated his impulses, and given style to his character. Kaufmann, *Nietzsche*, 309, 312–313, 316.

20. See, for example, Conway, "Overcoming *Übermensch*," 214.

CHAPTER 4

1. Leslie Paul Thiele, *Friedrich Nietzsche and the Politics of the Soul* (Princeton: Princeton University Press, 1990), 131, 134.
2. Ibid., 135.
3. See, for example, Alexander Nehamas, *Nietzsche: Life as Literature* (Cambridge: Harvard University Press, 1985), 20–21; Laurence Lampert, *Nietzsche's Teaching* (New Haven: Yale University Press, 1986), 45; Walter Kaufmann, *Nietzsche: Philosopher, Psychologist, Antichrist*, 4th ed. (Princeton: Princeton University Press, 1974), 85; Michael Tanner, *Nietzsche* (New York: Oxford University Press, 1994), 57.
4. Patrick Gardiner, "Schopenhauer," in *The Encyclopedia of Philosophy*, ed. Paul Edwards, vol. 7 (New York: Macmillan, 1967), 328.
5. Ibid., 329.
6. Thiele, *Nietzsche and Politics*, 134.
7. Karl Jaspers, *Nietzsche: An Introduction to the Understanding of His Philosophical Activity*, trans. Charles F. Wallraff and Frederick J. Schmitz (Tucson: University of Arizona Press, 1965), 104–106.
8. Nehamas, *Nietzsche: Life as Literature*, 14, 15–16, 19, 27.
9. Ibid., 23.
10. Jaspers, *Nietzsche*, 409, 411, 412.

CHAPTER 5

1. Walter Kaufmann, *Nietzsche: Philosopher, Psychologist, Antichrist*, 4th ed. (Princeton: Princeton University Press, 1974), 281.

2. Ibid., 153.

3. Ibid., 281–282.

4. Bruce Detwiler, *Nietzsche and the Politics of Aristocratic Radicalism* (Chicago: University of Chicago Press, 1990), 147–148.

5. Ibid., 148.

6. Ibid., 162–163.

7. Ibid., 165–166, 168.

8. Kaufmann, *Nietzsche*, 123, 158.

9. Ibid., 418.

10. Ibid., 40–41.

11. Ibid., 58; Karl Jaspers, *Nietzsche: An Introduction to the Understanding of His Philosophical Activity*, trans. Charles F. Wallraff and Frederick J. Schmitz (Tucson: University of Arizona Press, 1965), 254–256.

12. See, for example, Keith Ansell-Pearson, *An Introduction to Nietzsche as Political Thinker* (Cambridge: Cambridge University Press, 1994), 6–7 90–91.

13. Jaspers, *Nietzsche*, 277.

14. W. Johnson, "ARARARARARAGH!" *Sports Illustrated*, 3 March 1969, 28–33.

15. See, for example, Robert C. Solomon, *The Passions* (Indianapolis: Hackett, 1993), 280–281.

16. Ibid., 290.

17. See, for example, Leslie Paul Thiele, "Love and Judgement: Nietzsche's Dilemma," *Nietzsche-Studien* 20 (1991): 88–89.

18. Ibid., 90.

19. See, for example, Raymond A. Belliotti, *Seeking Identity: Individualism versus Community in an Ethnic Context* (Lawrence: University Press of Kansas, 1995).

20. Alasdair MacIntyre, *After Virtue*, 2d ed. (Notre Dame: University of Notre Dame Press, 1984), 257–259.

21. William R. Schroeder, "Nietzschean Philosophers," *International Studies in Philosophy* 24 (1992): 107–108.

22. Thomas Hurka, *Perfectionism* (New York: Oxford University Press, 1993), 70.

23. Ibid., 76–77.

24. See, for example, Abraham Maslow, *Toward a Psychology of Being* (Princeton: Van Nostrand, 1962); Abraham Maslow, *The Farther Reaches of Human Nature* (New York: Penguin Books, 1971).

25. See, for example, Tony Schwartz, *What Really Matters* (New York: Bantam Books, 1995), 205.

26. Sigmund Freud, *A General Introduction to Psychoanalysis* (New York: Pocket Books, 1971); Sigmund Freud, *Civilization and Its Discontents* (New York: Norton, 1930).

27. Roberto Unger, *Passion: An Essay on Personality* (New York: Free Press, 1984); Roberto Unger, *Social Theory: Its Situation and Its Task* (Cambridge: Cambridge University Press, 1987); Roberto Unger, *False Necessity: Anti-Necessitarian So-*

cial Theory in the Service of Radical Democracy (Cambridge: Cambridge University Press, 1987); Roberto Unger, *Plasticity into Power* (Cambridge: Cambridge University Press, 1987); Roberto Unger, "The Critical Legal Studies Movement," *Harvard Law Review* 96 (1983): 561. For accounts critical of Unger's work, see Belliotti, *Seeking Identity*, 104–116; James Boyle, "Modernist Social Theory," *Harvard Law Review* 98 (1985): 1066; Drucilla Cornell, "Toward a Modern/Postmodern Reconstruction of Ethics," *University of Pennsylvania Law Review* 133 (1985): 291; Bernard Yack, "Book Review. Toward a Free Marketplace of Social Institutions: Roberto Unger's 'Super-Liberal' Theory of Emancipation," *Harvard Law Review* 101 (1988): 1961; and Cornel West, "Between Dewey and Gramsci: Unger's Emancipatory Experimentalism," *Northwestern University Law Review* 81 (1987): 941.

28. Robert C. Solomon, "Always the Philosopher," in *Falling in Love with Wisdom*, ed. David D. Karnos and Robert G. Shoemaker (New York: Oxford University Press, 1993), 156.

BIBLIOGRAPHY

BOOKS

Ansell-Pearson, Keith. *An Introduction to Nietzsche as Political Thinker*. Cambridge: Cambridge University Press, 1994.

Belliotti, Raymond Angelo. *Justifying Law*. Philadelphia: Temple University Press, 1992.

―――. *Seeking Identity: Individualism versus Community in an Ethnic Context*. Lawrence: University Press of Kansas, 1995.

Berkowitz, Peter. *Nietzsche*. Cambridge: Harvard University Press, 1995.

Camus, Albert. *The Rebel*. New York: Vantage Books, 1956.

Copleston, Frederick. *A History of Philosophy*. Vol. 7, pt. 2. Garden City, N.Y.: Doubleday, 1946–1965.

Danto, Arthur C. *Nietzsche as Philosopher*. New York: Columbia University Press, 1965.

de Man, Paul. *Allegories of Reading: Figural Language in Rousseau, Nietzsche, Rilke, and Proust*. New Haven: Yale University Press, 1979.

Derrida, Jacques. *Spurs: Nietzsche's Styles*. Chicago: University of Chicago Press, 1979.

Detwiler, Bruce. *Nietzsche and the Politics of Aristocratic Radicalism*. Chicago: University of Chicago Press, 1990.

Freud, Sigmund. *Civilization and Its Discontents*. New York: Norton, 1930.

―――. *A General Introduction to Psychoanalysis*. New York: Pocket Books, 1971.

Higgins, Kathleen. *Nietzsche's Zarathustra*. Philadelphia: Temple University Press, 1987.

Hurka, Thomas. *Perfectionism*. New York: Oxford University Press, 1993.

Jaspers, Karl. *Nietzsche: An Introduction to the Understanding of His Philosophical Activity*. Translated by Charles F. Wallraff and Frederick J. Schmitz. Tucson: University of Arizona Press, 1965.

Kaufmann, Walter. *Nietzsche: Philosopher, Psychologist, Antichrist*. 4th ed. Princeton: Princeton University Press, 1974.

Kosko, Bart. *Fuzzy Thinking: The New Science of Fuzzy Logic*. New York: Hyperion, 1993.

Lampert, Laurence. *Nietzsche's Teaching*. New Haven: Yale University Press, 1986.

MacIntyre, Alasdair. *After Virtue*. 2d ed. Notre Dame: University of Notre Dame Press, 1984.

Maslow, Abraham. *Toward a Psychology of Being*. Princeton: Van Nostrand, 1962.

———. *The Farther Reaches of Human Nature*. New York: Penguin Books, 1971.

Middleton, Christopher, ed. and trans. *Selected Letters of Friedrich Nietzsche*. Indianapolis: Hackett, 1996.

Nehamas, Alexander. *Nietzsche: Life as Literature*. Cambridge: Harvard University Press, 1985.

Parent, David J., trans. *Conversations with Nietzsche*. New York: Oxford University Press, 1987.

Rorty, Richard. *Consequences of Pragmatism*. Minneapolis: University of Minnesota Press, 1982.

Rosen, Stanley. *The Limits of Analysis*. New York: Basic Books, 1980.

Russell, Bertrand. *A History of Western Philosophy*. New York: Simon & Schuster, 1945.

Schwartz, Tony. *What Really Matters*. New York: Bantam Books, 1995.

Solomon, Robert C. *From Hegel to Existentialism*. New York: Oxford University Press, 1987.

———. *The Passions*. Indianapolis: Hackett, 1993.

Tanner, Michael. *Nietzsche*. New York: Oxford University Press, 1994.

Thiele, Leslie Paul. *Friedrich Nietzsche and the Politics of the Soul*. Princeton: Princeton University Press, 1990.

Unger, Roberto. *Passion: An Essay on Personality*. New York: Free Press, 1984.

———. *False Necessity: Anti-Necessitarian Social Theory in the Service of Radical Democracy*. Cambridge: Cambridge University Press, 1987.

———. *Plasticity into Power*. Cambridge: Cambridge University Press, 1987.

———. *Social Theory: Its Situation and Its Task*. Cambridge: Cambridge University Press, 1987.

Wilcox, John T. *Truth and Value in Nietzsche*. Washington, D.C.: University Press of America, 1982.

ARTICLES

Altieri, Charles. "Ecce Homo." In *Why Nietzsche Now?* edited by Daniel T. O'Hara. Bloomington: Indiana University Press, 1985.

Ansell-Pearson, Keith. "Toward the *Übermensch*." *Nietzsche-Studien* 23 (1994): 123–145.

Boyle, James. "Modernist Social Theory." *Harvard Law Review* 98 (1985): 1066–1097.

Combee, Jerry H. "Nietzsche as Cosmologist." *Interpretation* 4 (1974): 38–47.

Conway, Daniel W. "Overcoming the *Übermensch*: Nietzsche's Revaluation of Values." *Journal of the British Society for Phenomenology* 20 (1989): 211–224.

Cornell, Drucilla. "Toward a Modern/Postmodern Reconstruction of Ethics." *University of Pennsylvania Law Review* 133 (1985): 291–314.

Galston, William A. "False Universality." *Northwestern University Law Review* 81 (1987): 751–765.

Gardiner, Patrick. "Schopenhauer." In *The Encyclopedia of Philosophy*, edited by Paul Edwards. Vol. 7. New York: Macmillan, 1967.

Gemes, Ken. "Nietzsche's Critique of Truth." *Philosophy and Phenomenological Research* 52 (1992): 47–65.

Geuss, Raymond. "Nietzsche and Genealogy." *European Journal of Philosophy* 2 (1994): 274–292.

Hales, Steven D., and Robert C. Welshon. "Truth, Paradox, and Nietzschean Perspectivism." *History of Philosophy Quarterly* 11 (1994): 101–119.

Heidegger, Martin. "Tragedy, Satyr-Play, and Telling Silence in Nietzsche's Thought of Eternal Recurrence," translated by David Krell. In *Why Nietzsche Now?* edited by Daniel T. O'Hara. Bloomington: Indiana University Press, 1985.

Heller, Peter. "Nietzsche's 'Will to Power' *Nachlass*." *International Studies in Philosophy* 22 (1990): 35–44.

Hunt, Lester H. "The Eternal Recurrence and Nietzsche's Ethic of Virtue." *International Studies in Philosophy* 25 (1993): 3–11.

Johnson, W. "ARARARARARAGH!" *Sports Illustrated*, 3 March 1969, 28–32.

Kemal, S. "Some Problems of Genealogy." *Nietzsche-Studien* 19 (1990): 30–42.

Leiter, Brian. "Morality in the Pejorative Sense: On the Logic of Nietzsche's Critique of Morality." *The British Journal of the History of Philosophy* 3 (1995): 112–145.

Loeb, Paul S. "Is There a Genetic Fallacy in Nietzsche's Genealogy of Morals?" *International Studies in Philosophy* 27 (1995): 125–141.

Nehamas, Alexander. "Who Are 'The Philosophers of the Future?'" In *Reading Nietzsche*, edited by Robert Solomon and Kathleen Higgins. New York: Oxford, 1988.

Redding, Paul. "Nietzschean Perspectivism and the Logic of Practical Reason." *The Philosophical Forum* 22 (1990): 72–88.

Roth, Robin. "Nietzsche's Metaperspectivism." *International Studies in Philosophy* 22 (1990): 66–77.

Schatzki, Theodore R. "Ancient and Naturalistic Themes in Nietzsche's Ethics." *Nietzsche-Studien* 23 (1994): 146–167.

Schlag, Pierre. "Missing Pieces: A Cognitive Approach to Law." *Texas Law Review* 67 (1989): 1195–1247.

Schrift, Alan. "Putting Nietzsche to Work." In *Nietzsche: A Critical Reader*, edited by Peter R. Sedgwick. Cambridge, Mass.: Blackwell, 1995.

Schroeder, William R. "Nietzschean Philosophers." *International Studies in Philosophy* 24 (1992): 107–114.

Small, Robin. "Three Interpretations of Eternal Recurrence." *Dialogue* 22 (1983): 91–112.

Solomon, Robert. "Always the Philosopher." In *Falling in Love with Wisdom*, edited by David D. Karnos and Robert G. Shoemaker. New York: Oxford University Press, 1993.

Thiele, Leslie Paul. "Love and Judgement: Nietzsche's Dilemma." *Nietzsche-Studien* 20 (1991): 88–108.
Unger, Roberto. "The Critical Legal Studies Movement." *Harvard Law Review* 96 (1983): 561–675.
West, Cornel. "Between Dewey and Gramsci: Unger's Emancipatory Experimentalism." *Northwestern University Law Review* 81 (1987): 941–951.
White, Richard. "Zarathustra and the Progress of Sovereignty." *International Studies in Philosophy* 26 (1994): 107–115.
Yack, Bernard. "Book Review. Toward a Free Marketplace of Social Institutions: Roberto Unger's 'Super-Liberal' Theory of Emancipation." *Harvard Law Review* 101 (1988): 1961–1996.

INDEX